Microsoft WORD 6 for Windows

Step by Step

Catapult

MicrosoftPress

PUBLISHED BY
Microsoft Press
A Division of Microsoft Corporation
One Microsoft Way
Redmond, Washington 98052-6399

Library of Congress Cataloging-in-Publication Data pending.

Printed and bound in the United States of America.

11 12 13 14 15 MLML 9 8 7 6

Distributed to the book trade in Canada by Macmillan of Canada, a division of Canada Publishing Corporation.

Distributed to the book trade outside the United States and Canada by Penguin Books Ltd.

Penguin Books Ltd., Harmondsworth, Middlesex, England
Penguin Books Australia Ltd., Ringwood, Victoria, Australia
Penguin Books N.Z. Ltd., 182-190 Wairau Road, Auckland 10, New Zealand

British Cataloging-in-Publication Data pending.

Macintosh is a registered trademark of Apple Computer, Inc. Microsoft, MS, and MS-DOS are registered trademarks and Windows is a trademark of Microsoft Corporation. Arial is a registered trademark of The Monotype Corporation PLC. WordPerfect is a registered trademark of WordPerfect Corporation. Paintbrush is a trademark of ZSoft Corporation.

For Catapult, Inc.
Managing Editor: Donald Elman
Author: Marie L. Swanson
Associate Editor: Ann T. Rosenthal
Layout Editor: Jeanne K. Hunt

For Microsoft Press
Acquisitions Editors: Marjorie Schlaikjer and Lucinda Rowley
Technical Editor: Bettijean Collins
Project Editor: Casey D. Doyle

Catapult, Inc. is a national software training company dedicated to providing the highest quality application software training. Years of PC and Macintosh instruction for major corporations and government institutions provide the models used in building Catapult's exclusive Performance-Based Training program. Based on the principles of adult learning, Performance-Based Training materials ensure that training participants leave the classroom with the confidence and ability to apply skills acquired during the training day. Both visual design and textual content are planned to motivate the adult learner to accomplish specific course objectives. This approach presents the required information about concepts and commands, allows for practice of newly learned skills, and provides additional follow-up to ensure skills retention. Catapult's adherence to Performance-Based Training is the basis for the approach Catapult brings to the Microsoft Press *Step by Step* series.

Catapult's development team builds into every *Step by Step* tutorial the knowledge gained from training hundreds of thousands of students. After gathering classroom feedback from individual entrepreneurs, session evaluations from employees of Fortune 500 companies, and input from decision makers at state and government agencies nationwide, Catapult analyzes the data to determine which skills can provide increased productivity. This information is applied to each *Step by Step* model. Then, working directly with software developers at Microsoft, Catapult's development team creates effective lessons and exercises that enhance skills to solve specific needs by utilizing the full power of your Microsoft applications and operating systems.

The Product Development group at Catapult is pleased to share their training experience with a wider audience through the *Step by Step* series. *Microsoft Word for Windows Step by Step* is the eighth in this series to be produced by Catapult Press. This book and others in the collection will help you to develop the confidence necessary to achieve increased productivity with your Microsoft products.

Catapult Software Training Centers provide instructor-led Performance-Based Training nationwide in their open-enrollment classrooms or as dedicated classes at customer sites. Catapult's corporate headquarters are in Bellevue, Washington.

WE'VE CHOSEN THIS SPECIAL LAY-FLAT BINDING

to make it easier for you to work through the step-by-step lessons while you're at your computer.

With little effort, you can make this book lie flat when you open it to any page. Simply press down on the inside (where the paper meets the binding) of any left-hand page, and the book will stay open to that page. You can open the book this way every time. The lay-flat binding will not weaken or crack over time.

It's tough, flexible, sturdy—and designed to last.

Contents

Part 1   Basic Skills

Part 3   Arranging Text and Graphics

About This Book

Microsoft Word for Windows is a full-featured word processor designed to help you work more efficiently—whether you spend several hours a day at the computer or use word-processing software only occasionally.

Microsoft Word for Windows Step by Step shows you how Microsoft Word can make your everyday work easy. You can use *Step by Step* in a classroom setting, or use it as a tutorial to learn Word at your own pace and at your own convenience. Most lessons provide a sample document to work through the steps.

The lessons in this book show you how to create effective documents using the features in Microsoft Word. Each lesson takes approximately 30 to 45 minutes, with an optional practice exercise at the end of each lesson.

Finding the Best Starting Point for You

This book is designed both for new users who are learning Microsoft Word for the first time, and for experienced users who want to learn about the new features in Word for Windows version 6.0. If you are familiar with other Microsoft Word products, such as Word for the Macintosh, Word for Windows version 2.0, or Word 5.5 for the PC, you'll have a head start on the basics of this new version of Word for Windows. Among the new features you'll want to learn about are the alternative toolbars, which give you easy access to the features you use the most, and the enhanced "smart drag and drop" feature, with which you can copy or move selected text by dragging and dropping it where you want. It's called "smart" because it automatically adjusts spacing around words. You can learn more about the new features in "New Features in Word for Windows 6.0."

The modular design of this book offers you considerable flexibility in customizing your learning. Lessons 1 through 4 teach basic skills. To help you decide whether you need to work through those lessons, review the Lesson Summary at the end of each one. You can go through the other lessons in any order, skip lessons, and repeat lessons later to brush up on specific skills.

The following table provides recommended starting points based on your word-processing experience.

If you are	Follow these steps
New to word processing	Read "If You are New to Word Processing," in "Getting Ready," later in this book. Next work through Lessons 1–4 in order. Work through the other lessons in any order.
New to the mouse	Read "If You are New to the Mouse," in "Getting Ready," later in this book. Next work through Lessons 1–4 in order. Work through the other lessons in any order. Note that the sample documents in the lessons often provide special tips for keyboard users.
New to Word for Windows, and unfamiliar with other Microsoft Word products	Work through Lessons 1–4 in order. Work through the other lessons in any order.
Familiar with Word for the Macintosh or Word 5.5 for the PC	Read the summaries at the end of Lessons 1, 2, 3, and 4. You may not need to work through these lessons. Work through the other lessons in any order. Even if you are familiar with using the mouse, you'll want to explore how to use the right mouse button.
An experienced Word for Windows user	Read "Getting Ready" and "New Features in Word 6.0," for information about new features and techniques you can try, and cross references to where these new features are covered in the book. Read the summaries at the end of Lessons 1, 2, 3, and 4. Note the new toolbars and toolbar buttons. Work through the other lessons in any order. Even if you are familiar with using the mouse, you'll want to explore how to use the right mouse button.

Using This Book As a Classroom Aid

If you're an instructor, you can use *Microsoft Word Step by Step* for teaching Word to novice users and for teaching the new features of Word for Windows version 6.0 to experienced users. You can choose from the lessons to customize courses for your students.

If you plan to teach the entire contents of this book, you should probably allow one and one-half to two days of classroom time to allow for discussion, questions, and any customized practice you might create. You can also obtain the Instructor Kit to get materials and information you need to prepare a Microsoft Word class. Order the Instructor Kit by completing the order form in the back of this book, or by calling 1-800-MSPRESS.

Conventions Used in This Book

Keyboard Conventions

If you get unexpected results as you work
Look for a note near the step in the left margin, as shown here. Additional information about getting the same results shown in the exercises is located in the Appendix, "Matching the Exercises."

- Names of keys are in small capital letters; for example, TAB and SHIFT.

- A plus sign (+) between two key names means that you must press those keys at the same time. For example, "Press SHIFT+SPACEBAR" means that you hold down the SHIFT key while you press the SPACEBAR.

- A comma (,) between two key names means that you must press those keys sequentially. For example, "Press ALT, F, O" means that you first press and release the ALT key, and then the F key, and then the O key.

Other Features of This Book

- As you work through the lessons in this book, you can imagine yourself working for a company called West Coast Sales (a wholesale supplier of down products, outdoor clothing, and upscale linen and bedding). In addition to your regular responsibilities there, you have become known as the resident word processing resource.

- You'll find optional "One Step Further" exercises at the end of each lesson. These exercises build on the skills and topics covered in the lesson, often exploring a new option or shortcut technique.

- The lessons in the book are divided into four parts. At the end of each part is an optional "Review & Practice" scenario. These less structured activities allow you to build your confidence with the features you learned about in the lesson using real life situations. You'll be introduced to problems and provided with general guidelines for solving them on your own.

Print

- You can carry out many commands by clicking a button at the top of the Word window. If a procedure instructs you to click a button, a picture of the button appears in the left margin, as the Print button does here.

- Text in the left margin summarizes main points, gives tips, or provides additional useful information.

- In the Appendix, "Matching the Exercises," you can review the options used in this book to get the results you see in the illustrations. Refer to this section of the book when your screen does not match the illustrations or when you get unexpected results as you work through the exercises.

Cross-References to Microsoft Word Documentation

Microsoft Word Step by Step will help you learn about your Word documentation. At the end of each lesson, you'll find references to the documentation that comes with Word. If you work through a lesson that teaches skills you use frequently and want to know more about the skills, check the chapter or online lesson referenced at the end of the lesson. You'll find cross-references to the following Word documentation and features:

- *Microsoft Word Quick Results* describes the features in Word, explains how to set up Word on your computer system, how to start and quit Word, and how to get the most out of the documentation provided with Word.

- *Microsoft Word User's Guide* contains background information, procedures, and examples for using the basic and advanced features in Word.

- *Online Examples and Demos* provide information about Word features and give instructions on performing specific tasks. Online Help also has documentation on WordBasic macros and fields, as well as information for users switching from WordPerfect to Word. When the WordArt feature is running, WordArt Help displays complete documentation about creating special effects in your documents.

- *Wizards* coach you through the steps for performing more challenging word processing activities, such as creating forms and merging documents. Use a wizard when you want to explore a new feature with your own text and documents.

- *Templates* help produce different kinds of documents, such as letters, memos, and business reports. Templates are located in the directory where you installed Word. For information on using templates, see Chapter 10, "Document Templates," in the *Microsoft Word User's Guide.*

- *Clip Art* provides graphics that you can paste directly into Word or edit by using the tools on the drawing toolbar. These graphics are located in the CLIPART subdirectory under the directory where you installed Word.

Getting Ready

This section of the book prepares you for your first steps into the Microsoft Word environment. There are several things you need to do before you begin the lessons. You will learn how to install the practice files on your computer's hard disk and how to start both Windows and Microsoft Word. You will also review some useful Microsoft Windows techniques, as well as terms and concepts that are important to understand as you learn to use Microsoft Word.

If you have not yet installed Windows or Microsoft Word, you'll need to do that before you continue with the lessons. If you need instructions for installing Windows, see your Windows documentation. If you need instructions for installing Microsoft Word version 6.0, see your Microsoft Word documentation.

You will learn how to:

- Install the practice files onto your computer's hard disk.
- Start Microsoft Windows.
- Start Microsoft Word.
- Use basic Windows features such as windows, menus, and dialog boxes in the Microsoft Word environment.
- Use Microsoft Word Help.

Installing the Step by Step Practice Files

Inside this book, you'll find a disk labeled "Microsoft Word for Windows Step by Step Practice Files." A special program on the Practice Files disk copies these files onto your hard drive into a directory named PRACTICE. Copy the practice files onto your hard drive.

1 Turn on your computer.

2 Insert the Practice Files disk into drive A or B of your computer.

3 If Windows is already running, open the Program Manager and choose Run from the File menu. If you have not started Windows yet, skip to step 5.

4 In the Command Line box, type **a:\install** (or **b:\install**) and click OK.

Do not type a space between the drive letter and the slash. Follow the instructions on the screen to complete the installation process and skip steps 5 and 6.

5 At the MS-DOS command prompt (usually "C:\>") type **a:\install** (or **b:\install**) and press ENTER.

Do not type a space between the drive letter and the slash.

6   Follow the instructions on the screen to complete the installation process.

The Step by Step setup program copies the practice files from the floppy disk onto your hard disk in a subdirectory (called PRACTICE) of the Microsoft Word home directory (often called WINWORD or WINWORD6). You'll need to remember the name of the drive and directory where the practice files are stored so that you can open a file for each lesson.

Using the Practice Files

As you work through the lessons using the practice files, be sure to follow the instructions for saving and giving the files new names. In general, each practice file name begins with the lesson number. When you save or create a file, you can specify a name that ends with the lesson number. Renaming the practice files this way allows you to make changes, experiment, and observe results without affecting the original practice files. With the practice files intact, you can reuse the original files later if you want to repeat a lesson or try a new option. Using the conventions for saving and naming documents described in the lessons makes it easy for you to quickly identify the original files and the files you create and modify.

Lesson Background

For these lessons, imagine that you work for a company called West Coast Sales. In addition to your regular responsibilities, you are also leading the effort to introduce new technologies into the organization. Part of this effort involves learning all about Microsoft Word and using it every day. As you learn new features, you have many opportunities to create different kinds of documents that will demonstrate the power and flexibility of Microsoft Word to your colleagues.

Starting Microsoft Word

You start Microsoft Word from within Windows. If Windows is not running, start Windows first, then start Word.

To start Windows

Follow these steps to start Windows from the MS-DOS prompt (usually C:\>). After you are in the Windows environment, you can start Microsoft Word.

1   At the MS-DOS prompt, type **win**

2   Press ENTER.

When Windows is active, everything on your screen is displayed in a *window*. In later lessons, you'll learn to make each window the size you want and move it anywhere you want on your screen.

Start Microsoft Word from Program Manager

Microsoft Office

Microsoft Word

The following steps show the sequence for starting Microsoft Word from within Windows. If you do not see the icon shown in step 2, look for the icon shown in step 3.

1 Double-click the Program Manager icon to display the Program Manager window.

2 Double-click the Microsoft Office group icon shown at the left to display the group window. (Or open whichever group contains Word 6.0.)

3 To start Microsoft Word, double-click the Microsoft Word icon shown at the left.

If You Are New to Microsoft Windows

Microsoft Windows provides a powerful work environment that streamlines many tasks and gives you a great deal of control over the way you work. With Windows, you can use Microsoft Word and other applications at the same time. Within Microsoft Word, you can display more than one document at a time. You can also arrange windows on the screen, just as you move papers around on a desk.

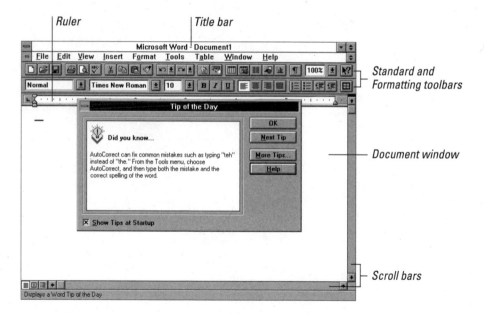

A window is a rectangular area on your screen in which you work on a document. By using a mouse, you can open, move, size, scroll through, switch between, or close windows—just as you might spread out or leaf through books and papers on your desk and put them aside when you're finished with them.

If You Are New to Using the Mouse

The toolbars and ruler were designed for working with the mouse. The mouse controls a pointer on the screen. When you move the mouse, the pointer moves too. Sometimes you need to press the mouse button while you're moving the mouse. If you run out of room to move the mouse, lift it and then put it down. The pointer doesn't move unless the mouse is touching a flat surface. When you press the mouse button, something happens at the location of the pointer.

When the mouse pointer passes over different parts of the Microsoft Word window, it changes shape, indicating what it will do at that point. You'll work with the following mouse shapes during the lessons.

This pointer	Appears when you
I	Point in the text area. This is sometimes called the "I-beam" pointer. In italic text, this pointer slants to make positioning and selecting easier. You use this pointer to indicate where you want to begin typing.
⬐	Point to the menus, inactive windows, scroll bars, ruler, or toolbars. You can use this pointer to choose a menu and command, click a button, or drag a tab stop marker.
⬑	Point in the selection bar or the style name bar along the window's left edge. You can use this pointer to select a line, paragraph, or the entire document. This pointer also appears in table selection bars.
⬐?	Press the Help key (SHIFT+F1). You can use this pointer to display help information. With this pointer, point to a command name or a region on the screen and click to view a Help topic about the item you clicked.
⬍	Point to a top or bottom window border. You can use this pointer to change the size of a window vertically. A similar, black sizing pointer appears at the edge of a graphic or frame.
⬌	Point to the left or right window border. You can change the size of a window horizontally. A similar, black sizing pointer appears at the edge of a graphic or frame.
⬂	Point to a corner of a window. You can use this pointer to change the size of a window horizontally and vertically. A similar, black sizing pointer appears at the corner of a graphic or frame.

This pointer	Appears when you
	Point near a frame, indicating that you can drag the frame to a new position.
	Point near the top of a column in a table. Click to select the column.
	Point to selected text and click the mouse button. This pointer indicates that you can drag the selected text to a new location, where you can either "drop" or insert it.

Using the mouse pointer

There are four basic mouse actions that you will use to move around in Word.

Pointing   Moving the mouse to place the pointer on an item is called pointing.

Clicking   Pointing to an item on your screen and then quickly pressing and releasing the mouse button is called clicking. You select items on the screen and move around in a document by clicking. When you click with the right mouse button, you get a short menu of commands that are available in the location where you clicked.

Double-clicking   Pointing to an item and quickly pressing and releasing the mouse button twice. Double-clicking executes an action immediately. This is a convenient shortcut for many of the tasks you'll do in Microsoft Word.

Dragging   Holding down the mouse button as you move the pointer is called dragging. You can use this technique to select text in documents. Sometimes you'll be instructed to hold down SHIFT or CTRL or ALT when you drag to take advantage of other dragging features.

Experiment with the mouse

Take a moment to test drive the mouse by moving the pointer and clicking the mouse in the window.

If you want to see the Tip of the Day
You have the option to see the Tip of the Day every time you start Microsoft Word. From the Help menu, choose Tip Of The Day.

The Tip Of The Day dialog box that you see when you first start Microsoft Word provides useful hints and tips for working in Word. If you do not see the Tip Of The Day dialog box, it means that the option to display the tip is turned off. In this case, skip step 1 and continue with step 2.

1   After you read the tip, click the OK button.

The dialog box disappears and a blank window appears.

2   Slide the mouse until the pointer is over the buttons at the top of the screen. Note the left-pointing arrow.

3   Slide the mouse around the large open area in the center of the screen, called the *document window*. This is the area in which you type text. Note that the pointer looks like an I-beam.

4   Slide the mouse so the pointer is on the left edge of the document window. Note the right-pointing arrow. In Lesson 1, you'll learn a shortcut that uses this right-pointing arrow.

5   Click the right mouse button anywhere in the document window.

If you click in the document area, you see a shortcut menu with commands relating to the item you are working with, as in the following illustration.

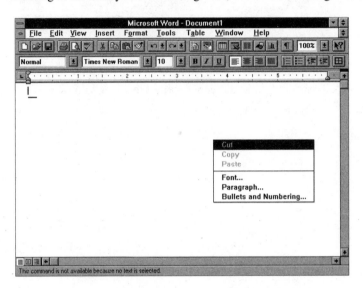

6   With the left mouse button, click anywhere outside of the menu in the document window to make the menu disappear.

Working in Microsoft Word

When you start Microsoft Word, a new (and empty) document appears in a *document window*. The document window is the Microsoft Word equivalent of a sheet of paper in a typewriter—it is where you type your text. The buttons and ruler you see at the top of the window offer easy ways to work on your documents. By using the mouse to click a button, select an option from a list, or adjust margins and indents on the ruler, you can change the way your document looks, check spelling, or perform any number of other common word processing tasks.

The rows of buttons and the ruler near the top of the Word window are really three separate items. You can display or hide them independently of each other if you need more viewing room on your screen. They are designed to speed your work by helping you perform the tasks you use most often. You will find it most convenient to display all three.

 — *Standard toolbar*

*Click Standard toolbar buttons to carry out commands such as
opening, saving, and printing documents.*

 — *Formatting toolbar*

*Use the Formatting toolbar to format text and paragraphs, for
example, to bold or center text.*

 — *Ruler*

Use the ruler to set tabs or adjust margins and indents.

Within the Word window, each Word document you open is displayed in its own
window. You can make a document window smaller and display several documents at
one time within the Word application window.

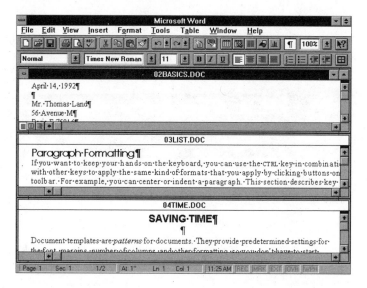

Document windows have a Minimize button (as do application windows). The
Minimize button shrinks a Word document to an icon, so that you can open other
document windows inside Microsoft Word without having all the documents displayed. You can then quickly return to the document you want by double-clicking its
minimized document window icon.

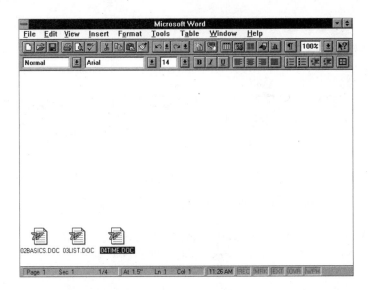

The button on the far right changes depending on the size of the window. If the window is as large as possible, the button with the up and down triangles is called the Restore button. Clicking it restores the window to its previous, smaller size, and the Restore button changes to an up arrow.

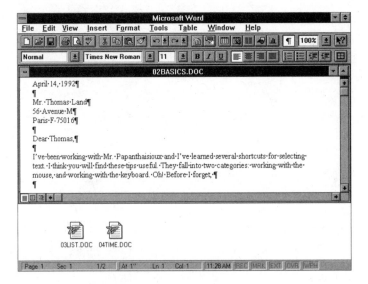

If the window is less than its maximum size, the Maximize button quickly enlarges the window to the largest possible size.

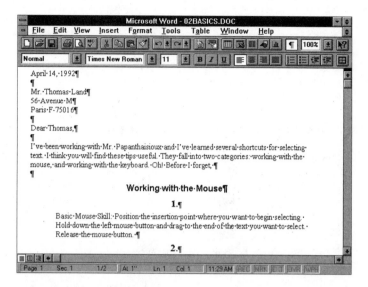

Working with Menus and Dialog Boxes

Microsoft Word commands are grouped together in *menus*. To choose a command, you click a menu to display its available commands and then choose one from the list. Many commands provide further choices. For example, if you choose the Font command from the Format menu, you can select numerous characteristics about the appearance of text. You make these selections in dialog boxes. A *dialog box* contains related options for a specific command. Commands that display a dialog box are followed by an ellipsis (...) on the menu.

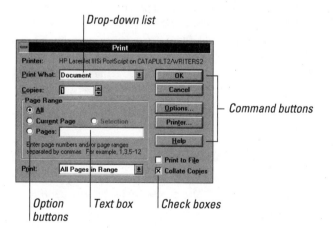

After you select or type the options you want Microsoft Word to use, you choose the command button—usually the OK button—that tells Microsoft Word to carry out the command with the options you specified. Or, if you change your mind while the dialog box is displayed, you can choose the Cancel button, and Microsoft Word will not carry out the command. When you choose the Cancel button, no change is made to the document.

Using Keys to Make Selections

This book teaches the mouse method for working with Microsoft Word. But if your hands are already on the keyboard, you may prefer to use the keyboard instead of the mouse to choose commands and dialog box options. Work through the following procedure to learn the keyboard method for working in Microsoft Word.

Use keys to choose commands and options

1   Take a moment to look at the menu bar and note the underlined letters in menu names, such as Table and Format.

2   Click the Format menu to see that underlined letters also appear in command names, such as Font.

3   Click the Font command to see underlined letters in the names of the dialog box options, such as Font, Size, and Small Caps.

   Holding down the ALT key and pressing an underlined letter chooses that menu, command, or option.

4   Press ALT+S to access options from the Size list.

5   Press the DOWN ARROW key on the keyboard to select an item from the list.

6   Press ALT plus another underlined letter to move to another location in the dialog box, or press ENTER to complete the command; or to close the dialog box without completing the command, press ESC.

Note   The instructions in these lessons show the underlined keys for menus and commands, so you can use the mouse or the keyboard to choose them, whichever you prefer.

Working with Toolbars

The toolbars provide the buttons for the features you use most often. A new feature in Microsoft Word version 6.0 allows you to display several toolbars at one time. For example, you can display the Borders toolbar if you want to put borders around your text. You can customize toolbars to display specific buttons from other toolbars you use often. You can also display other toolbars by choosing the Toolbars command from the View menu.

Take a quick guided tour of the Standard toolbar

Take a moment to get acquainted with the buttons on the Standard toolbar. If you accidentally click a button, you can press the ESC key or click the Undo button on the Standard toolbar.

▶ Move the pointer over a tool, and wait.

After a moment, the name of the tool appears. In addition, a brief description of the tool appears in the status bar at the bottom of the window.

If you do not see the tool name

From the View menu, choose Toolbars. Click the ToolTips check box.

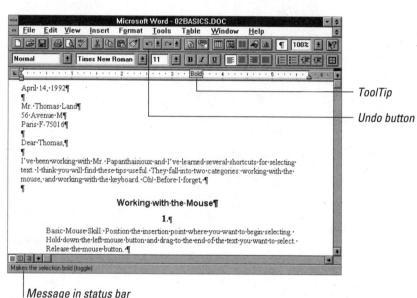

ToolTip

Undo button

Message in status bar

Using Wizards

Wizards (a new feature in Microsoft Word version 6.0) are friendly assistants that guide you through the steps of creating specific types of documents in Microsoft Word. Wizards are available for creating a variety of documents, such as resumes, letters, memos, or meeting agendas. When you run a wizard, the wizard asks you for information and text that will be incorporated in the document. Then the wizard uses attractive formatting to produce the document according to your specifications. You can always modify the documents the wizards produce for you, but wizards provide a great way to get started. You will explore numerous wizards throughout this book.

Locating Information in Help

With online Help in Microsoft Word, there are several ways you can get more information about using a feature. When you want general information, you can choose the Contents command from the Help menu. This Help window works like a table of contents to give you access to the entire online help system. When you want to look up information about a specific command, you can use the Search For Help On command. This Help window works like an index in which you enter a word or phrase, and then you select from a list of related topics that you want to see. In addition, when you are in a dialog box, you can press the F1 key to see information about the currently open dialog box.

Search for a topic in Help

You can quickly search the online Help topics for the information that you need. Once you display a topic, you can click any phrases that have solid underlines to jump to related topics. You can click a button to retrace your path through Help, backtracking through the topics you have viewed.

1   Press the F1 key.

Pressing F1 (when you are not in a dialog box) displays the Help window. This is the same as choosing Contents from the Help menu.

You can click any of the underlined topics and browse for information, but it's often faster to have Microsoft Word search for what you need.

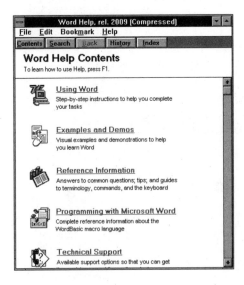

2   Click the Search button.

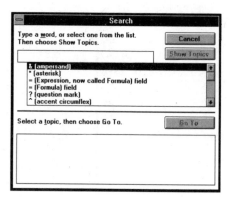

Clicking the Search button is the same as choosing the Search For Help On command from the Help menu. You'll begin your search at the top of this dialog box and work your way toward the bottom of the dialog box.

3 Type **indent** but do not press ENTER.

As you type, Microsoft Word searches for categories of information associated with the word "indent," and displays those categories in the center list box.

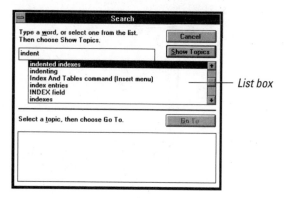

List box

4 In the list box, click the category "indenting" if it's not already selected.

5 Click the Show Topics button to show a list of topics related to indenting.

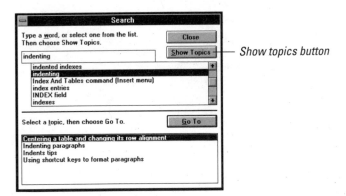

Show topics button

6   In the list of related topics, click "Indenting paragraphs," and then click the Go To button.

Information about indenting a paragraph appears.

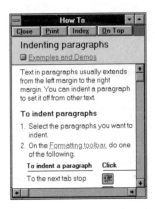

7   Use the down scroll arrow in the Help window to view information about indenting paragraphs.

Online Help appears in its own window. Because you can size and move your windows, you can display step-by-step instructions as you work in a document or a dialog box. You can close a Help window (as you would close any window) by double-clicking the Control-menu box in the window.

Jump to a related topic

If the information you need does not appear in a Help window, you can click any underlined phrase to jump to related information.

1   Click the down scroll arrow to scroll through the Help window text until you see the green underlined phrase "Formatting Paragraphs" at the bottom of the window.

2   To jump to this related topic, point to the phrase. When the mouse pointer changes to resemble a hand, click the underlined phrase.

Information about the topic appears. Take a moment to scroll through the topic, reading any definitions.

Return to the previous topic

You can easily backtrack through the Help topics that you've displayed if you want to recall previous topics.

1   Click the Back button in the Help window.

The previous topic appears.

2   When you finish reading the topic, but expect to return to this Help window shortly, click in the document to hide the Help window.

If you have finished using Help for the time being, you can close the Help window by double-clicking its Control-menu box.

Tip   From the Help window Help menu, you can choose Always On Top to display the Help window on top of the document window, even as you work in the document. It stays on top until you click the button again or until you close the Help window.

Get Help about dialog box options

F1 is the Help key.

When you are working in a dialog box, you can read about the available options by pressing the F1 key. Start this exercise by opening the Font dialog box.

1   From the Format menu, choose Font.

The Font dialog box appears.

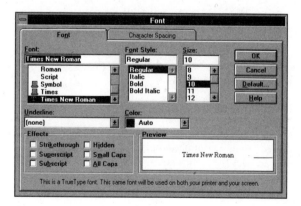

2 With the Font dialog box open, press the F1 key.

Microsoft Word displays a Help window that describes the command and the dialog box options.

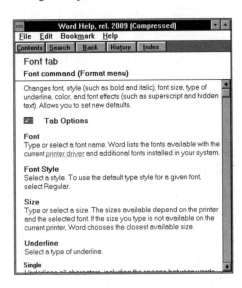

3 In the Help window, point to the phrase "printer driver." When the mouse pointer changes to resemble a hand, click the mouse button to display a definition of the term.

4 Click again to clear the definition.

5 Click the down arrow on the Help window scroll bar to read more about the dialog box options.

6 To hide the Help window, click in the document window, not in the dialog box. If the Help window completely fills the screen, you can hold down the ALT key and press F4 to close the Help window.

If you accidentally click the dialog box, click the Help window again and then click the document window.

Get information about a command

Help

The Microsoft Word online Help system contains a description of every command. You can read about a command before you actually use it. Use the following procedure to learn about the Zoom command.

1 Click the Help button on the Standard toolbar.

The Help button adds a question mark to the mouse pointer, indicating that you will choose a command for information only.

Tip You can also press SHIFT+F1to display the Help pointer.

---

2 Click the <u>V</u>iew menu.

3 Click <u>Z</u>oom.

Microsoft Word displays a Help window that describes the Zoom command and shortcuts or options related to that command. The Help window has its own scroll bars, separate from the document window scroll bars. You can scroll through the Help window in the same way you scroll through a document window.

4 Click the down scroll arrow in the Help window to read more about the Zoom command.

5 When you finish reading about the Zoom command, click in the document text. If the Help window fills the screen, hold down the ALT key and press F4. Either method hides the Help window. Click the Close button to close the topic window.

If You Are Familiar with WordPerfect Commands

If you are accustomed to working in WordPerfect, the Microsoft Word online Help system can ease the transition to Microsoft Word. In the Help system, you can choose a WordPerfect command name to read about the corresponding Microsoft Word procedure, or you can watch as Microsoft Word demonstrates the appropriate procedure.

Find the Microsoft Word equivalent of a WordPerfect command

1 From the <u>H</u>elp menu, choose <u>W</u>ordPerfect Help.

2 In the Command Keys box, click "Indent->." You might need to scroll through the list to see this command.

Help displays information about the Indent command.

3 For a demonstration of the command, click the Demo button.

Tip The dialog box that appears when you choose WordPerfect Help from the Help menu includes a button labeled Options. You can click this button to see special options for WordPerfect users. These options include using WordPerfect key combinations to perform commands and choosing the type of Help—demo or text—that you want to view.

If You Are New to Word Processing

Each time you start Microsoft Word, you will either create a new document—a letter, memo, report—or work on a document that you or someone else has already created. There are several basic stages to creating a document. You perform steps 1, 2a, 2b, and 2c a little at a time, alternating between them.

Step 1   Typing

Typing text in Microsoft Word is very similar to typing on a typewriter. There are, however, some important differences that can save you time. For example, when you type enough words to reach the end of a line, Microsoft Word automatically moves to the next line. This is called *wordwrap*. With wordwrap, you do not have to watch for the end of the line. You will not need to press ENTER unless you want to start a new paragraph or create a blank line in the document. If a complete word will not fit when you reach the end of a line, Microsoft Word automatically moves the last whole word you typed to the next line.

If you often type columns of numbers, you will find Microsoft Word much easier to use than a typewriter. You do not need to set up tabs to create the columns. Microsoft Word has a table feature that displays a grid of columns and rows on the screen. You type your information into the boxes that you see on the screen to organize the information automatically in columns and rows. The grid does not print; it simply helps you organize information.

Step 2a   Editing

Great writers often say their secret to success lies in rewriting their text, changing their mind, trying out a different word—in other words, *editing* the text. This is where a word processor is a great asset. If you change your mind after you write something, you can replace what you've written, add text, or delete the text you do not want. Whichever the case, Microsoft Word adjusts the spacing of the text—making more room for text that you add and closing up empty spaces that are left when you remove text. Your reader will never know a change was made. That's the beauty of word processing.

Step 2b   Formatting

Formatting means controlling the appearance of the document. Formatting in Microsoft Word includes several features available on many typewriters, such as applying bold, italic, or underlining, as well as centering text. It also includes other changes that Microsoft Word makes easy, such as changing the number of columns in the document or even the orientation of a page.

Step 2c   Adding special touches

Microsoft Word makes it easy to dress up a document. For example, you can add pictures and charts, create special effects with text, or type text once and have Microsoft Word automatically insert the text in the top or bottom margin of every page in your document.

Step 3   Checking the spelling and grammar

Microsoft Word can quickly compare each word in your document to a standard
dictionary and highlight words that are not found. It can also highlight possible
grammatical errors. You can accept or ignore suggestions for correcting both types of
errors. You can also make your own changes.

Step 4   Storing the document for safekeeping

When you create a new document, the information you type exists only in your
computer's memory until you save it on the hard disk that is built into your computer
or on a floppy disk that can be inserted and removed from your computer. Information
held in memory can be lost if the power to your computer goes off, but saving a
document stores it indefinitely on disk.

Step 5   Printing

You'll have many opportunities to print documents during these lessons.

Step 6   Removing the document from the screen

When you are through working on a document, you save it on a disk and, if you are
ready, you can also print it. Then you can *close* the document; that is, remove it from
the computer screen. Although you'll no longer see it on the screen, it remains stored
on the hard disk until you open it again.

Step 7   Displaying the document on the screen again

Perhaps you need to do more work to a document, or perhaps you want to use some of
the text in another document. (Sharing text between documents is another way word
processors can save you time.) To display a document on the screen, you *open* it. This
puts a copy of the document on the screen. The original document remains safe on
your hard disk.

After you make changes to the copy of the safely stored document, you have a choice.
You can either replace the original with your new version—this is called *overwrit-
ing*—or you can save your version with a different name. If you save your version
with a different name, you will have two versions of the document—the original and
the revised document with the new name.

This completes the cycle. Every time you begin work in Microsoft Word, you will
either create a new document, as in step 1, or you will open an existing document, as
in step 7, and then move on to step 2.

New Features in Word 6.0

The following table lists the major new features in Microsoft Word for Windows version 6.0 that are covered in this book. The table shows the lesson in which you can learn about each feature. For more information about new features, see the *Microsoft Word User's Guide*.

To learn how to	See in this *Step by Step* book
View useful Microsoft Word facts and tips with the Tip of the Day.	Getting Ready
Display context-sensitive menus with the right mouse button.	Getting Ready
Use new toolbars for easy access to the commands and features you use most often for specific Word features, such as Borders, Outlining, Drawing, Forms, and Databases.	Lessons 1, 10, 12, 13, and 15
Use multiple level undo and redo options to reverse or reapply the last several changes you made.	Lesson 1
Use context-sensitive drag-and-drop editing to avoid extra spaces and moved text.	Lesson 1
Use AutoCorrect to correct your spelling.	Lessons 2 and 5
Preview your entire document in the Print Preview window.	Lesson 4
Print non-sequential pages.	Lesson 4
Use AutoText (in place of glossaries in Word 2.0) to insert any amount of boilerplate text or graphics in a document.	Lesson 5
Use new search and replace features.	Lesson 5
Add page numbers to facing pages.	Lesson 7
Use AutoFormat to improve the appearance of your document automatically. AutoFormat also creates and applies styles for efficient formatting.	Lesson 9

To learn how to	See in this *Step by Step* book
Create character styles to apply consistent character formatting to words and phrases.	Lesson 8
Use wizards as a fast way to create basic business and personal documents. You provide the basic information for the document and the wizard creates the document for you.	Lesson 9
Use the Table AutoFormat feature to create attractive tables automatically. Select one of several table and list styles, and Microsoft Word automatically applies borders, shading, and even character formatting to improve the appearance of your tables.	Lesson 10
Use new column options to create columns of unequal width.	Lesson 11
Use Drop Caps to create special formatting effects in paragraphs.	Lesson 12
Use drag-and-drop techniques to copy or move text across several open documents.	Lesson 14
Create online forms using the Forms toolbar.	Lesson 15
Use the new Mail Merge Helper to merge documents containing boilerplate text with documents that contain customized information.	Lesson 16

1 Basic Skills

Creating a Document

If you are new to word processing, see "Getting Ready," earlier in this book.

In Microsoft Word, it's easy to create documents and make them look the way you want. In this lesson, you will type a short document and then use many of the formatting and editing options that are available with a simple click of the mouse button. You will apply formatting to an address in a letter to create and save a personalized company letterhead. At the end of the lesson, your document will look similar to the following illustration.

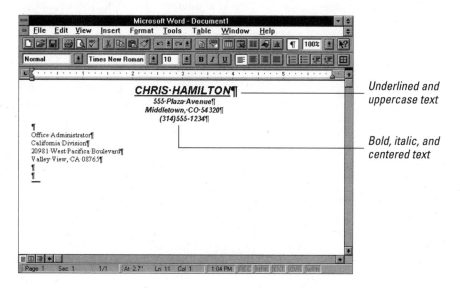

Underlined and uppercase text

Bold, italic, and centered text

You will learn how to:

- Type text in a new document window.
- Select text to edit or format.
- Use the Standard toolbar to perform common word processing tasks.
- Delete, replace, and move text.
- Change the appearance of text and its position on the page.
- Name and save your document for future use.
- End your Microsoft Word session.

Estimated lesson time: 40 minutes

The Document Window

When you start Microsoft Word, you see the application window with a new, empty document automatically opened for you. The new document assumes you are using standard 8.5-by-11-inch paper, with 1.25-inch left and right margins, and 1-inch top and bottom margins.

Typing Text

You can begin typing in the empty document window, just as you would on a clean sheet of paper. The blinking insertion point, which is already positioned for you at the top of the window, shows where the text you type will appear. As you type, the insertion point moves to the right, leaving behind a stream of text.

Type the sender's name and address

Follow the instructions below to begin this document as you would begin a typical letter. If you make a typing mistake, press the BACKSPACE key to delete the mistake, and then type the correct text. The first few lines of the document contain the sender's name and address. This text will become part of the letterhead you can use when you create any correspondence.

1   Type **chris hamilton** and press ENTER.

Do not capitalize the sender's name. Later in this lesson, you learn to use the Change Case feature to modify the case for you.

2   Type **555 Plaza Avenue** and press ENTER.

3   Type **Middletown, CO 54320** and press ENTER.

4   Press ENTER to create a blank line.

Type the recipient's name and address

Continue typing the rest of the document by including the recipient's name and address.

1   Type **Office Administrator** and press ENTER.

2   Type **California Division** and press ENTER.

3   Type **20981 West Pacifica Boulevard** and press ENTER.

4   Type **Valley View, CA 08765** and press ENTER.

5   Press ENTER to create a blank line.

6   Type **Dear Office Administrator,** and press ENTER.

7   Press ENTER to create another blank line.

Your screen should look like the following.

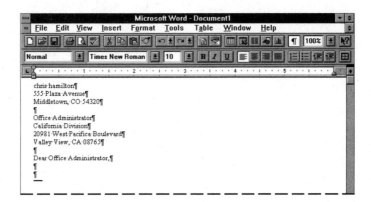

Type a paragraph of text

When you type paragraphs that are longer than one line, do not press ENTER at the end of each line. Instead, just keep typing. When the insertion point approaches the right margin, it automatically moves to the next line as you continue typing. This is known as *wordwrap*. Press ENTER to begin a new paragraph or to create a blank line.

▶ Type the paragraph below without pressing ENTER. If you make a typing mistake, press the BACKSPACE key to delete the mistake and then type the correct text, or simply ignore the mistake and correct it later.

West Coast Sales is getting bigger and better all the time. To help us move into the 21st century, the company is using the best tools available: from the telephone technology in Customer Service to the word processing technology in our offices. There are many features you are sure to appreciate. If you liked version 2.0, you'll be inspired to new heights of productivity with Microsoft Word 6.0. I'll be heading up the effort to get everyone up to speed right away. Look for communications from me every week.

Display paragraph marks and special symbols

Show/Hide ¶

When you typed the address for the letter, Microsoft Word inserted a paragraph mark (¶) each time you pressed ENTER. If you cannot see the paragraph marks, you can display them by clicking the Show/Hide button.

▶ Click the Show/Hide ¶ button.

In Word, a paragraph can be any amount of text that ends with a paragraph mark, from a word or two, as in your name, to several lines. Even a blank line is a paragraph; it's called an *empty paragraph*. Microsoft Word also displays small dots that represent the spaces between words, created when you press the SPACEBAR. Paragraph marks and dots are nonprinting symbols. They will not appear in printed documents. Your document should look similar to the following illustration.

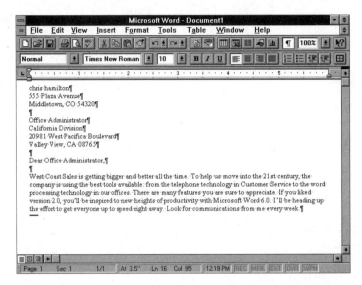

You can work with the paragraph marks and space marks displayed or hidden, simply by clicking the Show/Hide ¶ button. With the marks displayed, you can see how many empty paragraphs fall between lines of text.

Insert text into the practice paragraph

You can easily insert new text anywhere in a document.

1 Position the pointer just before the word "telephone" as shown in the following illustration, and then click. If you are working with paragraph and space marks displayed, click immediately to the right of the space mark.

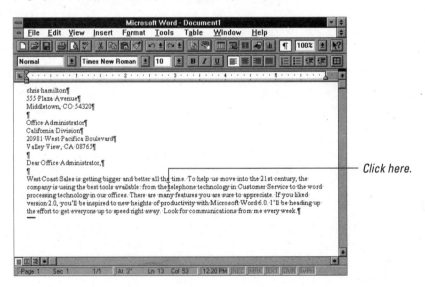

— *Click here.*

2   Type **latest** and then press SPACEBAR to insert a space between the two words.

Microsoft Word makes room in the document for the new word.

Deleting and Replacing Text

You can delete and replace text in your document. To indicate which text you want to change, you must first *select* it. Once you've selected the text, you can click a button to do something to the text. Selected text is highlighted, that is, shown in white letters against a dark background, depending on your Windows settings.

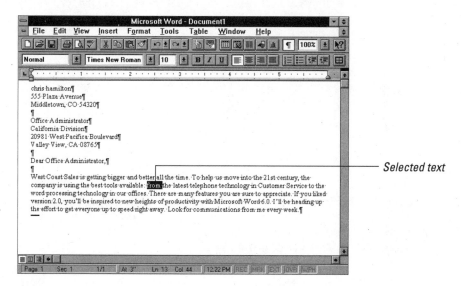

Selected text

Select and delete a word

You can always press BACKSPACE to delete characters if you make a mistake as you type. Of course, it would be cumbersome to backspace through an entire document. Instead you can delete, or "cut," mistakes, whether the mistake is one word or many paragraphs.

1   In the second line of the practice paragraph, place the pointer in the word "from."

2   Double-click to select the word and the space that follows it. This keeps the spacing correct after you delete a word.

3   On the Standard toolbar, click the Cut button to remove the word from the text.

The text in the document moves over to fill the space left by the deleted text.

Cut

Reversing Your Changes

A handy feature in Microsoft Word is the Undo button, which reverses or "erases" your last actions. For example, clicking the Undo button will put the word that you just cut back into your document. Whenever something happens that is confusing or is not what you intended, click the Undo button as your *next* action.

Change your mind

Undo

▶ On the Standard toolbar, click the Undo button to reverse your last change.

If this did not put the word back in the paragraph, you might have pressed another key before you clicked the Undo button. Clicking Undo once reverses only the last change.

Undo more changes

You can also click the arrow next to the Undo button to see a list of actions you can reverse. For example, if you want to return the document to the way it looked before you made the last two changes, you can scroll to that action in the Undo list and select it.

▶ On the Standard toolbar, click the arrow next to the Undo button, and then select the second change in the list to undo your last two actions.

All of the changes you made between then and now are reversed. Because several changes in sequence often depend on preceding changes, you cannot select an individual action without undoing all the actions that appear above it in the list.

Change your mind again

The Redo button on the Standard toolbar allows you to reverse an undo action. Reverse the results of the last change by clicking the Redo button.

▶ On the Standard toolbar, click the Redo button to undo your last action.

Redo

Select text and replace it

Double-clicking a word selects it, but you can select any amount of text by dragging across it with the mouse. Once you've selected text, the next text you type—regardless of its length—replaces the selection.

1   In the practice paragraph, drag to select the sentence, "There are many features you are sure to appreciate."

Tip   If you didn't select the amount of text that you wanted, click outside the selection, and then try again. As you drag, keep the mouse pointer in the line of the text that you want to select.

---

2   Type the following words: **That's why I'm writing this letter in the new version of Microsoft Word.**

3   Check the spacing before and after the new text you typed. To add a space, position the insertion point and press the SPACEBAR.

4   Click the Undo button to return to the original wording.

Moving and Copying Text

You can also re-use text, as well as rearrange text in your documents. The "drag and drop" feature in Microsoft Word allows you to copy and move text to a new location simply by dragging it where you want it.

Select text and move it

The following procedure shows how to move the second sentence to the end of the paragraph by selecting and dragging it.

1   Select the sentence, "If you liked version 2.0, you'll be inspired to new heights of productivity with Microsoft Word version 6.0." Be sure you select the period and the space that follows the sentence.

Tip   You might find it easier to click where you want the selection to begin, and then, while holding down the SHIFT key, click where you want the selection to end. Microsoft Word selects everything between the first place you clicked and the second place you clicked. This technique is useful when you want to select a large amount text that does not appear on the screen at one time.

---

2   Position the mouse pointer over the selection until the pointer turns into a left-pointing arrow.

3   Hold down the left mouse button. A small, dotted box and a dotted insertion point appear. Drag until the dotted insertion point is at the end of the paragraph. Then release the mouse button.

4   Click anywhere outside the selected text to remove the highlighting. Then click in front of the sentence you just moved, and press the SPACEBAR to insert a space if no space exists already.

Your moved text should look like the following illustration.

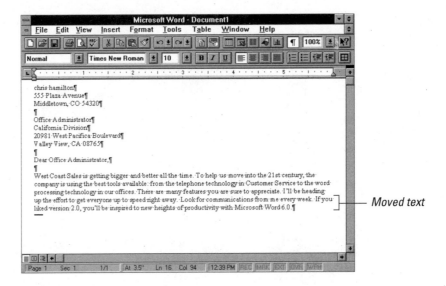

Moved text

Copy text using the mouse

Copying text with the mouse is similar to moving text with the mouse. For example, you can quickly copy the text "Microsoft Word" and insert it at another location in the paragraph.

1 Drag to select "Microsoft Word" in the last sentence (the one you just moved).

2 Hold down the CTRL key on the keyboard, point to the selected text, and then hold down the mouse button.

3 Drag the dotted insertion point to the place immediately before the word "version." Release the CTRL key and the mouse button.

A copy of the selected text is inserted; the original remains where it was, unchanged.

4 Click anywhere outside the selected text to remove the highlighting.

5 Click in front of the text you just copied, and press the SPACEBAR to insert a space, if necessary.

Your screen should look like the following picture.

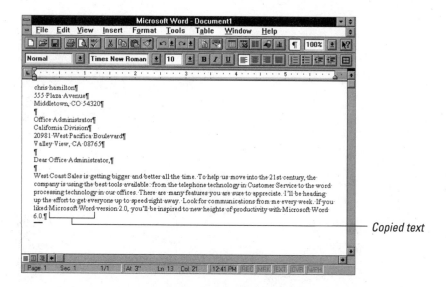

Copied text

Using Context-Sensitive Drag and Drop

As you noticed, when you double-click to select a word, the space after the word is
automatically selected. When you move your selection to a new location in the middle
of a sentence, you don't need to type a space to separate it from the other words.
However, there are times (at the end of a sentence, for example) when you do not
want this space in the new location. With Microsoft Word, you have the option to
automatically eliminate the space before a period when you move a selection to the
end of a sentence. With the smart-cut-and-paste feature turned on, you don't have to
remember to add or delete extra spaces between words or at the end of sentences.

Activate the smart-cut-and-paste feature

The smart-cut-and-paste feature allows you to enable context-sensitive drag-and-drop
editing. Use the Options command from the Tools menu to enable this feature.

1   From the <u>T</u>ools menu, choose <u>O</u>ptions.

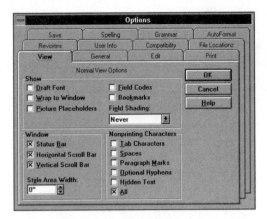

2   In the Options dialog box, click the Edit tab.

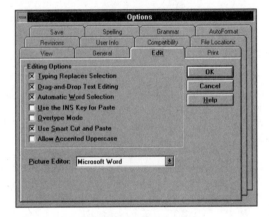

3   Click the Use Smart Cut And Paste check box.

If this check box already has a check in it, it means that the smart-cut-and-paste feature was already turned on. If you clear the check box, you turn off this setting, so leave it checked.

4   Click OK to return to your document.

Select text and move it

With the smart-cut-and-paste feature turned on, you don't have to remember to add or delete extra spaces between words or at the end of sentences.

1   Select the words "every week" in the second to the last sentence.

2   Position the mouse pointer over the selection until the pointer turns into a left-pointing arrow.

3   Hold down the left mouse button. A small, dotted box and a dotted insertion point appear. Drag until the dotted insertion point is in front of the word "from." Then release the mouse button.

Notice that no space appears between the last word and the period. The remaining lessons in this book assume you have selected the smart-cut-and-paste option.

Changing the Look of Your Text

When you change the appearance of text—by centering it or making it bold or italic, for example—you are *formatting* it. The concept of "select then do" is important in formatting. You first select the text you want to format, and then you apply one or more formats to it.

Bold, italic, and underlining are formats you can apply or remove quickly by clicking buttons on the Formatting toolbar. For example, you can select text, and then click the Bold button to apply bold formatting. If you select the text, and then click the Bold button again, you remove the formatting. Other character formats are available in the Font dialog box.

Note   Your printer might not be able to print both underlining and bold, or other combinations of formatting, if they are applied to the same word. Check your printer documentation for any limitations.

Display the Formatting toolbar

To format your text quickly, you need to display the Formatting toolbar. Follow these steps if the Formatting toolbar is not already displayed.

1   From the View menu, choose Toolbars.

2   In the Toolbars dialog box, select the Formatting toolbar check box, if it is not already selected.

3   Click the OK button.

The Formatting toolbar appears below the Standard toolbar.

Selecting lines of text

At the left of every paragraph, there's an invisible selection bar. By clicking in the selection bar, you can select an entire line. You can also drag the mouse pointer down the selection bar to select several lines at once. For the following steps, you need to select the name and address.

1   Position the mouse pointer to the left of the name "chris hamilton."

When the mouse pointer is in the selection bar, the pointer changes to a right-pointing arrow.

2   Click to select the line.

3   With the first line selected, hold down the mouse button, and drag down the selection bar to select both lines of the address. Release the mouse button when all three lines are selected.

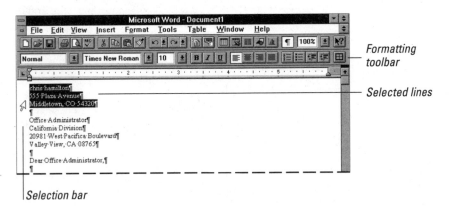

Formatting toolbar

Selected lines

Selection bar

Change the look of the text

Bold

Italic

1   With the first three lines of the document selected, click the Bold and Italic buttons on the Formatting toolbar.

The Bold, Italic, and Underline buttons each apply formatting the first time you click them, and then remove the formatting when you click them again. The formatted text looks like the following illustration.

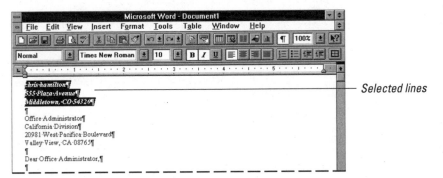

Selected lines

2   Click in the selection bar for the first line of the document.

This unselects the second and third lines, while selecting the first line.

3   Click the Underline button on the Formatting toolbar.

The formatted text looks like the following illustration.

Underline

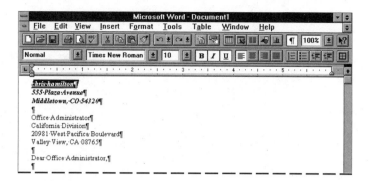

Change the design and size of text

Microsoft Word displays your text in the *font* and *point size* in which it will print. The font is the design of the text characters (letters and numbers); the point size is their size. You can change the font and point size for selected text by making selections from the Font and Size lists in the Formatting toolbar.

1   With the first line selected, hold down the mouse button, and drag down the selection bar to select the remaining lines of the address. Release the mouse button when all three lines are selected.

2   To display the list of fonts, click the down arrow next to the Font box.

   The font names in your list may be different from those in this illustration.

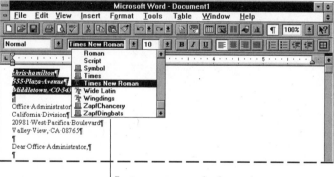

Fonts you can use for formatting text

If you see symbols or lines instead of "chris"

You selected a font that converts your text to symbols or lines. To see the name again, select another font.

3   Click Arial from the list of font names.

   You might have to scroll through the list to find it. All three lines change to the Arial font.

4   Select the first line again.

5   To display a list of point sizes for the font you've selected, click the down arrow next to the Font Size box.

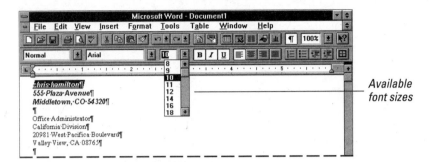

Available font sizes

6   Click 16 from the list of point sizes.

Note   A point is a standard measurement used in the publishing industry. There are 72 points in an inch, 36 points in one-half inch, and 18 points in one-quarter inch.

Change the case of the text

Microsoft Word makes it easy to change the capitalization of the characters in your selection. The Change Case command gives you the option to select from four standard capitalization schemes. In this exercise, you change the first character of each word to appear in uppercase. This is called *title case*.

1   Select the first line if it is not already selected.

2   From the Format menu, choose Change Case.

The Change Case dialog box appears.

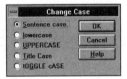

3   Click the Title Case option button.

4   Click the OK button to return to your document.

The first line appears in title case.

Select another case style

The uppercase style formats all selected characters in uppercase. This style creates a more dramatic appearance for a document, such as company stationery.

1   Select the first line if it is not already selected.

2   From the Format menu, choose Change Case.

3   In the Change Case dialog box, click the Uppercase check box.

4   Click the OK button to return to your document.

Your document looks like the following illustration.

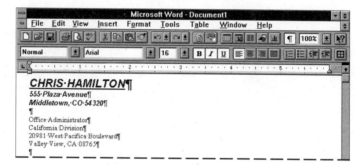

Change the alignment

1   Select all three lines of the address.

2   Click the Center button on the Formatting toolbar.

The address is now centered horizontally on the page. Your document looks like the following illustration.

Center

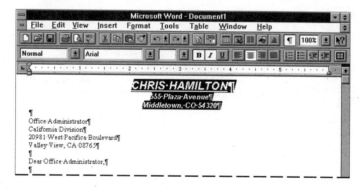

Add a new paragraph

Microsoft Word "stores" formatting information in the paragraph mark at the end of each paragraph. Pressing ENTER in front of a paragraph mark copies the paragraph mark to the next line and carries the paragraph formatting into the new paragraph.

Tip If you do not want a new paragraph to have the formatting of the one preceding it, press CTRL+SPACEBAR before you begin typing the new paragraph. This removes, or *clears,* the formatting.

1 Move the insertion point to the end of the last line of the address, as shown in the following illustration.

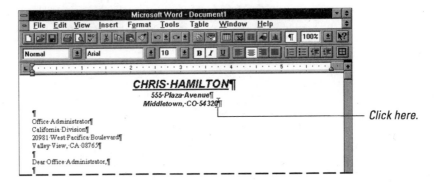

— Click here.

2 Press ENTER.

3 Type **(314) 555-1234**

Note that the phone number has the same formatting as the paragraph above it.

Delete the practice paragraph and salutation

1 Double-click in the selection bar to the left of the practice paragraph to select the entire paragraph. Hold the mouse button down after you double-click.

Tip Another way to select an entire paragraph is to triple-click anywhere in the paragraph.

2 Drag upward to select the salutation.

3 On the Standard toolbar, click the Cut button to delete the paragraph from the document.

Your completed document looks like the following illustration.

Cut

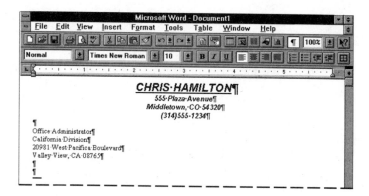

The work you've done is currently stored in the computer's memory. To save the work for future use, you must give the document a name and store it on a disk. After you save it, the letterhead document is available each time you want to use it as stationery for a letter.

Save the document

When you save a document, you must give it a name and specify where you want to store it. For the documents you use in this book, it is a good idea to save the documents in the same directory as the Step by Step practice files. You specify how you want to save your file in the Save As dialog box.

Save

1   On the Standard toolbar, click the Save button.

Microsoft Word displays the Save As dialog box. The insertion point is automatically positioned in the File Name box, ready for you to type a name for the document.

Document names can be no more than eight letters long. They cannot have spaces in them. You can use either uppercase or lowercase letters.

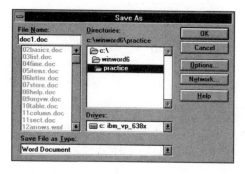

2   Type **letter01**

Microsoft Word automatically provides the DOC filename extension. All Microsoft Word documents are saved with this extension.

3   In the Drives box, verify that drive C is selected, if this is where you stored your Step by Step practice files. If you need assistance, see "Getting Ready," earlier in this book.

4   In the Directories list, check to be sure that the PRACTICE directory is the current directory and that its name appears above the Drive list. If it does not, double-click PRACTICE to make it the current directory.

   If you can't locate the PRACTICE directory, be sure you are in the Microsoft Word home directory.

5   To close the dialog box and save the document as you've specified, click the OK button, or press ENTER. It is best to name and save a document soon after you start working on it. After that, you should continue to save the document as you work. The Save button on the Standard toolbar makes this quick and easy to do. It's a good idea to save a document every 15 minutes or so as you work. This ensures that only 15 minutes of work would be lost if the power to your computer is interrupted.

One Step Further

The Standard and Formatting toolbars provide the basic tools you need to format and edit documents. After using various formatting combinations in your document, you can save time by reapplying formats with the Format Painter button.

1   With the insertion point after the name "Chris Hamilton," press ENTER.

2   Type **West Coast Sales**

3   Select the line you just entered.

4   Click the Underline button on the Formatting toolbar to remove the underlining for this selected text.

5   Click to place the insertion point in the first line, which reads "Chris Hamilton."

Format Painter

6   On the Standard toolbar, click the Format Painter button to temporarily store formatting information.

7   Move the insertion point to the start of the line containing the phone number.

8   Drag the Format Painter button across the line to apply the formatting from the first line to this line as well.

If You Want to Continue to the Next Lesson

1   From the File menu, choose Close.

2   If a message appears asking whether to save changes, click the Yes button.

   Choosing this command closes the active document; it does not exit the Microsoft Word application.

If You Want to Quit Microsoft Word for Now

1 From the File menu, choose Exit.

This command closes both the document and the Microsoft Word application.

2 If a message appears asking whether to save changes, click the Yes button.

Microsoft Word will prompt you to save your changes if you attempt to close the document or the application before you save your most recent changes.

Lesson Summary

To	Do this	Button
Create a new paragraph or blank line	Press ENTER.	
Insert text into existing text	Position the insertion point where you want the new text, and then type.	
Display or hide paragraph marks	Click the Show/Hide ¶ button on the Formatting toolbar.	¶
Select a word	Double-click the word you want to select.	
Select any amount of text	Drag over the text you want to select, or click where you want the selection to begin, hold down SHIFT, and then click where you want the selection to end.	
Select entire lines	Point to the left of the line in the selection bar, and then click. To select more than one line, select a line, and then drag up or down in the selection bar.	
Select a paragraph	Double-click while the pointer is pointing to the left of the paragraph in the selection bar. Or triple-click in the paragraph.	
Delete text	Select the text, and then click the Cut button on the Standard toolbar.	✂
Replace text	Select the text, and then type new text.	
Move or copy text	Select the text, and then drag the selection to a new location. To copy text, hold down CTRL while dragging the text.	
Activate the smart-cut-and-paste feature	From the Tools menu, choose Options. Click the Edit tab, and then select the Smart Cut And Paste option. Click OK.	

To	Do this	Button
Apply bold, italic, or underlining	Select the text, and then click buttons on the Formatting toolbar.	**B** *I* U
Change a font or point size	Select the text, click the down arrow next to the Font or Points list box, and then click a font or point size.	
Change the case of text	Select the text to change. From the Format menu, choose Change Case. Select the desired case option. Click OK.	
Reverse an action	Click the Undo button immediately after an action.	
Reverse an undo action	Click the Redo button immediately after an action.	
Center text	Select the text and click the Center button on the Formatting toolbar.	
Save a new document	Click the Save button, and then type a name that has a maximum of eight letters.	
End a Microsoft Word session	Choose Exit from the File menu.	

For more information on	See
Creating and formatting a simple document	Chapter 4, "Creating your First Document" in *Microsoft Word Quick Results*
The Microsoft Word window	Chapter 1, "The Word Workplace" in *Microsoft Word User's Guide*
Opening and saving documents	Chapter 21, "Opening, Saving, and Protecting Documents" in *Microsoft Word User's Guide*
Typing and editing text	Chapter 2, "Typing and Editing" in *Microsoft Word User's Guide*

Preview of the Next Lesson

In the next lesson, you'll open an existing document and learn how to take advantage of work that's already done by copying useful text and changing it. You'll also learn how to move text by using the buttons on the Standard toolbar. At the end of the lesson, you'll use the Microsoft Word spelling checker.

Moving Around in a Document

By copying and moving text, you can easily take advantage of work you've already done. For example, you can copy text, move it to a different location, and edit it. In this lesson, you'll copy and move text within a document using buttons on the Standard toolbar. You'll also check the spelling in the document using the Microsoft Word spelling checker.

You will learn how to:

- Open an existing document.

- Move text to a new location in a document.

- Copy text to a new location in a document.

- Scroll through a document.

- Check and correct spelling.

Estimated lesson time: 30 minutes

If you left Microsoft Word at the end of the last lesson

For additional instructions about starting Microsoft Word, see "Getting Ready," earlier in this book.

If you haven't already started Microsoft Word, do the following.

1   At the C:\ prompt, type **win** and press ENTER.

2   Double-click the Program Manager icon if the window is not open.

3   Double-click the Microsoft Word group icon if the group is not open.

4   Double-click the Microsoft Word icon.

5   If you see the Tip Of The Day dialog box, click the OK button or click the Show Tips At Start Up check box if you no longer want to see the Tip dialog box when you first start Microsoft Word.

Note   The remaining lessons in this book assume you have turned off the Tip Of The Day option.

Opening a Document

As you learned in Lesson 1, a new, empty document window is displayed when you start Microsoft Word. You can also open an existing document and work on it in the same way you work on a new document. To open an existing document, you click the Open button on the Standard toolbar and specify the name of the document and where it's located.

Open a sample document

Open

1   On the Standard toolbar, click the Open button.

A dialog box appears where you can select the name of the document you want. Depending on where the Step by Step files are stored, your dialog box might look different from the following.

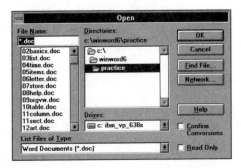

2   In the Drives list, be sure the drive displayed is the one where the Step by Step practice files are stored. Click the down arrow next to the list box to see and select other drives.

3   In the Directories list, double-click PRACTICE. This is the subdirectory where the Step by Step practice files are stored.

If you do not see PRACTICE in the list of directories, see the Appendix, "Matching the Exercises."

4   In the File Name list, click 02BASICS.DOC.

5   Click the OK button.

Microsoft Word closes the dialog box and displays the document 02BASICS.DOC. Ignore any spelling errors for now. At the end of this lesson, you'll use the Microsoft Word spelling checker to correct them.

If you share your computer with others who use Microsoft Word, the screen display might have changed since your last lesson. For the illustrations in this lesson, the ruler is hidden to display additional lines of text. You do not need to hide the ruler as you work. If your screen does not look similar to the following illustration—with the exception of the ruler—see the Appendix, "Matching the Exercises."

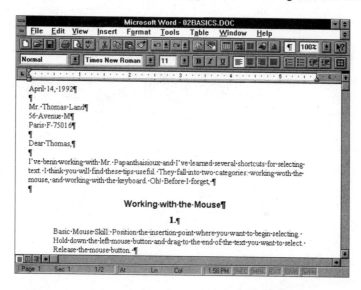

Save the document with a new name

To choose a command, click the menu name at the top of the window, and then click the name of the command.

In this lesson and the ones that follow, you will begin by giving the practice document a new name. When you rename a document, any changes you make do not affect the original. This way, if you want to repeat a lesson, the original practice document will still be intact.

1   From the File menu, choose Save As.

2   In the File Name box, type **basics02**

3   Click the OK button.

Display paragraph marks

Show/Hide ¶

▶   If paragraph marks are not displayed on your screen, click the Show/Hide ¶ button on the Standard toolbar.

Scrolling Through a Document

To prevent acciden-
tally saving changes
in the original
practice document
Be sure the
AutoSave option is
not turned on. From
the Tools menu,
choose Options.
Click the Save tab,
and clear the
Automatic Save
check box. Click the
OK button to return to
the document.

The sample document you're working on contains more text than you can see on the screen at one time. To see the rest of the text, you need to *scroll* through the document. Scrolling means moving text over the screen to bring the text that's currently above or below the window into view. You use the *scroll arrows* and *scroll box* located on the *vertical scroll bar* to move the document text through the window.

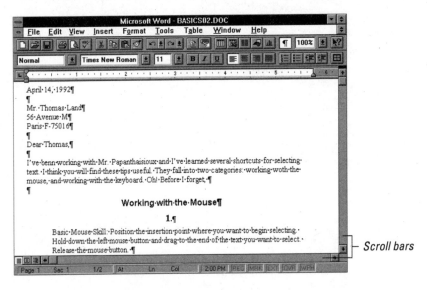
— Scroll bars

If a solid line appears
across the window
Double-clicking the
split box, located at
the top of the scroll
bar, divides the
document window.
To remove the
horizontal line, point
to the solid black bar
in the middle of the
scroll bar (the split
box) between the
two scroll arrows.
When the mouse
pointer changes to a
double-headed
arrow, double-click.

You can use any of three methods for scrolling, depending on how quickly you want to move through the document. You can scroll line by line, window by window, or you can jump immediately to the beginning, middle, or end of the document.

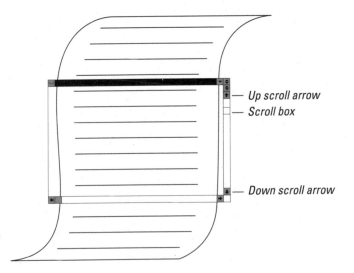
— Up scroll arrow
— Scroll box
— Down scroll arrow

Scroll line by line

Each time you click a scroll arrow, Microsoft Word changes the screen to show you one more line.

1   Click the down scroll arrow once to see the line of text that is currently below the window display. Click the down scroll arrow a few more times.

2   Click the up scroll arrow a few times to see the text that is currently above the window display.

3   Point to the down scroll arrow and hold down the mouse button.

Text will "roll" by very quickly line by line. To stop scrolling, release the mouse button. As you scroll to the end of the document, you might notice a dotted line that extends across the page. This line indicates a page break. Microsoft Word adjusts the page break as you add and delete text.

Scroll window by window

To see text in the window area above or below the text currently displayed, simply click in the area above or below the scroll box.

1   To see the window of text above what you are currently viewing, click in the scroll bar above the scroll box.

2   To see the window of text below what you are currently viewing, click in the scroll bar below the scroll box.

3   Scroll to the beginning of the document.

Jump to a different part of the document

Dragging the scroll box to any location on the scroll bar is a quick way to jump to the beginning, middle, or end of a document, or anywhere in between. For example, if you want to work on text that is in the middle of the document, drag the scroll box halfway down the scroll bar.

1   To see the end of the document, drag the scroll box to the bottom of the scroll bar.

2   Drag the scroll box to the top of the scroll bar. (You cannot drag it off the scroll bar.)

The beginning of the document appears.

Moving and Copying Text Using the Standard Toolbar

In Lesson 1, you learned a quick way to move and copy text using the mouse, but in both cases, you could see the final destination for the text on the screen. If you need to move or copy text to a location you cannot see in the document, you can use buttons on the Standard toolbar to store the text until you display the new location.

The following illustration shows how you can use the Copy and Paste buttons on the Standard toolbar to insert text in a new location. When you copy text, Microsoft Word stores the copy on the *Clipboard* —a temporary storage area. The text remains on the Clipboard until you cut or copy other text, or until you exit Windows.

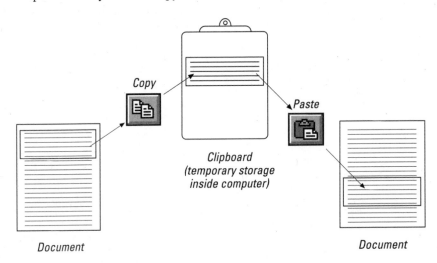

Clipboard
(temporary storage
inside computer)

Document

Document

Copy and edit a heading

*Remember, the area
to the left of the text
is called the
selection bar.*

By copying and editing existing text, you save time and reduce errors. If you copy the heading "Working with the Mouse" and insert the text in a new location, you only need to revise the last word to have a new heading, "Working with the Keyboard." Its formatting is identical to the original heading.

1   Select the text "Working with the Mouse." Be sure to include the paragraph mark.

2   On the Standard toolbar, click the Copy button.

Copy

You see no change in the document, but a copy of the selected text is placed on the Clipboard.

3   Click the down scroll arrow repeatedly to scroll line by line. Stop when the "4" is in the middle of the screen.

4   Position the insertion point in front of the "4."

Paste

5   On the Standard toolbar, click the Paste button.

Microsoft Word inserts a copy of the heading. The copied text is centered because the original centered paragraph mark, which stores paragraph formatting, was included in the selection.

Edit the new heading

▶ Double-click "Mouse" in the new heading, and type **Keyboard** to complete the new heading, as shown in the following illustration.

If text is inserted next to the selection, be sure the Typing Replaces Selection option is checked. For more information, see *Edit Options* in the Appendix, "Matching the Exercises."

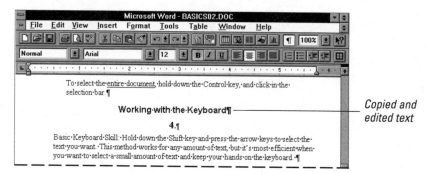

Copied and edited text

Moving Text Over a Long Distance

Moving text a long distance is similar to copying text a long distance, as you just did. The Standard toolbar provides buttons to make this easy. The difference is that instead of copying the text, you remove the text from the document and store it on the Clipboard. Then you scroll to where you want to insert the text and paste it back into the document.

Move text from the end of the document to the beginning

Use the following procedure to move the last sentence in the document to the beginning of the document.

1   Click the down scroll arrow until you can see "Sincerely."

2   Select the line that begins "I'm enclosing five sets of tips."

3   On the Standard toolbar, click the Cut button.

The text from the document is removed and stored on the Clipboard.

4   Drag the scroll box to the top of the scroll bar to move quickly to the top of the document.

5   Position the insertion point in front of the bold heading "Working with the Mouse."

Cut

Paste

6 On the Standard toolbar, click the Paste button to insert the text from the Clip-board.

The "Working with the Mouse" heading moves downward to make room for the text you insert.

Your document should look similar to the following illustration.

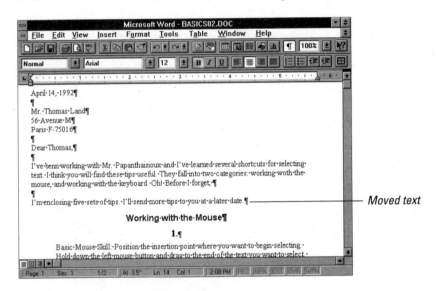

Moved text

Save the document

Save

▶ On the Standard toolbar, click the Save button.

The current version replaces the previous version. You will not see any change to the document. The status bar, however, displays a brief message indicating your document is being saved, and a thermometer-style display indicates its progress.

Checking the Spelling in a Document

Before you complete any document, you'll want to check for typographical and spelling errors. With the Microsoft Word spelling checker, you can do a quick and thorough job of *proofing* the document.

When you check the spelling in a document, the check begins at the insertion point and proceeds downward from there. Microsoft Word compares each word in the document to a standard, built-in dictionary. The spelling checker might find words such as your name, your company name, or a technical term that are spelled correctly but that are not in the standard dictionary. You can ignore these words as you check the spelling. In Lesson 6, you'll learn how to add such words to a custom dictionary.

Microsoft Word not only displays the misspelled word in the dialog box, but also highlights the word in the document. You can read the surrounding text to determine the correct spelling. If a word is spelled incorrectly, you have two choices for correcting it: You can re-type it, or you can select the correct spelling from a list.

Check the spelling

1 Scroll to the beginning of the document and position the insertion point in front of the first line (the date).

Tip You can also press CTRL+HOME to move the insertion point to the start of the document.

Spelling

2 On the Standard toolbar, click the Spelling button.

The Spelling dialog box appears when the spelling checker finds a word that is not in its dictionary.

3 In the selected misspelling, "benn" should be "been." The suggested spelling appears in the Change To box. Click the Change button.

Microsoft Word corrects the spelling in the document and selects the next misspelled word.

4 "Papanthaisioux" is a proper name that is spelled correctly. To have Microsoft Word ignore this instance of the name and all future instances in this document, click the Ignore All button.

5 Continue checking and correcting the spelling in the document.

For this word	Do this
woth	Click "with" in the list of suggested spellings, and then click the Change button. Because this can be a frequent mistake, you can also click the AutoCorrect button (you need to do this before you click the Change button). The next time you type "woth" followed by a space, Microsoft Word will automatically enter the correct spelling. (For more information, see Lesson 5.)
many	Note that the label in the dialog box has changed to "Repeated Word." The sentence contains two instances of the word "many" in a row. Click the Delete button.

For this word	Do this
arow	The spelling you want is the first suggested spelling. Click the Change button.
youneed	In the Change To box, correct the text. Because you make this mistake frequently, click the AutoCorrect button. Click the Change button to continue. The next time you type "youneed" and a space, Word will automatically correct the spelling for you.

6   Click the OK button when the spelling check is complete.

Save the document

Save

▶ On the Standard toolbar, click the Save button.

Microsoft Word saves the current version of this document in place of the previous version.

One Step Further

You might realize that you must make changes to your document after you have already checked its spelling. So that you don't have to spell check the entire document again, you can restrict the spelling check to only the text you select.

Add some new text to your document. Now that you have made a few AutoCorrect entries in your spelling dictionary, you can see for yourself how useful the AutoCorrect feature can be. After you enter the paragraph, check the spelling of the new text for additional typographical errors you might have made.

1   Move the insertion point to the end of the document. You can scroll or press CTRL+END.

2   Press ENTER to create a new paragraph.

3   Type the following text. Allow yourself to misspell the words as indicated so you can see AutoCorrect make corrections for you.

When youneed to move around quickly in a document, use the Ctrl key woth the Home and End keys. Press Crtl and Home to move the insettion point to the very beginning of the document. Press Ctrl woth the End key, if youneed to move the insertion point to the very end.

4   Limit the spelling check to the new text you added by selecting the paragraph first.

5   On the Standard toolbar, click the Spelling button.

Spelling

6   Microsoft Word checks the spelling in this paragraph only. Respond to each correction that appears in the Spelling dialog box.

For this word	Do this
Crtl	Select the text in the Change To box, and type Ctrl. Then click the Change button.
insettion	Click "insertion" in the list of suggested spellings, and then click the Change button.

7   Click the OK button when the spelling check is complete.

8   Click the No button when you see the message asking whether you want to continue checking from the beginning of the document.

If You Want to Continue to the Next Lesson

1   From the File menu, choose Close.

Remember, click the File menu, and then click the Close command.

2   If a message appears asking whether you want to save changes, check the Yes button.

Choosing this command closes the active document; it does not exit the Microsoft Word application.

If You Want to Quit Microsoft Word for Now

1   From the File menu, choose Exit.

2   If a message appears asking whether you want to save changes, check the No button.

Lesson Summary

To	Do this	Button
Open an existing document	On the Standard toolbar, click the Open button, and then select the document name from the File Name list. If you don't see the document name, check to make sure the correct drive and directory are selected.	
Scroll through a document	Click the scroll arrows on the scroll bar, drag the scroll box, or click above or below the scroll box.	

To	Do this	Button
Move text to a location not currently visible	Select the text, and click the Cut or Copy button on the Standard toolbar. Scroll to the new location, and click to place the insertion point. Click the Paste button to insert the selection.	
Check and correct the spelling in a document	On the Standard toolbar, click the Spelling button, and then change or ignore words as Microsoft Word selects them.	

For more information on	See in the *Microsoft Word User's Guide*
Opening and saving documents	Chapter 21, "Opening, Saving, and Protecting Documents"
Moving and copying text	Chapter 2, "Typing and Revising"
Scrolling through a document	Chapter 1, "The Word Workplace"
Checking the spelling of a document	Chapter 5, "Editing and Proofing Tools"

Preview of the Next Lesson

In the next lesson, you'll learn to add bullets or numbers to lists. You'll also learn how to indent paragraphs and how to set page margins. At the end of the lesson, you'll have another document for your quick reference notebook.

Formatting Paragraphs

Just as you can change the appearance of text using the toolbars, you can change the appearance of paragraphs. In this lesson, you'll learn about using the Formatting toolbar to indent text, adjust the margins, create tables, and add bullets and numbers to lists. Using commands from the menu, you'll further customize the appearance of paragraphs by changing line spacing and sorting lists. When you complete this lesson, your document will look like the following illustration.

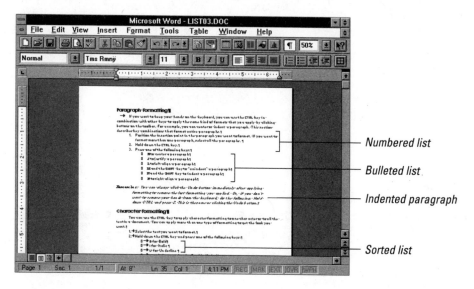

You will learn how to:

- Set left, right, and first-line indents.
- Create bulleted and numbered lists.
- Create a table.
- Sort a list.
- Change the size of the margins.
- Change the line spacing in a paragraph and between paragraphs.
- View an entire page on the screen.

Estimated lesson time: 35 minutes

If you left Microsoft Word at the end of the last lesson

For instructions about starting Microsoft Word, see "Getting Ready," earlier in this book.

If you haven't already started Microsoft Word, do the following.

1 At the C:\ prompt, type **win** and press ENTER.

2 Double-click the Program Manager icon if the window is not open.

3 Double-click the Microsoft Word group icon if the group is not open.

4 Double-click the Microsoft Word icon.

Open a sample document

Open

1 On the Standard toolbar, click the Open button.

2 In the Directories list, be sure the PRACTICE directory is open. If it is not, select the drive and directory for the Microsoft Word home directory, and click each subsequent directory until you locate PRACTICE.

3 In the File Name list, click 03LIST.DOC.

If you do not see 03LIST.DOC in the list of file names, check to be sure the correct drive and directory are open. If you need help, see "Getting Ready."

For information about opening a sample document, see Lesson 2.

4 Click the OK button.

If you share your computer with others who use Microsoft Word, the screen display might have changed since your last lesson. If your screen does not look similar to the following illustration, see the Appendix, "Matching the Exercises."

If you can't see all the text at the right margin
Depending on your display settings, you might need to adjust the magnification of your document. From the Zoom Control drop-down list at the right end of the Standard toolbar, select Page Width. This setting reduces the magnification so that you can see the entire width of the page.

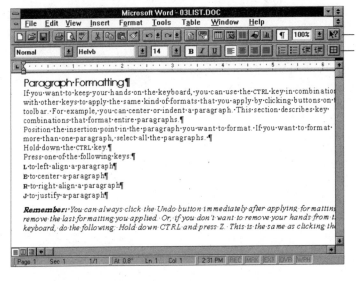

Standard toolbar
Formatting toolbar

Save the document with a new name

Give the document a new name so the changes you make in this lesson will not overwrite the original practice file.

1   From the File menu, choose Save As.

2   In the File Name box, type **list03**

3   Click the OK button.

Using the Tab Key to Indent Text

The basic way to indent a single line of text is with the TAB key. You can insert a tab in front of the first character you want to indent. If you are entering new text, you can press TAB before typing your text.

Use a tab to indent a line

1   Move the insertion point in front of the word "If" in the first paragraph.

2   Press TAB.

Your paragraph should look like the following illustration.

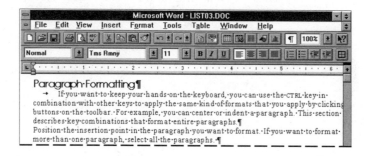

Setting Indents and Creating Lists

If you cannot see the Formatting toolbar Click a gray area on the Standard toolbar with the right mouse button. Select Formatting from the menu.

You can quickly indent the left edge of one or more paragraphs simply by clicking a button on the Formatting toolbar. You can also use the Formatting toolbar buttons to automatically add bullets or numbers to lists.

Using the Formatting Toolbar to Set Indents

With buttons on the Formatting toolbar, you can quickly indent one or more paragraphs. Each time you click the Increase Indent button, Microsoft Word indents the selected paragraph (or the paragraph containing the insertion point) one-half inch.

Microsoft Word has preset, or *default,* tab stops every one-half inch, so you are actually indenting to the next tab stop. The Formatting toolbar also has a Decrease Indent button if you've indented a paragraph too far.

 — *Formatting toolbar*

Use the indent buttons

1   Be sure the insertion point is still in the first paragraph below the heading "Paragraph Formatting."

2   On the Formatting toolbar, click the Increase Indent button.

Increase Indent

Your indented paragraph looks like the following illustration.

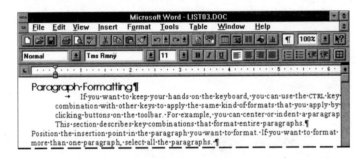

3   Click the Increase Indent button two more times.

Each time you click the button, the paragraph indents one-half inch and the text wraps in the paragraph to fit.

4   On the Formatting toolbar, click the Decrease Indent button to move the paragraph to the left. Continue clicking until the paragraph reaches the left margin—it will not move beyond the margin.

Decrease Indent

Indent several paragraphs

1   Select the next three paragraphs of the sample document, starting with the text "Position the insertion point" and ending with "Press one of the following keys:"

2   On the Formatting toolbar, click the Increase Indent button to indent the selected paragraphs one-half inch, as shown in the following illustration.

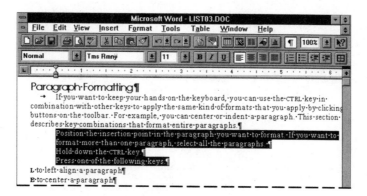

3   Select the next group of paragraphs, beginning with "L to left align" and ending with "J to justify."

4   On the Formatting toolbar, click the Increase Indent button twice to indent the selected items 1 inch.

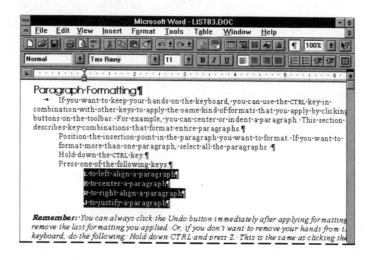

Creating Bulleted and Numbered Lists

Bulleted and numbered lists are common elements in many documents. Bullets clearly separate listed items from one another, emphasizing each point; numbers show sequence. Using buttons on the Formatting toolbar, you can quickly turn a series of paragraphs into a bulleted or numbered list.

Create a bulleted list

1   Be sure the group of paragraphs that begins "L to left align" is still selected.

2   On the Formatting toolbar, click the Bullets button.

Bullets

***If you see codes
instead of bullets***

*If you do not see
bullets, but see
{symbol ...} instead,
you are viewing the
codes that produce
the bullets. To see
the bullets, select
Options from the
Tools menu. On the
View tab, clear the
Field Codes check
box.*

A bullet appears in front of each selected paragraph and the indents adjust to separate the text from the bullets.

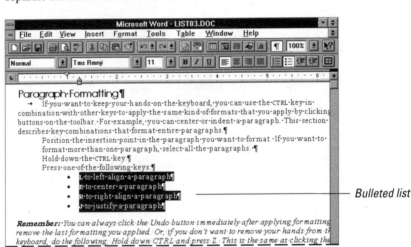

—— *Bulleted list*

Create a numbered list

1   Select the three paragraphs directly above the bulleted list.

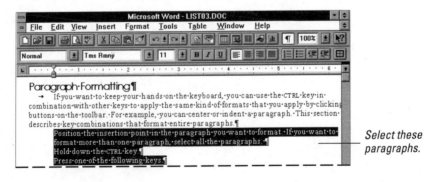

—— *Select these
paragraphs.*

Numbering

2   On the Formatting toolbar, click the Numbering button.

The list is numbered and the indents adjust to separate the text from the numbers. Notice that when the paragraph is longer than one line, as it is in step 1, and the second line of text aligns with the one above, as shown in the following illustration.

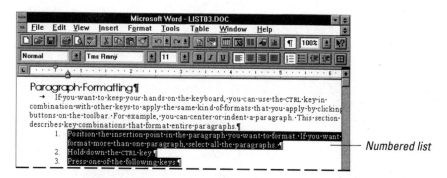

Numbered list

Tip   Although the Formatting toolbar buttons are the quickest way to create a numbered or bulleted list, many more options are available with the Bullets And Numbering command on the Format menu.

Setting Custom Indents

Clicking the Formatting toolbar buttons is the fastest way to adjust a left indent in one-half inch increments. Sometimes, however, you might want to use different settings in your document. You can use the ruler at the top of your screen to set custom indents. The ruler is preset to show inches, and each inch is divided into eighths.

The triangular markers on the ruler control the indents of the current paragraph (the one you've selected or the one that contains the insertion point). The left side of the ruler has three icons. The top triangle controls the first line of the paragraph; the bottom triangle controls the remaining lines of the paragraph. The small square under the bottom triangle, called the *paragraph indent marker,* controls the entire left edge of the paragraph. The triangle on the right side of the ruler controls the right edge of the paragraph.

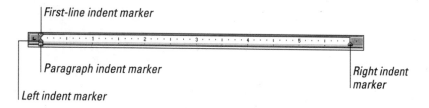

First-line indent marker

Paragraph indent marker

Right indent marker

Left indent marker

Display the ruler

To complete this lesson, you will need to display the ruler. Do this step if your ruler is not already displayed.

▶ From the View menu, choose Ruler.

Set a custom left indent

In the following procedure, you'll drag the paragraph indent marker to adjust the entire left edge of the paragraph, including the first line.

Clicking the scroll arrow scrolls the document line by line.

1 Click the down arrow of the vertical scroll bar until the paragraph that begins with "Remember" is near the top of the window. The insertion point should be somewhere in the paragraph.

2 Drag the paragraph indent marker just past the one-half inch mark on the ruler and then release the mouse button.

Both the top and bottom triangles move with the square. A dotted line appears to help you see where the new indent will be. When you release the mouse button, the text moves to align with the paragraph indent marker.

If a triangle moves

Both the bottom and top markers should move when you drag the square. If only one marker moves, it means the mouse pointer dragged a triangle instead of the square. On the Standard toolbar, click the Undo button. Then point to the square and try again.

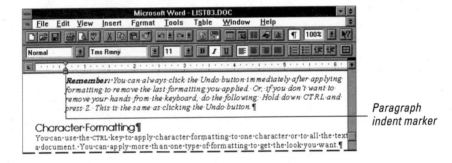

Paragraph indent marker

Set a right indent

▶ With the insertion point still in the paragraph, drag the *right indent marker* (the triangle at the right end of the ruler) to the 5.5-inch mark.

You might need to scroll to the right to see the right indent marker, and then scroll back to the left edge when you are done.

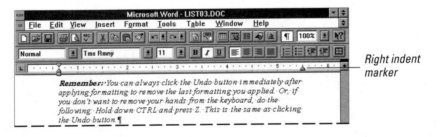

Right indent marker

Set a hanging indent

The top triangle on the left is called the *first-line indent marker*. This marker controls only the first line of a paragraph.

If both triangles moved

Only the top, or first-line indent, marker should move. If both markers move, it means the mouse pointer dragged the square instead of the top triangle. On the Standard toolbar, click the Undo button. Then point to the top triangle and try again.

▶   With the insertion point still positioned in the italic paragraph, drag the first-line indent marker to the far left edge of the ruler.

The first line extends to the left of the paragraph, with the rest of the paragraph "hanging" below it. This creates what is called a *hanging indent*.

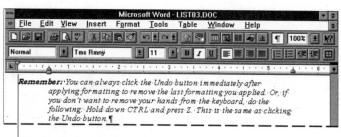

First-line indent marker

Indent the first line

1   Click in the paragraph under the heading "Character Formatting."

2   Drag the first-line indent marker (the top triangle) to the one-half inch mark.

The paragraph should look similar to the following illustration.

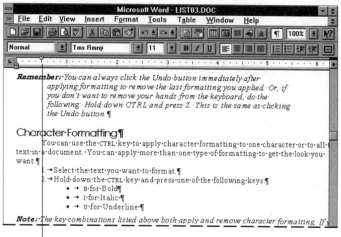

First-line indent marker

Indent another paragraph

1   Scroll downward to display all of the paragraph that begins with the word "Note," and then click in that paragraph.

2   Drag the paragraph indent marker (the square) just past the one-half inch mark.

3   Drag the right indent marker to the 5.25-inch mark.

Further customize the left indent

1   Be sure the insertion point is still in the paragraph that begins "Note."

2   Drag the bottom-left indent marker to 1 inch.

The first line does not move. The paragraph should look similar to the following.

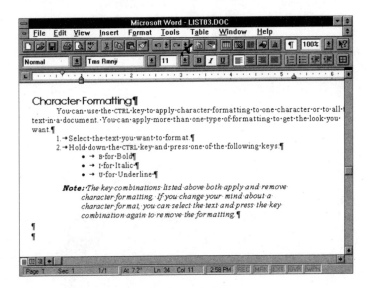

Tip   If you know the exact measurements that you need for indents and you prefer to enter the measurements in a dialog box instead of dragging markers on the ruler, use the Paragraph command on the Format menu.

Sorting a List

Sorting a list in alphabetical order helps organize information in your document. You can sort a list by selecting all the items in the list you want sorted and choosing the Sort Text command on the Table menu. These steps show you how easily you can perform simple sorting in a list. Later in this book, you learn about additional sorting options and features.

Sort a list

1 Select the bulleted list of keyboard shortcuts that begins with "L to left align a paragraph."

2 From the Table menu, choose Sort Text.

The dialog box appears and displays different sorting options from which you can choose. Because you want to sort the list in alphabetical order (from A to Z) you don't need to make any changes in this dialog box.

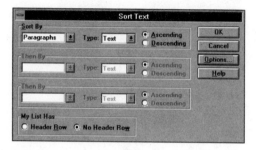

3 Click the OK button.

Your list is sorted alphabetically by the first character in the paragraph.

Changing Paragraph Formatting

In addition to formatting with the ruler and toolbars, you can change the appearance of paragraphs with the Paragraph command on the Format menu. In the Paragraph dialog box, you can change the line spacing of a paragraph and the space between paragraphs, as well as indentation and alignment. Options you set with this command affect entire paragraphs, as does formatting you specify with the toolbars.

If you know the exact measurement you want for indents, the Paragraph dialog box provides an opportunity for greater precision in comparison to what is available on the Formatting toolbar and ruler. For instance, you can specify exact measurements and preview the effect on a sample paragraph displayed in the dialog box.

1 Place the insertion point in the paragraph that begins with "Remember."

2 From the Format menu, choose Paragraph.

Word displays the Paragraph dialog box. In the Preview box, you see a preview of the options as you set them. This dialog box shows you the formatting of the current paragraph.

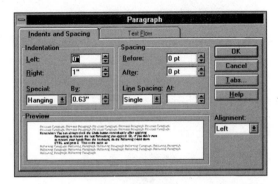

3   In the Indentation area, click the down arrow next to the Right box until 0.7"
appears.

Note that the Preview box changes to reflect the new setting.

4   From the Alignment drop-down list, select Justified.

5   Click the OK button to return to the document.

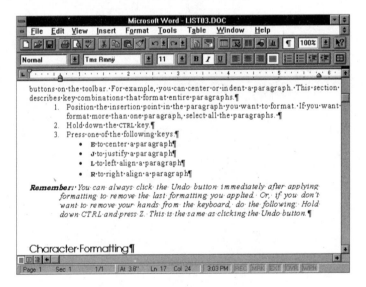

Add spacing before the paragraph

Instead of pressing ENTER to add blank lines before and after a heading or text
paragraph, you can make the spacing part of the paragraph's formatting. Later, if you
need to move the paragraph to another location in the document, the correct spacing
travels with it. This method also gives you more flexibility and precision, because you
can increase spacing by a fraction of a line, for example, by 1.5 or 1.75 lines.

1   From the F_ormat menu, choose _Paragraph.

2   In the Spacing area, click the up arrow in the Before box until "12 pt" appears.

Remember to check the sample in the Preview box to see the results.

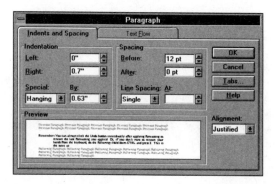

3   Click the OK button to return to the document.

Change the line spacing within a paragraph

Microsoft Word is preset to create single-spaced lines. If you prefer a different line spacing, you can change the setting.

1   Place the insertion point anywhere in the paragraph at the end of the document that begins with "Note," and then from the F_ormat menu, choose _Paragraph.

2   Click the down arrow under Line Spacing to display the spacing options.

3   Select 1.5 Lines.

4   Click the OK button to apply the formatting and close the dialog box.

Your paragraph now looks like the following illustration.

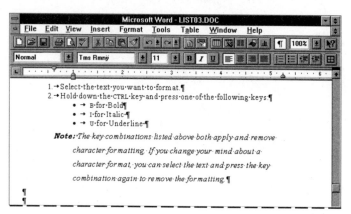

> **Tip**   If you want to change the line spacing for an entire document, use the Select All command on the Edit menu to select the entire document, and then choose the Paragraph command and set the spacing.

Creating a Table with the Standard Toolbar

When you want to create paragraphs that should appear side by side, you can use the Insert Table button on the Standard toolbar. With this button, you can create a grid of any size. For example, if you want to create a table containing two columns and four rows, click the Insert Table button and drag to create a table that contains the number of rows and columns you want. In each cell of the grid, you can enter text of any length. Microsoft Word handles all the formatting.

Create a table

1   Place the insertion point after the last paragraph mark in the document.

2   Press ENTER to create a blank line.

Insert Table

3   From the Standard toolbar, click the Insert Table button and drag to highlight a group of cells that is two columns wide and three rows long.

When you release the mouse button, your screen looks like the following illustration.

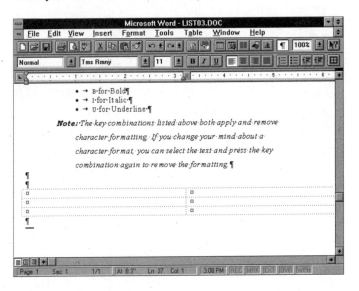

Enter text in the table

1 With the insertion point in the first cell of the left column, type **Position** and press TAB.

The insertion point moves to the first cell in the right column.

2 Type **Press Ctrl and this key** and press TAB.

The insertion point moves to the second cell in the left column.

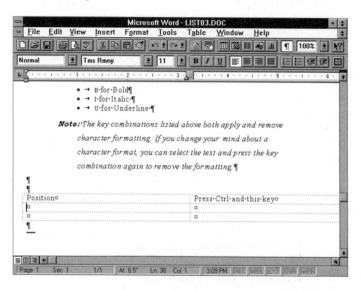

3 Type **If you want to place the insertion point at the start of the document** and press TAB.

The insertion point moves to the second cell in the right column.

4 Type **Home** and press TAB.

The insertion point moves to the third cell in the left column.

5 Type **If you want to place the insertion point at the end of the document** and press TAB.

The insertion point moves to the third cell in the right column.

6 Type **End**

Your completed table looks like the following illustration.

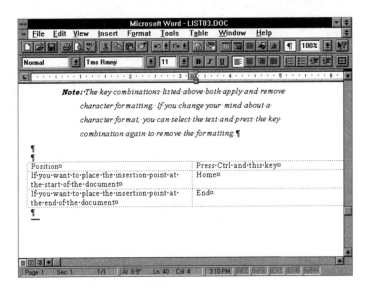

7   Click the insertion point anywhere outside of the table to prepare for the rest of the lesson.

This introduction to tables is intended to help you see how easy it is to make tables in Microsoft Word. In Lesson 10 of this book, you will learn more about working in tables.

Setting Margins with the Ruler

You've seen how you can use the ruler to set indents. In page layout view, the ruler can also display margin markers, which you can drag to change the page margins. In this view, you can see the effect that changing the margins has on the layout of the entire page. You can also quickly switch between normal and page layout views by clicking the buttons to the left of the horizontal scroll bar.

Change to page layout view

Page Layout View

In page layout view, you can see the edge of the page to better see the changes to your margins. This view reflects how your page appears when you print your document.

▶   From the View menu, choose Page Layout.

Display the margin boundaries on the ruler

You can also click the Page Layout View button to the left of the horizontal scroll bar.

When you display indents on the ruler, the numbers indicate inches from the left margin. On the other hand, margins are measured in inches from the left edge of the page. Just as you can adjust indents from the ruler, you can adjust the margins on the ruler. After adjusting your margins, you can switch to page layout view and change the magnification to see your changes.

1 Position the pointer near the left edge of the ruler until the pointer changes to a two-sided arrow, as shown in the following illustration.

Arrow

2 To adjust the left margin, drag to the right to the 1.5-inch mark on the scale.

3 Scroll to the left to see the 1.5-inch margin you created.

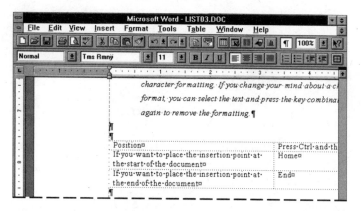

4 Drag the right margin marker to the left until you see the 6.5-inch mark on the scale. The paper is 8.5 inches wide, so this creates a one-half inch right margin.

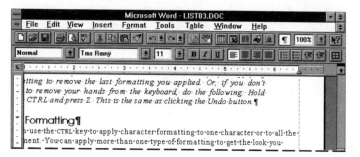

Change the magnification

As in normal view, you can adjust the magnification in page layout view to get an overall view of the page.

▶ In the Zoom Control drop-down list, select 50%.

Your document looks like the following illustration.

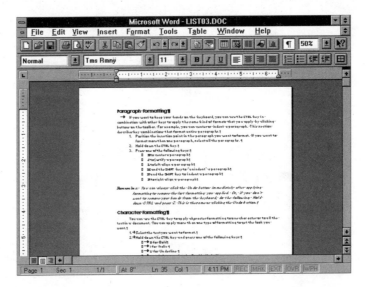

Switch back to normal view

Normal View

▶ Click the Normal View button to return to normal view.

Note   If you know the exact measurements that you want for your document's margins, you can choose the Page Setup command on the File menu and enter them in the dialog box. You can also divide the document into sections and set different margins for each. For more information about setting margins, see Chapter 11, "Page Setup: Margins, Page Numbers, and Other Items," in the *Microsoft Word User's Guide*.

Save

Save the changes

▶ On the Standard toolbar, click the Save button. Microsoft Word saves this version of the document in place of the previous version.

One Step Further

Earlier in this lesson, you sorted a list. With the list sorted the way you want, you can select a vertical block of text and apply a character format to it to better emphasize each point.

1   In your document, position the cursor in front of the text that begins with "E to center a paragraph."

2   Hold the ALT key and the mouse button to drag and select the first letter in each line.

When you release the mouse, the first letter in each line is selected.

Underline

3 On the Formatting toolbar, click the Underline button.

The first character of each line in your list appears underlined.

If You Want to Continue to the Next Lesson

1 From the File menu, choose Close.

2 If a message appears asking whether you want to save changes, click the Yes button.

Choosing this command closes the active document; it does not exit the Microsoft Word application.

If You Want to Quit Microsoft Word for Now

1 From the File menu, choose Exit.

2 If a message appears asking whether you want to save changes, click the Yes button.

Lesson Summary

To	Do this	Button
Set indents	Click the Increase Indent or Decrease Indent button.	
Create bulleted lists	Select the paragraphs to format, and click the Bullets button.	
Create numbered lists	Select the paragraphs to format, and click the Numbering button.	
Set custom indents	Drag the triangular indent markers on the ruler to set the first-line, left, and right indents.	
Sort text in a list	From the Table menu, choose Sort Text.	
Adjust spacing between paragraphs	From the Format menu, choose Paragraph. Select the spacing you want in the Spacing area.	
Adjust line spacing within a paragraph	From the Format menu, choose Paragraph. Select the line spacing you want in the Line Spacing area.	
Create a table	Click the Insert Table button and drag a grid the size and shape you want for your table.	
Set margins	In page layout view, drag the left and right edges of the ruler to the measurement you want.	

To	Do this	Button
View an entire page	From the View menu, choose Page Layout. *or* Click the Page Layout View button.	
Return to normal view	Click the Normal View button.	

For more information on	See in the *Microsoft Word User's Guide*
Setting indents	Chapter 7, "Formatting Paragraphs"
Creating bulleted or numbered lists	Chapter 7, "Formatting Paragraphs"
Setting margins	Chapter 11, "Page Setup: Margins, Page Numbers, and Other Items"

Preview of the Next Lesson

In the next lesson, you'll prepare to print a document. You'll first view your document in Print Preview to examine it before you print it. Then you will select a printer and print the document.

Printing Your Document

After creating documents and getting them to look the way you want, you can print the results of your labors. In this lesson, you'll use buttons on the Standard toolbar to examine the document. After changing the margins and inserting manual page breaks, you'll print your document, if you have a printer available. If not, you can still preview your document, and see how it will look when you are able to print it.

In the Print Preview window, you can see what your document will look like before you print it.

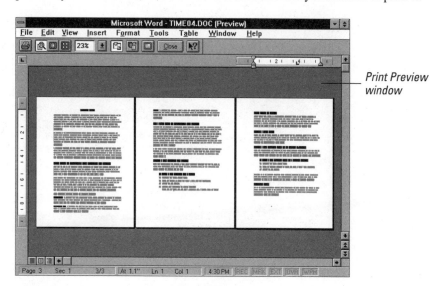

Print Preview window

You will learn how to:

For instructions about starting Microsoft Word, see "Getting Ready," earlier in this book.

- Examine one or more pages of a document in the Print Preview window.
- Change the margins in the Print Preview window.
- Insert page breaks.
- Repaginate a document.
- Print your document from the Standard toolbar and from the menu.

Estimated lesson time: 30 minutes

Open a sample document

Open

1   On the Standard toolbar, click the Open button.

2   In the Directories list, be sure the PRACTICE directory is open. If it is not, select the drive and directory for the Microsoft Word home directory, and click each subdirectory until you locate PRACTICE.

For information about opening a sample document, see Lesson 2.

3   In the File Names list, click 04TIME.DOC.

If you do not see 04TIME.DOC in the list of file names, check to be sure the correct drive and directory are open. If you need help, see "Getting Ready."

4   Click the OK button.

If you share your computer with others who use Microsoft Word, the screen display might have changed since your last lesson. If your screen does not look similar to the following illustration, see the Appendix, "Matching the Exercises."

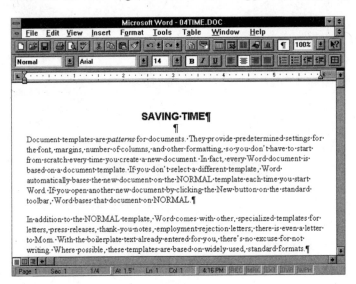

Save the document with a new name

Give the document a new name so the changes you make in this lesson will not overwrite the original practice file.

1   From the File menu, choose Save As.

2   In the File Name box, type **time04**

3   Click the OK button.

Previewing Your Document

To get a better idea of how your document will look when you print it, you can use the Print Preview window. In this window, you can see the overall appearance of one page or all the pages. You can see where text falls on a page before it continues on to the next. After you examine your document, you can make more adjustments to get everything just right. Previewing the document can save you time, because it reduces the number of times you print the document before it looks exactly the way you want. Previewing saves paper, too.

Preview the document

Print Preview

▶ On the Standard toolbar, click the Print Preview button.

Your document in the Print Preview window looks like the following illustration.

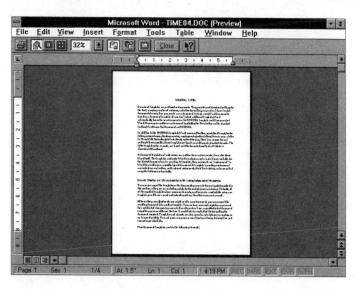

Microsoft Word displays the current page of your document in the Print Preview window. A toolbar contains the buttons you can use in this window. The menu bar still contains the usual Microsoft Word menu items.

View other pages

Multiple Pages

▶ On the Print Preview toolbar, click the Multiple Pages button, and then drag across four boxes.

Now you can see all pages of your document side by side.

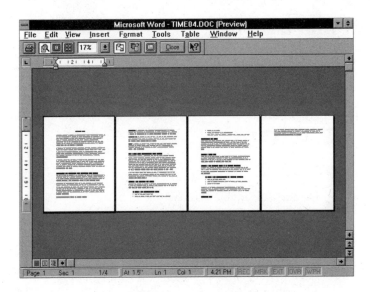

Adjust document length

Page four of the document contains only a short paragraph. You can adjust your margins in the Print Preview window to fit the document on three pages, or you can accomplish the same thing by clicking the Shrink To Fit button on the Print Preview toolbar.

Shrink To Fit

▶ Click the Shrink To Fit button.

  Your document now fits on three pages.

Adjust document margins

The document looks better, but by adjusting the margins yourself, you can improve the appearance even more. To do this, begin by displaying the rulers. You can display the rulers in the Print Preview window by clicking the View Rulers button on the Print Preview toolbar.

In addition, you might find it easier to adjust your margins if you display the document in a single page view first.

One Page

1 Click the One Page button to return to a single page view.

2 Click the View Ruler button to display the rulers and the margins for your document, if they are not already displayed.

View Ruler

3 Position the pointer near the top edge of the vertical ruler until the pointer changes its shape, and drag up to the 1-inch mark.

Tip You can hold down the ALT key while you drag to see the measurements for the margins as you adjust them in the ruler.

---

4   Position the pointer near the bottom edge of the vertical ruler until the pointer changes its shape, and then drag down to the 9-inch mark.

5   Click the Multiple Pages button to display all three pages of the document.

Your Print Preview window looks like the following illustration.

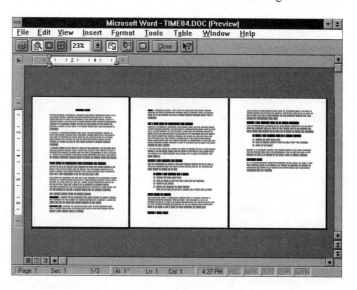

Inserting Page Breaks

You have improved the appearance of the overall document, but you can improve the balance of the text on the last two pages by telling Word where you want the page to break. Begin by returning to normal view in the document window.

▶   On the Print Preview toolbar, click the Close button.

Insert a page break

1   Scroll to the bottom of the second page and place the insertion point immediately in front of the line that reads "Quick Starts on Letters."

2   Press CTRL+ENTER.

Microsoft Word inserts a page break just above the insertion point and places the text after the insertion point on the next page. The page break is represented by a dotted line labeled Page Break. Neither the line nor the label appear when you print the document.

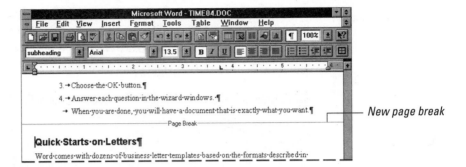

— *New page break*

Preview your document

Print Preview

1   On the Standard toolbar, click the Print Preview button.

In the Print Preview window, the text breaks appropriately over the pages. Microsoft Word automatically repaginates the document after you insert or delete a break. This means that the text flows from page to page throughout the document without requiring you to reposition the text on each page.

Your Print Preview window looks like the following illustration.

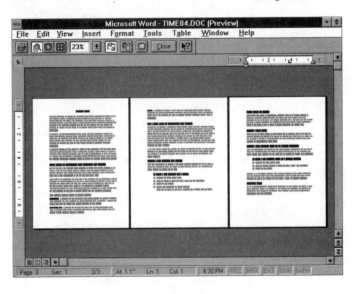

2   On the Print Preview toolbar, click the Close button.

Save the changes

▶   On the Standard toolbar, click the Save button.

Save

Printing Your Document

Now that you are satisfied with the appearance of your document, you are ready to print it. If you don't have a printer connected to your computer, you can skip the remainder of this lesson.

Before You Begin Printing

If you are the only person who uses this computer and you have not printed a document using a Windows-based application, you might not have installed or selected a printer. For complete instructions about installing and setting up a printer, see your Windows documentation. If you share this computer with others, it's likely that a printer is installed and ready to use.

Print a document from the Standard toolbar

The Print button prints all pages of the currently active document on the default printer connected to your computer.

1   Be sure the printer is on.

2   On the Standard toolbar, click the Print button.

A message tells you that the document is being printed.

Print

Print a document from the menu

You can also print a document directly from the Print Preview window using the Print button on the Print Preview toolbar.

Clicking the Print button on the Standard toolbar always prints the entire document. Occasionally, you might want to print just a page or two from a long document, instead of printing all the pages. One of the printing options you can select is to print only the page that currently contains the insertion point.

1   Be sure the printer is turned on.

2   Double-click anywhere in the status bar, and then type **3** in the Go To dialog box.

3   Click Go To to move to page 3 of your document, and then click Close.

4   From the File menu, choose Print.

The Print dialog box appears.

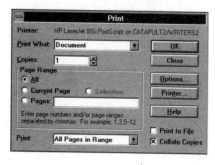

5   In the Page Range area, click the Current Page option button.

6   Click OK to begin printing.

One Step Further

Suppose that after printing your document, you discover that someone else has used your printer, accidentally taking the first and last pages of your document. Instead of printing the entire document again, you can specify the pages you want to print. These pages do not need to be sequential.

1   Be sure the printer is on.

2   From the File menu, choose Print.

The Print dialog box appears.

3   In the Pages box of the Page Range area, type **1, 3**

The status bar indicates that your document contains 3 pages, so page 3 is the last page of your document.

If you are not connected to a printer, you will not be able to continue to the next step. Click Cancel to return to your document.

4   Click OK to begin printing.

If You Want to Continue to the Next Lesson

1   From the File menu, choose Close.

2   If a message appears asking whether you want to save changes, click the No button. You do not need to save the changes you made to the document after you printed it.

Choosing this command closes the active document; it does not exit the Microsoft Word application.

If You Want to Quit Microsoft Word for Now

1   From the File menu, choose Exit.

2   If a message appears asking whether you want to save changes, click the No button.

You do not need to save the changes you made to the document after it was printed.

Lesson Summary

To	Do this	Button
Display a document in Print Preview	On the Standard toolbar, click the Print Preview button.	
Change margins in the Print Preview window	Use the Ruler in the Print Preview window to change margins in selected paragraphs.	
See multiple pages of the document at one time	On the Print Preview toolbar, click the Multiple Pages button. Drag across the number of pages you want to see.	
Adjust document length	In the Print Preview window, click the Shrink To Fit button on the Print Preview toolbar.	
See one page of a document in Print Preview	On the Print Preview toolbar, click the One Page button.	
Print a document from the Print Preview window	On the Print Preview toolbar, click the Print button.	
Print a document from a document window (default printer and all pages)	On the Standard toolbar, click the Print button. *or* Click the Print button in the Page Preview window.	
Print selected pages	From the File menu, choose Print. In the Print dialog box, enter the specific pages you want to print in the Pages area.	

For more information on	See in the *Microsoft Word User's Guide*
Previewing and printing text	Chapter 23, "Printing"

Preview of the Next Lessons

The lessons in the next part of the book will show you how to get the most out of Microsoft Word. You'll learn how to increase your productivity by using styles to quickly format text and paragraphs. In the next lesson, you'll use such editing productivity tools as search and replace, AutoText, and AutoCorrect. In later lessons, you'll use proofing tools to check your spelling and grammar, and use the online Thesaurus. Finally, you'll learn how templates and master pages save you time when you create documents that use similar formatting.

Review & Practice

The lessons in Part 1 helped acquaint you with basic word processing and editing skills. If you want to practice these skills and test your understanding before you proceed with the lessons in Part 2, you can work through the Review & Practice section following this lesson. This less structured activity allows you to increase your confidence using many of the features introduced so far.

Part 1 Review & Practice

In this Review & Practice, you have an opportunity to fine-tune the basic editing and word processing skills you learned in Part 1 of this book. Use what you have learned about selecting, moving, and copying text to rearrange and reformat the text in the practice document.

Scenario

For instructions about starting Microsoft Word, see "Getting Ready," earlier in this book.

In this Review & Practice section, you will complete a cover letter that was started by an associate. This letter is going to accompany an annual report package for West Coast Sales. While your colleagues in the marketing department are working on the annual report itself, the task of making this cover letter more attractive has fallen to you. Most of the text was already entered, so you can focus on formatting text and paragraphs to give the letter more impact.

You will review and practice how to:

- Open and modify a document.
- Save a document.
- Edit a document.
- Check the spelling in a document.
- Format characters and paragraphs.

Estimated practice time: 20 minutes

Step 1: Open and Modify a Document

1 Open the document called P1REVIEW.DOC.

2 Place the insertion point at the beginning of the fifth line and press ENTER.

3 At the insertion point, type the following paragraph. Be sure to make the typing mistakes as written so you can practice using the spelling feature.

Enclosed is your copy of West Coast Sales Annual Report. The Annual Report contains all the details about major progress and achievements at West Coast Sales. The accompanying Executive Summary provides a brief overview of the past year's highlights.

For more information on	See
Opening a document	Lesson 2
Typing text	Lesson 1

Step 2:   Save a Document

▶ Save your letter with the name REVIEW01.DOC.

For more information on	See
Saving a document with a new name	Lesson 2

Step 3:   Edit a Document

1   Delete the text "your copy of" in the first sentence, and replace it with "the."

2   In the first paragraph, move the third sentence in front of the second sentence.

3   Copy the text "West Coast Sales" in front of "Annual Report" throughout the letter.

4   Add this sentence to the end of the last paragraph, before the closing:

Thank you for your continued support and interest in West Coast Sales.

For more information on	See
Deleting text	Lesson 1
Copying text	Lesson 2

Step 4:   Check a Document's Spelling

1   Click the Spelling button on the Standard toolbar.

2   Add all proper names to the dictionary, and add AutoCorrect entries for words you misspell frequently.

3   After you have finished spell checking the document, save your document.

For more information on	See
Checking spelling	Lesson 2

Step 5:   **Format Characters and Paragraphs in a Document**

Use the following illustration as a guide for the kind of formatting you can apply to characters and paragraphs. When you have completed formatting, your document should look like the following.

Chris Hamilton
West Coast Sales
555 Plaza Avenue
Franklin, CO 54320

Enclosed is the **West Coast Sales** *Annual Report*. The accompanying Executive Summary provides a brief overview of the past year's highlights. The **West Coast Sales** *Annual Report* contains all the details about major progress and achievements at **West Coast Sales**. Year-end financial results are also included. But here is a quick overview:

- We moved our corporate headquarters to the renovated Elliott building in Franklin.
- After a year-long search and interviewing many highly qualified candidates, we hired a new director of Quality and Customer Satisfaction, Lisa Martinez, formerly of Sweet Lil's Bonbons.
- This year we increased profitability by 17% over last year, a fact that pleases shareholders and employees alike.

If you would like to continue to receive regular updates about our company, you need to complete the enclosed subscription card and return it to new our corporate offices in Franklin.

West Coast Sales
555 Plaza Avenue
Franklin, CO 54320

Be sure to indicate whether you want to receive the **West Coast Sales** *Annual Report*, the Executive Summary, or both. If you do not complete the card, you will no longer receive the **West Coast Sales** *Annual Report*. Thank you for your continued support and interest in West Coast Sales.

Sincerely,

Chris Hamilton
President/CEO
West Coast Sales

▶ When you have completed formatting your document, preview the document. If you have a printer connected to your computer, you can print your document and then save it.

For more information on	See
Formatting characters	Lesson 1
Formatting paragraphs	Lesson 3
Previewing and printing a document	Lesson 4

If You Want to Continue to the Next Lesson

1   From the File menu, choose Close.

2   If a message appears asking whether you want to save changes, click the Yes button.

If You Want to Quit Microsoft Word for Now

1   From the File menu, choose Exit.

2   If a message appears asking whether you want to save changes, click the Yes button.

2 Everyday Tasks Made Easy

Increasing Editing Productivity

After you have created a few documents, you might notice that you often use the same text throughout a given document. In this lesson, you learn different ways to work more productively by using the Word Find And Replace, AutoCorrect, and AutoText features. These features reduce the amount of repetitive typing or actions you take in a document, so you can produce documents more quickly and with fewer errors.

You will learn how to:

For instructions about starting Microsoft Word, see "Getting Ready," earlier in this book.

- Locate and replace text.
- Locate and replace formatting.
- Use AutoCorrect to insert boilerplate text as you type.
- Use AutoText to insert boilerplate text when you wish.

Estimated lesson time: 30 minutes

Open a sample document

Open

1   On the Standard toolbar, click the Open button.

2   In the Directories list, be sure the PRACTICE directory is open. If it is not, select the drive and directory for the Microsoft Word home directory, and click each subsequent directory until you locate PRACTICE.

3   In the File Name list, double-click 05ITEMS.DOC.

If you share your computer with others who use Microsoft Word, the screen display might have changed since your last lesson. If your screen does not look similar to the following illustration, see the Appendix, "Matching the Exercises."

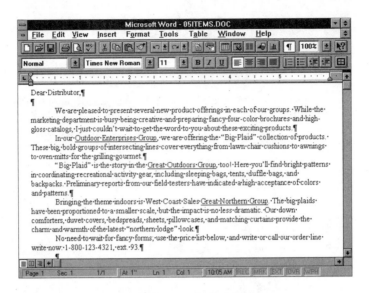

Save the document with a new name

Give the document a new name so the changes you make in this lesson will not overwrite the original practice file.

1 From the File menu, choose Save As.

2 In the File Name box, type **items05**

3 Click the OK button.

Show/Hide ¶

Display paragraph marks

▶ Click the Show/Hide ¶ button on the Standard toolbar to display paragraph marks and tab characters if they are not already displayed.

Finding and Replacing Text

When you need to review or change text in a document, use the Find and Replace commands on the Edit menu. With these commands, you can quickly find—and, if necessary, replace—all occurrences of a certain word or phrase. For example, you might want to find every instance of an outdated product name in a brochure and substitute its new name. You can change all instances at once, or you can accept or reject each change individually. Either method ensures that the change is made consistently throughout the document.

Identify text to find and replace

The sample document you opened refers to "groups" at West Coast Sales, but these should really be called "divisions." Use the Replace command to locate the word "group" and replace it with "division."

1   From the Edit menu, choose Replace.

2   In the Find What box, type **group**

If you share your computer with others who have used the Find command or the Replace command in the current work session, the text they last searched for might appear in the Find What box. You can select the text and type over it.

3   If the No Formatting button is not dimmed, click it so Word does not search for any formatting.

4   In the Replace With box, type **division**

If text is already in the Replace With box, select the text and type over it.

5   If the No Formatting button is not dimmed, click it so Word does not format the replacement text.

6   In the Search box, click the down arrow and select All, if it is not already selected.

Your completed dialog box looks like the following illustration.

Find and replace the text

1   To begin the search, click the Find Next button.

The word "group" is highlighted.

2   Click the Replace button.

The word "division" replaces the word "group," and the next occurrence of "group" is highlighted.

3 Click the Replace button.

The word "division" replaces the word "group," and the next occurrence of "group" is highlighted.

4 Because "group" is the word you want in this case, click the Find Next button.

The next occurrence of "group" is highlighted.

5 Click the Replace button for each of the remaining occurrences.

6 A message box appears when the end of document is reached and no more search items are found. Click the OK button to continue.

Replacing All Occurrences of Text

When you do not want to confirm each change, you can use the Replace All option in the Replace dialog box. This option makes changes without asking you to confirm each one. In this exercise, you change all occurrences of "we are" to "West Coast Sales is."

Identify text to replace

1 In the Find What box, type **we are**

The text you last searched for is selected in the Find What box. You can type over it.

2 In the Replace With box, select the existing text and type **West Coast Sales is**

Your completed dialog box looks like the following illustration.

Find and replace all occurrences

1 To replace all occurrences, click the Replace All button.

A dialog box indicates how many changes were made.

2 Click the OK button to return to the Replace dialog box.

3 Click the Close button to return to the document and see the changes.

Scroll through the document and note that "West Coast Sales is" is substituted throughout the document.

Finding and Replacing Formatting

You can locate text that has a specific format, such as bold or underlined, and change the formatting as well as the text. You can also search for and change only the formatting without changing the text. For example, suppose you underlined division names but then later changed your mind, deciding to make them italic and bold instead. With the Replace command, you can quickly find any underlined text and change the underline to italic and bold.

Specify which formatting to find and replace

You can press CTRL+HOME to quickly move the insertion point to the top of the document.

Throughout the sample document, the names of West Coast Sales divisions are underlined. Scroll through the document to view the formatting. Then return to the beginning and use the Replace command to change underlined text to italic and bold.

1   From the Edit menu, choose Replace.

2   Select the text in the Find What box and delete it by pressing the BACKSPACE key.

3   Click the Format button at the bottom of the dialog box, and select Font from the list.

   The Find Font dialog box looks like the Font dialog box in which you format characters.

4   Click the arrow next to the Underline drop-down list, and then select Single.

5   Click the OK button to return to the Replace dialog box.

6   Select the text in the Replace With box, and then press the BACKSPACE key.

7   Click the Format button again and select Font from the list.

8   Click the arrow next to the Underline drop-down list and select None.

9   In the Font Style list, select Bold Italic.

10   Click the OK button to return to the Replace dialog box.

   Your completed dialog box looks like the following illustration.

Now that you've specified the formatting to find and replace, you are ready to start the search.

Find and replace formatting

1   In the Replace dialog box, click the Replace All button.

A dialog box indicates how many changes were made.

2   Word tells you how many changes were made. Click the OK button to return to the Replace dialog box.

3   Click the Close button to return to the document and see the changes.

Scroll through the document and note that the text that was underlined is now italic and bold.

Inserting Text with AutoCorrect and AutoText

As you learned in Lesson 1, you can use the AutoCorrect feature in the Spelling dialog box to identify words that you often misspell. The next time you misspell that word and type a space, it is automatically corrected as you type. In addition, you can use AutoCorrect to insert words and phrases you use frequently, even if they are not misspelled. An AutoCorrect entry automatically inserts repeated text as you type.

Similarly, you can use the AutoText feature to insert repeated text only when you press the F3 key after typing the AutoText entry. Use the AutoText feature when you want greater control over when repeated text is inserted. AutoText entries are particularly useful when entering numbers or text that requires complicated formatting.

Creating an AutoCorrect Entry

Suppose you are creating a list of products in which each line begins with the same name. Instead of typing the repeated part of the product name each time, you can type the AutoCorrect entry followed by the rest of the name. Microsoft Word inserts the repeated text as you type.

Create an AutoCorrect entry

Product names appear in a table in the Price List section of this document. Each product name should begin with the text "Big Plaid" but, because you often misspell "plaid" as "pld," create an AutoCorrect entry to insert the correct spelling automatically when you type "pld" followed by a space. While you're at it, have the AutoCorrect entry also insert the word "Big." Now when you type "pld" and a space, the text "Big Plaid" is inserted automatically. You save time because you have to type less text.

1   Scroll to the price list near the end of the document.

2   In the first row of the price list, select the text "Big Plaid" by placing the insertion point after the "d" and holding down the SHIFT key while you press the LEFT ARROW key until both words are selected.

Note   Do not double-click to select the words. Double-clicking includes the space after the second word in the selection, and you do not want the extra space inserted when you use this AutoCorrect entry.

---

3   From the Tools menu, choose AutoCorrect.

The AutoCorrect dialog box appears.

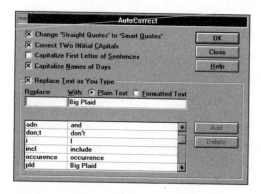

4   With the insertion point in the Replace box, type **pld**

5   Click the Add button.

The new entry is added to the list of AutoCorrect entries in the dialog box.

6   Click the OK button to return to the document.

Use AutoCorrect to insert text

Try your new AutoCorrect entry to insert the text "Big Plaid" in front of each product in the list. You can press TAB to move from cell to cell in the table. Press SHIFT+TAB to move to a previous cell. In Lesson 10, you will learn more about working in tables.

1   In the price list area of the document, place the insertion point in the second column and fourth row of the table.

2   Type **pld** and a space, and **Awning**

The text "Big Plaid" appears as soon as you type a space and start typing the next word, "Awning."

3   Place the insertion point in front of the word "Mountain" in the next group of products in the price list.

4   Type **pld** and a space.

The text "Big Plaid" appears in front of the word "Mountain."

5   Repeat step 4 for each product in the list.

When you have completed inserting text, your document should look like the following illustration.

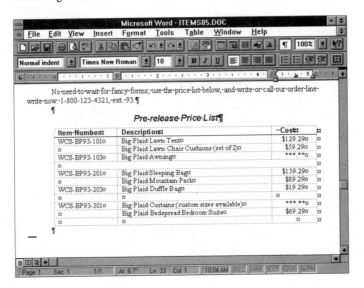

Creating an AutoText Entry

Suppose your list of products also includes item numbers that begin with the same characters. Instead of typing these item numbers for each product, you can type the AutoText entry followed by the F3 key, and Word inserts the rest.

Create an AutoText entry

The item number for each product should be listed under the Item Number heading in the price list. Each item number begins with the text "WCS-BP93-." Create an AutoText entry to insert this text when you type "wcs" followed by the F3 key.

1   In the first line of the price list, select the text "WCS-BP93-".

Be sure to include the second hyphen.

2   From the Edit menu, choose AutoText.

The AutoText dialog box appears.

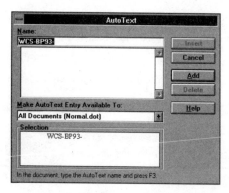

3   In the Name box, replace the existing text by typing **wcs**

4   Click the Add button to return to the document.

Use AutoText to insert text

Try your new AutoText entry to insert the text "WCS-BP93-" to begin item numbers in the list. After you insert this text, you can type in the rest of the missing numbers.

1   Place the insertion point in the third row of the first column in the table.

2   Type **wcs**

3   Press F3.

The text "WCS-BP93-" appears.

4   After the inserted text, type **102**

5   Repeat steps 3 and 4 for each product missing an item number in the price list. For example, for the second item in the next group of products, insert the AutoText entry followed by "202." For the second item in the third group of products, use the AutoText entry followed by "302."

Use AutoText and AutoCorrect to insert text

Compare both AutoCorrect and AutoText for inserting repeated text in a document by adding a new product to the price list. Remember, AutoCorrect entries are inserted as soon as you type a space; while AutoText entries are inserted only after you press F3.

1   Place the insertion point in the first cell of the last row in the table.

2   Type **wcs**

3   Press F3.

4   Type **303** and press TAB.

5   Type **pld Down Bedroom Suite** and press TAB.

6   Type **$89.29**

Your completed price list looks like the following illustration.

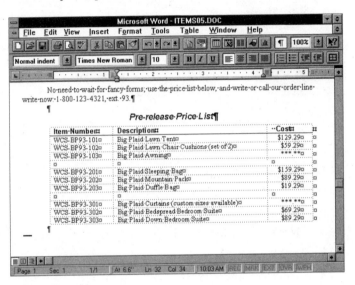

Save

Save your work

▶   Click the Save button on the Standard toolbar.

One Step Further

You can use the Find and Replace feature to help you review and proofread your document. Suppose you typically misuse the words "right" and "write." You can use the Sounds Like option with the Find command to locate words that sound alike. Once you review the word in a sentence, you can decide whether you should change it.

Identify the text to find and replace

1   From the Edit menu, choose Find.

2   In the Find What box, type **right**

3   Click the No Formatting button to clear any formatting specified from a previous search.

4   Click the arrow next to the Search drop-down list, and select Up.

This option searches backward through the document. Use this option when the insertion point is located at the end of the document.

5 Click the Sounds Like check box.

Find and replace the text

1 Click the Find Next button.

Word highlights the word "write."

In this sentence, this is not the correct word. You need to replace it.

2 Click the Replace button.

3 In the Replace With box, type **right** and click the No Formatting button to clear any formatting specified from a previous search.

4 Click the Replace button.

Word highlights the word "write." In this sentence, this is the correct word.

5 Click the Find Next button.

6 When you see the message box, click the Yes button to continue.

7 Click the Close button to return to the document.

If You Want to Continue to the Next Lesson

1 From the File menu, choose Close.

2 If a message appears asking whether you want to save changes, click the Yes button.

If You Want to Quit Microsoft Word for Now

1 From the File menu, choose Exit.

2 If a message appears asking whether you want to save changes, click the Yes button.

3 If you see the message asking whether you want to save changes to NORMAL.DOT, click the No button if you share your computer with others or are connected to a network. Your AutoText entries will not be saved.

Click the Yes button, if you are the only one who uses your computer, and you want to save the AutoText entries you created in this lesson.

Note   When you create an AutoText entry, it is stored in a template document called NORMAL.DOT. This document contains information about how you work with Microsoft Word. The options you enable (or disable) and your AutoText entries are saved in this template as well. This means that the AutoText entries you create in this document will be available in all your documents.

Lesson Summary

To	Do this
Find and replace text	From the Edit menu, choose Replace. In the Replace dialog box, type the text you want to find. Clear or select any formatting. Type the replacement text to use, and clear or select any formatting. Use the Find Next button to move to each occurrence. Click the Replace button to replace an occurrence and move to the next. Click Replace All to replace all occurrences at once.
Find and replace formatting	From the Edit menu, choose Replace. Use the buttons and options available in the Replace dialog box to specify the kind of formatting to find and the replacement formatting. Use the Find Next button to move to each occurrence. Click the Replace button to replace an occurrence and move to the next. Click Replace All to replace all occurrences at once.
Create an AutoCorrect entry	Select the text for the entry. From the Tools menu, choose AutoCorrect. With the insertion point in the Replace box, type the name of the entry. Click the Add button. Click the OK button to return to the document.
Insert an AutoCorrect entry	Type the name of the entry and a space.
Create an AutoText entry	Select the text for the entry. From the Edit menu, choose AutoText. With the insertion point in the Replace box, type the name of the entry. Click the Add button to return to the document.

To	Do this
Insert an AutoText entry	Type the name of the entry and press F3.
Find and replace words or phrases that sound alike	From the Edit menu, choose Find. Type the text you want to find, and clear any formatting. Click the Sounds Like check box. Click the Find Next button. Click the Replace button and enter the replacement text, and then click the Replace button. Continue using the Find Next and Replace buttons to replace text where needed. Click Close to return to your document.

For more information on	See in the *Microsoft Word User's Guide*
Finding and replacing text	Chapter 3, "Finding and Replacing"
Finding and replacing formatting	Chapter 3, "Finding and Replacing"
Inserting repeated text	Chapter 4, "AutoCorrect and AutoText: Reusing Text and Graphics"

Preview of the Next Lesson

In the next lesson, you'll learn to use and customize proofing tools that help improve the quality of your writing. You'll use the thesaurus to locate alternative words and write more precisely. You'll also customize the spelling checker dictionary to include special terms you use often. Finally, you'll use Microsoft Word to check your grammar and style in a document.

Proofing a Document

After you've written and formatted a document, you'll probably want to *proof,* or check, the document one last time to be sure no errors exist and that everything is in order. You've already seen how simple it is to check for spelling errors using the Spelling button on the toolbar. In this lesson, you'll learn how to specify special words you do not want identified as misspelled. You'll also learn how to use other proofing tools, such as the grammar checker, to locate common grammatical or stylistic errors, and you'll work with the thesaurus to add interest and precision to your writing by asking Microsoft Word to suggest synonyms for selected words.

You will learn how to:

For instructions about starting Microsoft Word, see "Getting Ready," earlier in this book.

- Find synonyms and related words using the thesaurus.
- Check grammar and spelling.
- Customize the spelling dictionary.

Estimated lesson time: 30 minutes

Open a sample document

Open

1 On the Standard toolbar, click the Open button.

2 In the Directories list, be sure the PRACTICE directory is open. If it is not, select the drive and directory for the Microsoft Word home directory, and click each subsequent directory until you locate PRACTICE.

3 In the File Name list, double-click 06LETTER.DOC.

If you share your computer with others who use Microsoft Word, the screen display might have changed since your last lesson. If your screen does not look similar to the following illustration, see the Appendix, "Matching the Exercises."

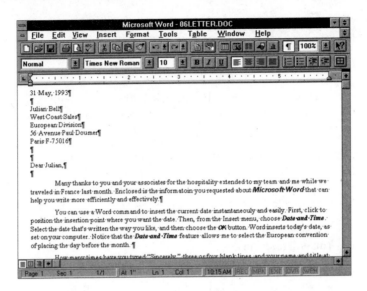

Save the document with a new name

Give the document a new name so the changes you make in this lesson will not
overwrite the original practice file.

1   From the File menu, choose Save As.

2   In the File Name box, type **letter06**

3   Click the OK button.

Important   The Setup program you use to install Microsoft Word on your computer gives you the
option to install or not install the Word proofing tools, which include the Thesaurus,
Grammar, and Spelling commands. You need to have installed these commands for
them to appear on the Tools menu. You can run the Word Setup program again and
specify that you want to install the proofing commands only. For more information on
the Setup program, see *Microsoft Word Quick Results*.

Using the Thesaurus

Using the thesaurus helps you add precision and variety to your writing. Like a printed
thesaurus, the Microsoft Word thesaurus provides synonyms (words with a similar
meaning) and sometimes antonyms (words with an opposite meaning) for a particular
word. It also provides lists of related words and different forms of the selected word.

For example, the word "work" can be used as a noun or as a verb; the thesaurus lists synonyms for both forms. When you select a word and then choose the Thesaurus command, the Thesaurus dialog box appears, where you can quickly search through a wide range of synonyms and related words until you find exactly the word you want.

Look up a word in the thesaurus

Suppose you want to find an alternative to the word "excellent" and insert it in the document. The following procedure shows you what to do. First you use the Find command to find the word "excellent;" then you use the Thesaurus command to select a synonym.

1   From the Edit menu, choose Find.

2   Type **excellent**

3   If the No Formatting button is not dimmed, select it.

4   Click the Find Next button.

The word "excellent" is found and highlighted.

5   Click the Cancel button to close the Find dialog box.

6   From the Tools menu, choose Thesaurus.

The Thesaurus dialog box appears.

7   In the Replace With Synonym box, click "premium" in the list, and then click the Replace button.

"Premium" replaces "excellent" and the dialog box closes.

Replace another word

This procedure shows how you can find an alternative to the word "suggestions."

1   In the second sentence that follows "premium," select the word "suggestions," as shown in the following illustration.

2 From the Tools menu, choose Thesaurus.

Note that Microsoft Word does not display alternatives for "suggestions." Instead, it displays the singular form of the word, "suggestion." This indicates that you can look up alternatives for the singular form.

3 Click the Look Up button to see alternatives for the singular form of this word.

Word lists the synonyms. The word "idea" would be a good alternative, but you'll need to add an "s" to the end of it.

4 Select "idea" to have Word copy it to the Replace With Synonym box.

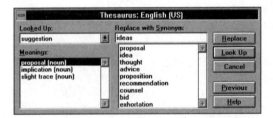

5 In the Replace With Synonym box, click at the end of "idea" and type **s**

6 Click the Replace button.

Word replaces "suggestions" with "ideas."

Checking Grammar and Spelling

The Grammar command identifies sentences in your document that have possible grammatical errors or a nonstandard writing style. For many types of errors, the Grammar command suggests ways to correct the sentence. You can choose the correction you want to make and have the sentence changed in your document. You can also make changes directly in your document and then continue checking.

While checking your document for grammatical errors, spelling is also checked. If a questionable word is found, the Spelling dialog box displays over the Grammar dialog box so you can correct the misspelling. Microsoft Word then continues checking the grammar.

The Grammar command provides a quick and convenient way to find many common grammatical errors. However, remember that no grammar checker can replace reading a document carefully.

Check the grammar and spelling

Microsoft Word normally checks all of your document, beginning at the insertion point. Although you can position the insertion point anywhere in the document, in this lesson you'll position it at the top.

Dragging the scroll box is a fast way to scroll.

1   Scroll to the top of the document.

2   Position the insertion point at the beginning of the line that shows the date.

3   From the Tools menu, choose Grammar.

This starts both the grammar checker and the spelling checker.

4   The spelling checker finds the street name "Doumer," which is correctly spelled. Click the Ignore button.

The next error is a spelling error: "informatoin." Microsoft Word displays the error and the suggested correction in the Spelling dialog box.

5   Click the Change button.

The word "informatoin" changes to "information" and the spell check continues.

6   The next error is a grammatical error. "Date and Time" is interpreted as two subjects in the sentence, when, in fact, "Date and Time" is the name of a single Word feature.

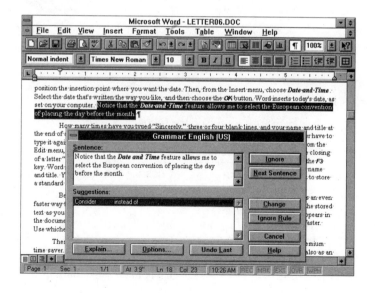

You can disable the spelling checker while doing a grammar check. From the Options menu, choose Tools, and then select the Grammar tab. Clear the "Check Spelling" check box, and close the dialog box. For purposes of this lesson, however, do not disable the spelling checker.

In this case, click Ignore to not use the suggested change. The correct form of the verb is "allows." The next error is the word "AutoText." By adding this word to the custom dictionary, this word will no longer be flagged as misspelled. In the next part of this lesson, you learn to add this word to your dictionary.

Note   Your dictionary might already include the words "AutoText" and "AutoCorrect." In this case, Word will not recognize these as errors. If this should occur, skip to step 3 in the following exercise.

Customizing the Dictionary

You often use words in your documents that are not likely to be in the Word dictionary—for example, specialized terms, product codes, acronyms and abbreviations, and proper names, such as your name and names of business associates. If you don't want Word to question such words during spelling checks, you can add them to a custom dictionary. You can use one or more custom dictionaries in addition to the standard main dictionary when you check your documents. Word can then check that the words entered in a custom dictionary are also correctly spelled.

Add words to a custom dictionary

You can have Word consult a custom dictionary when checking spelling. You can customize your dictionary as you work by clicking the Add button in the Spelling dialog box whenever a word is flagged as misspelled.

1   Click the Add button.

The next time you check a document that contains "AutoText," Word supplies the correct spelling.

The next error is the word "AutoCorrect." Add this word to the custom dictionary as well.

2   Click the Add button.

3   For each error found, do the following:

When Word suggests	Do this
Wordy expression. Consider "When" instead.	Click the Change button.
This sentence does not seem to contain a main clause.	In the Sentence box, click after the word "When" and type "you" and a space. Then click the change button.
Consider "make" instead of "makes."	Click the Change button.

When Word suggests	Do this
This word may be con-fused with "expedient."	Click the Ignore button. Later you can use the thesaurus to look up a better word.
Consider "effect" in-stead of "affect."	See the next exercise, "Get an explanation for a grammar rule."

Get an explanation for a grammar rule

Word provides explanations for the suggestions that it makes. The following proce-dure shows how to read about a grammar rule before you make a change in your document.

1   With "Consider effect instead of affect" still displayed in the Grammar dialog box, click the Explain button.

Word displays a window with an explanation of the grammar rule.

2   Scroll down to see more of the explanation.

3   When you finish reading about the grammar rule, double-click the Control-menu box in the upper-left corner of the explanation window.

4   Click the Change button.

Note   Each time the grammar checker finds a sentence with a possible error, you can click the Ignore button or the Next Sentence button if you don't want to change anything. If you click Ignore, Word ignores the "error" it flagged and continues checking the sentence. If you click Next Sentence, Word skips to the next sentence. You can also specify which grammatical and stylistic rules Word applies when checking your documents.

---

5   Continue checking, and choose Ignore for any other items that are flagged.

Viewing Readability Statistics

In the Readability Statistics dialog box that appears when the grammar check is finished, Microsoft Word displays information about the text that it checked. The readability statistics help you evaluate how easily the average adult reader can understand your writing. Most readability indexes assign a reading grade level. A grade level of 7, for example, indicates writing that can be understood by an average English-speaking reader who has completed seven years of education in the United States.

1 Note the grade level numbers in the dialog box before you continue.

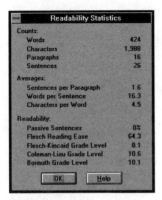

2 Click the OK button to return to your document.

Note If the Readability Statistics dialog box did not appear, it means the option has been cleared. To display the statistics the next time you run the grammar checker, choose Options from the Tools menu. Click the Grammar tab. Select the check box next to Show Readability Statistics, and then click OK.

One Step Further

You can improve the readability of your writing by using the thesaurus to substitute shorter words for the long words that make your document more difficult to read.

1 Find and select each of the following words in the document, and use the thesaurus to substitute a synonym that is shorter or has fewer syllables.

2 Click the Meanings button to see additional words you can use.

Although you might prefer to use different words, this example illustrates how you can affect the readability of a document by using shorter words.

Replace this word	With this word
efficiently	clearly
instantaneously	quickly
position	place
convention	custom
repeatedly	often
extensively	often

Replace this word	With this word
expeditious	fast
significant	good

2 From the Tools menu, choose Grammar.

3 Click the Ignore button in response to each suggestion until you see the readability statistics.

Note the readability statistics and compare these statistics with those you saw before you substituted the shorter words.

If You Want to Continue to the Next Lesson

1 From the File menu, choose Close.

2 If a message appears asking whether you want to save changes, click the No button. You do not need to save the changes you made while experimenting.

Choosing this command closes the active document; it does not exit the Microsoft Word application.

If You Want to Quit Microsoft Word for Now

1 From the File menu, choose Exit.

2 If a message appears asking whether you want to save changes, click the No button. You do not need to save any of the changes you made while experimenting.

Lesson Summary

To	Do this
Use the Word thesaurus	Select a word or phrase in the document, and then choose Thesaurus from the Tools menu to see synonyms, related words, and, sometimes, antonyms.
Check grammar and spelling	From the Tools menu, choose Grammar. As possible grammar or spelling errors are flagged, make the suggested changes or ignore them.
Add words to the custom dictionary	During a spelling or grammar check, click the Add button in the dialog box to add a correctly spelled word to a custom dictionary.

For more information on	See in the *Microsoft Word User's Guide*
Checking spelling and grammar, or using the thesaurus	Chapter 5, "Editing and Proofing Tools"

Preview of the Next Lesson

In the next lesson, you'll learn to number pages automatically. You'll also learn to add text, such as a company name or a chapter name, as well as a page number in the top or bottom margin of every page in the document. You'll work with two sample documents in the next lesson. Both describe ways Word can help you save time.

Establishing the Look of a Page

When you create multiple-page documents with Word, it is easy to give all the pages of your document a consistent and polished appearance. In this lesson, you first learn to set the margins and text that appear on every page in a document. Then you learn to print additional information on every page in headers and footers. Finally, you change the text that appears in headers and footers in different parts of the document.

You will learn how to:

For instructions about starting Microsoft Word, see "Getting Ready," earlier in this book.

- Establish margins, paper size, and orientation for the entire document.
- Insert page numbers in a document.
- Create a header or footer that prints on every page.
- Create different headers on different pages.

Estimated lesson time: 30 minutes

Open a sample document

Open

1   On the Standard toolbar, click the Open button.

2   In the Directories list, be sure the PRACTICE directory is open. If it is not, select the drive and directory for the Microsoft Word home directory, and click each subsequent directory until you locate PRACTICE.

3   In the File Name list, double-click 07STORE.DOC.

If you share your computer with others who use Microsoft Word, the screen display might have changed since your last lesson. If your screen does not look similar to the following illustration, see the Appendix, "Matching the Exercises."

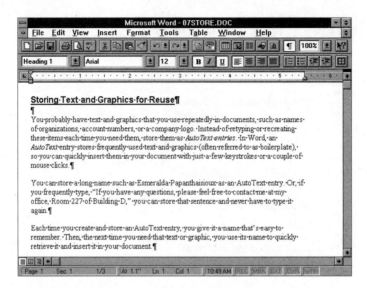

Save the document with a new name

Give the document a new name so the changes you make in this lesson will not overwrite the original practice file.

1   From the File menu, choose Save As.

2   In the File Name box, type **store07**

3   Click the OK button.

Setting Up Document Pages

With the Page Setup command on the File menu, you define the appearance of all the pages in your document. Unless you specifically change a page setup setting, such as the margins, paper size, or orientation for an individual page or section, all of the pages of the document will follow the settings you establish with the Page Setup command.

Establish document margins

1   From the File menu, choose Page Setup.

The Page Setup dialog box appears.

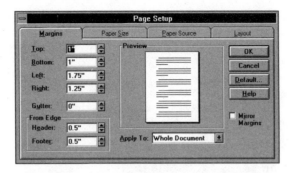

If your dialog box does not look like this, click the Margins tab to bring the Margins page to the front.

2   In the From Edge area, click or hold down the up arrow next to the Header box until 1" appears in the scroll box.

This setting increases the distance between the Header text and the top edge of the page.

Verify the paper size

In the Page Setup dialog, you can specify the size of paper on which your document is printed and the *orientation,* or position, of the text on the page.

1   Click the Paper Size tab and verify that all the settings look like those shown in the following illustration.

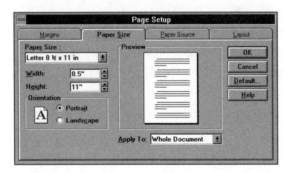

2   Click the OK button to return to the document.

Creating Headers and Footers

With the page setup established, you can specify the information you want to appear on every page. Using the Page Numbers command, you can insert page numbers. You can specify whether a page number should appear at the top of every page (in the *header*) or at the bottom of every page (in the *footer*). You can also position the page number so it is left-aligned, centered, or right-aligned. In addition, you can enter text or include other information that should appear on every page along with the page numbers.

Number all pages except the first

When you use the Page Number command, you have the option not to place a number on the first page. Instead, the numbering would begin with "2" on the second page. This is useful for letters, reports, and many other types of documents that normally do not number the first page. In the following exercise, you'll add page numbers to the upper-right corner of the page.

1 From the Insert menu, choose Page Numbers.

2 In the Position drop-down list, select Top Of Page (Header).

3 In the Alignment drop-down list, be sure that Right is selected.

You can view other alignment settings in the list.

4 Clear the Show Number On First Page check box (to remove the X).

5 Click the OK button.

6 Scroll to page 2 and place the insertion point anywhere on the page.

Viewing Headers and Footers

Word provides several *views*, or ways of looking at your document. You've been working in *normal view*, which is often the fastest view for typing and editing. In normal view, to work with page numbers, headers, and footers, you need to use the Header And Footer command on the View menu. The Header And Footer toolbar allows you to add and modify headers and footers quickly.

If you see the {Page} code instead of numbers

You are seeing field codes. To view the page numbers, from the Tools menu, choose Options. Select the View tab and clear the Field Codes check box.

View header and footer information

When you view headers and footers, you see the header and footer areas enclosed with a dotted line and the body text dimmed on the page. This means you cannot edit the body text while you are viewing and editing the headers or footers. You can use the buttons on the Header And Footer toolbar to switch between the header area and the footer area. Other buttons insert the date, time, and page number. There is also a button you can click to clear the grayed text if you find it distracting.

▶ From the <u>V</u>iew menu, choose <u>H</u>eader And Footer.

Your document looks like the following illustration.

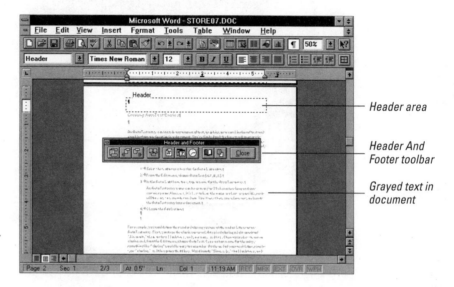

— Header area

— Header And Footer toolbar

— Grayed text in document

Tip If the Header And Footer toolbar appears in the middle of the screen, double-click a gray area in the Header And Footer toolbar. This places the toolbar above the ruler so it does not obscure your view of the Standard toolbar or of the page on the screen.

Enter text in a header

With the insertion point in the header area, you can type and format text that should appear with the page number.

1 Click the Align Right button on the Formatting toolbar.

2 Type **Page**

Align Right

Enter information in the footer

A date is another piece of information that is often included on every page in a document. In this exercise, you insert a date in the footer.

1   Click the Switch Between Header And Footer button in the Header And Footer toolbar.

The insertion point moves to the footer area.

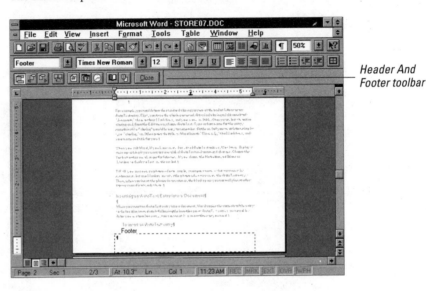

Header And
Footer toolbar

Center

2   Click the Center button on the Formatting toolbar.

3   With the insertion point in the center of the footer, click the Date button on the Header And Footer toolbar.

4   Click the Close button on the Header And Footer toolbar to return to normal view.

Date

Preview the document

1   Click the Print Preview button on the Standard toolbar.

2   Click the One Page button to display a single page of the document.

3   Scroll to the second page.

Print Preview

Your document looks like the following illustration.

One Page

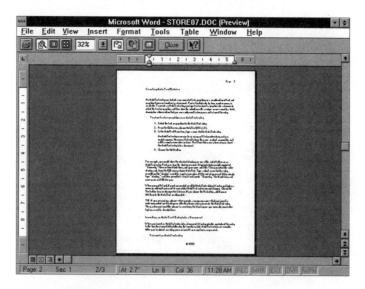

4   Click the Close button to return to normal view.

Creating Facing Pages

Facing pages are pages that you intend to print on both sides of a sheet of paper. For this kind of document, you want the page numbers to print differently on even-numbered and odd-numbered pages. For instance, on odd-numbered pages, the page number should appear at the right margin, and on even-numbered pages the page number should appear at the left margin. The following illustration shows an example of a document with facing pages.

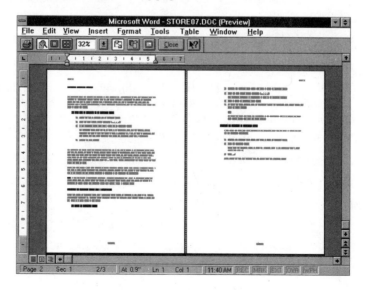

Establish facing pages in a document

1   From the File menu, choose Page Setup.

2   Click the Margins tab.

3   Click the Mirror Margins check box.

This option creates facing pages in the document. The Preview area reflects this change.

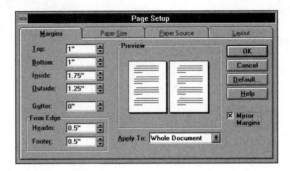

4   Click the OK button.

You won't see any change in your document until you view it in Print Preview.

Adjust a header for facing pages

1   From the Insert menu, choose Page Numbers.

2   In the Alignment drop-down list, select Outside.

This option instructs Word to place page numbers on the outside margin of every page.

3   Click the OK button.

Move text in a header

With the page number on the outside margin, you need to move the text "Page" to the left margin of the header for even-numbered pages. Before you edit the header, change the magnification to get a better view of the page.

1   In the Zoom Control box on the Standard toolbar, select 75%.

2   Place the insertion point anywhere in the second page of the document.

3   From the View menu, choose Header And Footer.

4   Select the text "Page" in the header.

5   Click the Cut button on the Standard toolbar.

Cut

You might need to drag the Header and Footer toolbar away from the Standard toolbar to see the Cut button.

6 In the header area, place the insertion point to the left of the number.

Paste

7 Click the Paste button on the Standard toolbar to insert the text in front of the page number.

Print Preview

8 Click the Close button on the Header and Footer toolbar to return to the document.

9 Click the Print Preview button on the Standard toolbar and click the Multiple Pages button to see what the document will look like when you print it.

Multiple Pages

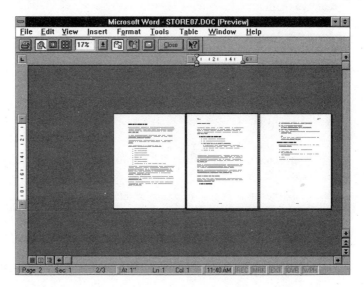

10 Click the text near the top of page 2 to examine the headers.

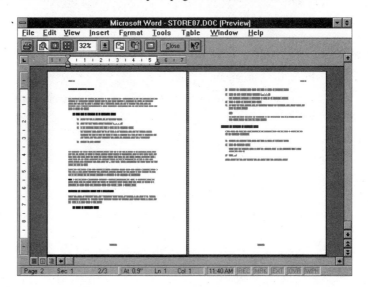

One Step Further

In addition to footers, *footnotes* are another kind of text that can appear at the bottom of a page. When you want to make a reference in a document, you insert a footnote reference mark (for which you have the option to have Word assign a number), and then you can enter the text. If you add or delete a footnote, Word automatically renumbers the footnotes. Although you don't see the footnotes in normal view, you can see them in page layout and print preview views, as well as when you print them.

Insert a footnote

1 Click the Normal View button to the left of the horizontal scroll bar.

2 Move the insertion point to the end of the first paragraph on page 2.

3 From the Insert menu, choose Footnote.

4 Click the OK button.

5 In the footnote area, type:
   Don't confuse this feature with AutoCorrect, which inserts stored text as you type.

6 Click the Close button to return to the text of the document.

7 Click the Print Preview button on the Standard toolbar to see how your document will look when it is printed.

If You Want to Continue to the Next Lesson

1 From the File menu, choose Close.

2 If a message appears asking whether you want to save changes, click the Yes button.

If You Want to Quit Microsoft Word for Now

1 From the File menu, choose Exit.

2 If a message appears asking whether you want to save changes, click the Yes button.

Lesson Summary

To	Do this
Number all pages except the first	From the Insert menu, choose Page Numbers. Clear the Show Number On First Page check box. Select additional options to format and position the page numbers. Click OK.
Create a header or footer	From the View menu, choose the Header and Footer command. In the header or footer area, type the text or click the buttons for the data you want to appear.
View page numbers and headers or footers	Choose Page Layout from the View menu or choose Print Preview from the File menu.
Alternate headers and footers for facing pages	From the File menu, choose Page Setup. On the Margins tab page, click the Mirror Margins check box.
Insert a footnote	Place the insertion point where you want the footnote reference to be. From the Insert menu, choose the Footnote command. Select a footnote option if you want, and click OK. In the footnote area, type the text of your footnote and click the Close button.

For more information on	See in the *Microsoft Word User's Guide*
Margins, page numbers, and headers and footers	Chapter 11, "Page Setup: Margins, Page Numbers, and Other Items"

Preview of the Next Lesson

In the next lesson, you'll learn how to use styles to take advantage of the text formatting you've already done in a document. Styles save you time because, in a single step, you can apply a set of formatting specifications to characters and paragraphs.

Using Styles

When creating documents, you might decide that all product names be in bold and italic; you might also decide that paragraphs in a list have a specific line spacing and right indent setting. You can save a lot of time by using styles to quickly apply a set of formatting specifications to text and paragraphs.

In this lesson, you'll learn how to store a collection of formatting specifications to create a *style*. You'll create and modify character styles to format characters, and you'll create and modify paragraph styles to format entire paragraphs. By applying styles, you can ensure fast and consistent formatting of text and paragraphs throughout your document.

You will learn how to:

For instructions about starting Microsoft Word, see "Getting Ready," earlier in this book.

- Store a combination of formats as a character style.
- Store a combination of formats as a paragraph style.
- Apply style to text and paragraphs.
- Change the definition of a style.

Estimated lesson time: 30 minutes

Open a sample document

Open

1   On the Standard toolbar, click the Open button.

2   In the Directories list, be sure the PRACTICE directory is open. If it is not, select the drive and directory for the Microsoft Word home directory, and click each subsequent directory until you locate PRACTICE.

3   In the File Name list, double-click 08HELP.DOC.

If you share your computer with others who use Microsoft Word, the screen display might have changed since your last lesson. If your screen does not look similar to the following illustration, see the Appendix, "Matching the Exercises."

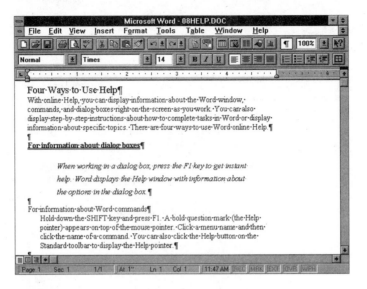

Save the document with a new name

Save the document with a new name so the changes you make in this lesson will not overwrite the original practice file.

1   From the File menu, choose Save As.

2   In the File Name box, type **help08**

3   Click the OK button.

Formatting with Character Styles

Suppose you are writing instructions for using Microsoft Word and you want to emphasize certain keys used in procedures. So that the key name looks different from the surrounding text, you might format the names of the keys in small caps, bold, and italics. You could specify all the formatting for each key name, but even using the Formatting toolbar, you might forget a format or two.

By storing combinations of character formats (such as bold, italic, underlined, font, and font size) as styles, you save time and ensure identical formatting throughout your document. The following procedure shows you how to store a combination of formats so that you can later apply a set of character formats to selected text with a click of the mouse.

Create a character style

The easiest way to create a style is to locate text that already contains most of the formatting you want. When you create the style, you can modify the formatting, if necessary.

1   Select the word "SHIFT" in the paragraph under "For information about Word commands."

Bold

2   In the Formatting toolbar, click both the Bold and the Italic buttons to change the the text to bold italic.

3   From the F_ormat menu, choose _Style.

Italic

The Style dialog box looks like the following illustration.

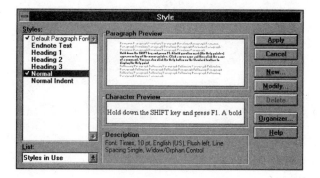

4   Click the New button to create a new style.

The New Style dialog box looks like the following illustration.

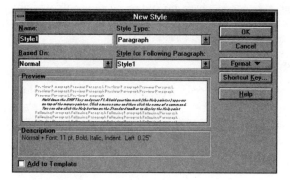

5   In the Name box, type **WCSKey**

Note   You can give your style a name that is up to 255 characters long, including numbers, letters, and spaces. Two styles cannot have the same name, but Microsoft Word does store uppercase and lowercase letters separately. As a result, you could have one style called "WCSKEY" and another called "wcskey."

---

6   From the Style Type drop-down list, select Character.

This selection ensures that your style will affect only selected text, not entire paragraphs.

7   Click the OK button to return to the Style dialog box.

Notice that your new style has been added to the list of styles in this document. Also notice that character styles do not appear in bold text in the list.

Your Style dialog box looks like the following illustration.

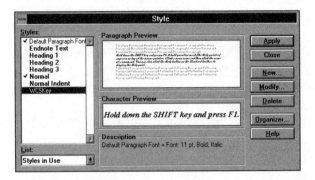

8   Click the Apply button to apply this new style to the selected text and return to your document.

Applying Character Styles

Once you've created a character style, you can apply it to any text you want formatted a specific way. After you apply a style, the selected text contains the same formatting of the text upon which you based the style.

Apply the key style

Locate another occurrence of a key name in the document and apply the new character style to it.

1   In the paragraph under the next heading, double-click the word "SHIFT" to select the word.

2   Click the down arrow next to the Style box at the far left of the Formatting toolbar.

3   Select the style called WCSKey.

You might need to scroll through the list to locate the style. When you release the mouse button, Microsoft Word applies the style to the selected text.

You can also press the repeat key F4 to repeat the last operation.

4   Locate all occurrences of the key names F1 and SHIFT in this document, and repeat steps 1 through 3 to apply this style to each one.

When you complete applying styles, your document looks like the following illustration.

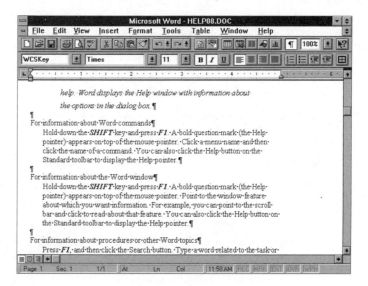

Formatting with Paragraph Styles

A paragraph style contains a collection of both paragraph and character formatting that you want to apply to the entire paragraph. This means that, in addition to specifying the appearance of text in a style, you can specify the alignment, spacing, and line spacing of paragraphs. You use paragraph styles when you want to ensure consistent paragraph formatting for different kinds of paragraphs in your document.

Like all paragraph formatting, paragraph styles are stored in paragraph marks at the end of paragraphs. When you work with paragraph styles, it is a good idea to display paragraph marks. This prevents accidentally deleting a paragraph mark and, with it, the paragraph's formatting.

Show/Hide ¶

▶   If paragraph marks are not currently displayed, click the Show/Hide ¶ button on the Standard toolbar.

Create a paragraph style for paragraph headings

Creating a paragraph style is quite similar to creating a character style. You simply specify a paragraph style type in the New Style dialog box. When creating paragraph styles, you can also use a procedure that does not require you to use the Style dialog box, so you can create paragraph styles more quickly. Use this technique to create two new paragraph styles: one for the headings of paragraphs and one for the body of the paragraphs.

1   Scroll near the top of the document and select the heading "For information about dialog boxes," which is formatted with a double underline.

2   In the Style box on the Formatting toolbar, double-click to select the current style name "Normal" so you can replace it with a new style name.

3   Name the style by typing **WCSHeading** in the box.

The text you type replaces the selected text.

4   Press ENTER.

You will not see a change in the document, but Word has stored the formatting of the paragraph as the WCSHeading style.

Create a paragraph style for the body of paragraphs

You can select an entire paragraph by double-clicking in the selection bar.

1   Select the next paragraph (the one in italic text, formatted with 1.5-line spacing).

2   In the Style box, drag to select the current style name for this paragraph, "Normal," so you can replace it with a new style name.

3   Type **WCSBody1.5** to remind you that this paragraph style indents the paragraph and changes the line spacing to 1.5 lines.

4   Press ENTER to store the formatting.

Applying Paragraph Styles

You can apply a paragraph style to any number of paragraphs in the document. Applying a paragraph style gives a paragraph the same formatting as the paragraph that served as the model for that style. Remember that paragraph styles affect entire paragraphs. If you want to add additional formatting to only a part of a paragraph, select the text, and then apply formatting with a character style or buttons on the Formatting toolbar.

Note   To create and modify character styles, use the Style command from the Format menu.

Apply the heading style

Apply the WCSHeading style to the next heading in the document.

1   To see more of the headings, scroll down until the formatted heading, "For information about dialog boxes," is at the top of the screen.

2   Select the next heading, "For information about Word commands," which appears after the italic paragraph.

3   Click the down arrow next to the Style box to display the list of styles.

This displays the styles you've created along with some of the standard styles that Word provides, for example, the Heading 1, Heading 2, and Heading 3 styles.

4   Select the WCSHeading style name.

Word applies the formats stored in this style—bold, double-underlining, 11-point font size—to the selected text. Click outside the selection for a better look at the formatting.

Your document looks like the following illustration.

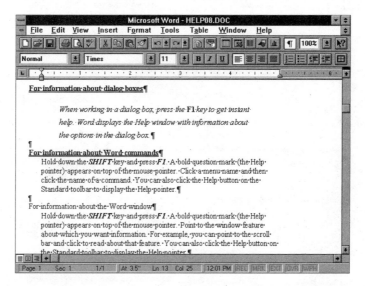

Apply another style

Apply the WCSBody1.5 style to the next paragraph in the document.

1   Select the paragraph that follows the heading "For information about Word commands."

2   Click the down arrow next to the Style box and then click the WCSBody1.5 style.

Word applies all the formats stored with the style name—italic, left and right indents, 1.5-line spacing, and space before the paragraph. Click outside the selection for a better look at the formatting.

Apply the styles to the rest of the document

1   Click the down scroll arrow on the vertical scroll bar until you see the last two headings and the paragraph that follows each of them.

2   Apply the WCSHeading style to each heading and the WCSBody1.5 style to the body paragraphs below each heading.

3   Click outside the selection for a better look at the formatting.

Your document looks like the following illustration.

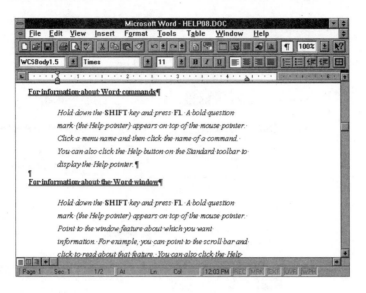

View the document

▶ Use the up scroll arrow to scroll line by line to the top of the document, noting the formatting as you go.

Changing a Style

Suppose that after viewing the document, you decide that the body paragraphs would look better with justified lines, no right indent, and no italic. Instead of reformatting every text paragraph separately, all you need to do is change the style. Redefining the style changes the formatting of every paragraph to which you applied that style.

Reformat a styled paragraph

In the next exercise, you'll make quick adjustments to the paragraph formatting before redefining the style.

1 Select the first body paragraph that has the WCSBody1.5 style.

Justify

2 On the Formatting toolbar, click the Justify button.

Word justifies the text, adding space between words as necessary to make the lines extend to the right indent.

Italic

3 On the Formatting toolbar, click the Italic button.

Word removes the italic formatting from the paragraph.

4 Drag the Right Indent marker to 5 inches on the ruler, as shown in the following illustration.

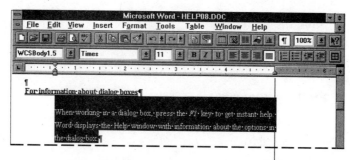

Right indent marker

Redefine the style

1 With the formatted paragraph still selected, select the name WCSBody1.5 in the Style box.

2 Press ENTER.

3 When you see the Reapply Style dialog box, be sure the first option button is selected, and then click the OK button.

Every paragraph with the WCSBody1.5 style changes to reflect the new formatting.

4 Click the down scroll arrow to scroll through the document line by line, viewing the results.

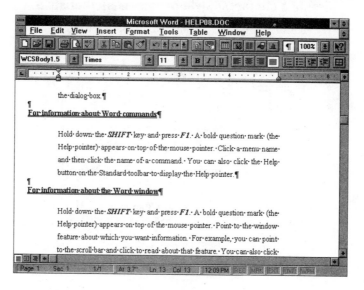

Save the document

Save

▶ On the Standard toolbar, click the Save button.

Word saves the current version of the document in place of the previous version.

Print the document

The sample document describes the online Help system and suggests ways to use it.

Print

1 Be sure the printer is on.

2 On the Standard toolbar, click the Print button.

Word prints one copy of the document.

One Step Further

Suppose you want to create another character style that uses a different font from the WCSKey style, but in all other respects is the same as the WCSKey style. By basing your new style on the WCSKey style, you can be sure the text will always have the same characteristics as the WCSKey style (except for the font), even if the WCSKey style changes.

To make applying styles even easier and faster, you can also specify a keyboard shortcut as an alternative to applying a style from the Formatting toolbar.

Create a character style based on another style

1 Select the text "Tip:" near the bottom of the page.

2 Apply the WCSKey style.

3 From the Font drop-down list in the Formatting toolbar, change the font of the text by selecting Arial.

4 From the Format menu, choose Style.

5 Click the New button to create a new style.

6 In the Name box, type **WCSTip**

7 In the Style Type drop-down list, select Character.

This selection ensures that your style will affect only selected text, and not entire paragraphs. When you select Character, the Based On box changes to display the style name of the currently selected text, "WCSKey."

Create a keyboard shortcut

1 In the New Style dialog box, click the Shortcut Key button to display the Customize dialog box.

2 With the insertion point in the Press New Shortcut Key box, press CTRL+SHIFT+E.

3 Click the Assign button to assign this keyboard shortcut to the character style.

4 Click the Close button to return to the New Style dialog box.

5 Click the OK button to return to the Style dialog box.

Notice that your new style has been added to the list of styles in this document. Also notice that character styles do not appear in bold text in the list.

Apply the style

1 In the Style dialog box, click the Apply button to apply this style to the currently selected text and return to your document.

2 Select each occurrence of the word "Tip:" and apply the WCSTip style to it using the keyboard shortcut, CTRL+SHIFT+E.

If You Want to Continue to the Next Lesson

1 From the File menu, choose Close.

2 If a message appears asking whether you want to save changes, click the Yes button.

Choosing this command closes the active document; it does not exit the Word application.

If You Want to Quit Word for Now

1 From the File menu, choose Exit.

2 If a message appears asking whether you want to save changes, choose the Yes button.

3 If a message appears asking whether you want to save changes to NORMAL.DOT, click the No button if you share your computer with others or are connected to a network. Your styles will be available only in this document.

Click the Yes button, if you are the only one who uses your computer and you want to save the styles you created in this lesson so that you can use them in other documents.

Lesson Summary

To	Do this
Create a character style	Select the formatted text and choose Style from the Format menu. Click the New button and enter a new style name in the Style Name box. Select the Character style type from the Style Type drop-down list. Click the OK button, and then click the Apply button.
Apply a character style	Select the text you want to format, and then select the style name in the Style drop-down list on the Formatting toolbar.
Create a paragraph style	Select the formatted paragraph, and then type the style name in the Style box on the Formatting toolbar.
Apply a paragraph style	Select the paragraphs you want to format. Select the style name in the Style drop-down list on the Formatting toolbar, and then press ENTER.
Redefine a paragraph style	Format one of the styled paragraphs the way you want it to look, select the style name, and then press ENTER. Choose the Yes button to redefine the style.
Create a character style based on another style	Select the formatted text containing the style you want to change. Modify the character formatting, and choose Style from the Format menu. Click the New button, and enter a new style name in the Style Name box. Select the Character style type from the Style Type drop-down list. Click the OK button, and then click the Apply button.

For more information on	See in the *Microsoft Word User's Guide*
Defining, naming, applying, and changing paragraph styles	Chapter 7, "Formatting Paragraphs"
Defining, naming, applying, and changing character styles	Chapter 9, "Automatic Formatting and Styles"

Preview of the Next Lesson

In the next lesson, you'll learn how to save time when creating and setting up documents by using templates. Templates store the standard formatting you apply to pages and paragraphs for specific documents, such as letters, memos, or reports. You'll learn how to create a template and use it to create a standard letter.

Saving Time with Wizards and Templates

If you use several kinds of documents in your work, each requiring its own set of formatting and styles, you can save a lot of time by using wizards and templates. This lesson has two parts. In the first part, you learn how to use a wizard to create a letter and its accompanying envelope. In the second part, you open a document that has already been formatted but does not have any styles applied to it. You create a template that can be used as a basis for other documents that require the same formatting.

You will learn how to:

- Use a wizard to create a letter.
- Create an envelope.
- Use AutoFormat to create formatting and styles for a new template.
- Create a document based on a template.

Estimated lesson time: 30 minutes

Using a Wizard to Create a Letter

A *wizard* guides you through the process of creating many different kinds of documents. You answer the questions posed by the wizard regarding style and other formatting options, and the wizard creates the document you requested. All the formatting, page setup information, and even styles are already created and applied for you.

Create a letter with a wizard

You start a wizard by choosing the New command on the File menu and selecting the kind of wizard you want. Use a wizard to create a letter to a West Coast Sales regional manager.

For instructions about starting Microsoft Word, see "Getting Ready," earlier in this book.

1 Be sure you are in Normal view. Then, from the File menu, choose New.

The New dialog box appears.

2   In the Template list, select Letter Wizard.

3   Click the OK button.

The first window of the wizard appears.

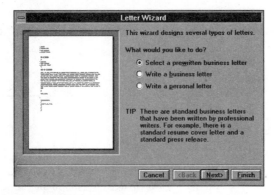

Answer wizard questions

The wizard gives you several choices as you create your letter. There is no wrong or right answer; what you select depends on your preferences. In this exercise, you create a classic business letter.

1   In the first wizard window, select the "Write a business letter" option.

2   Click the Next button to continue to the next window.

3   Select the Date and Enclosures check boxes, and clear any of the other check boxes that might already be selected.

The Letter Wizard presents options for you to indicate other information to be included with your letter, if you want.

4   Click the Next button to continue to the next window.

5   Select the "Plain paper" option button.

The Letter Wizard provides an option to allow room for a letterhead. In this case, you will not print the letter on letterhead.

6   Click the Next button to continue to the next window.

7   In the upper-right text box, select and delete any existing text, and then type:
Julia Stevens
Regional Manager
West Coast Sales
123 West Valley Drive
Riverdale, MT 75661

Be sure to press ENTER at the end of each line.

8   Press TAB to move to the return address box. With the existing name and address selected, type:
Chris Hamilton
West Coast Sales
555 Plaza Avenue
Franklin, CO 54320

9   After checking the accuracy of what you typed, click the Next button to continue to the next window.

10   Choose the Classic option button.

11   Click the Next button to continue to the next window.

The final window in the wizard looks like the following illustration.

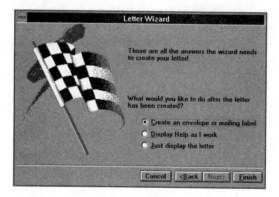

12   Be sure the "Create an envelope or mailing label" option button is selected.

This option prepares an envelope using the name and address of the recipient you entered for your letter. You can edit the recipient's address information, as well as the return address, if necessary.

13   Click the Finish button.

The Envelopes And Labels dialog box appears.

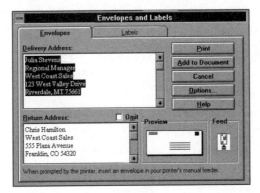

14 Click the Add To Document button.

This selection ensures that the envelope prints each time you print this letter. When you print the document, the envelope prints first. Your printer will pause until you supply an envelope, and then it will resume printing.

15 When you see the message box asking whether you want the return address information to be saved as the default return address, click the No button.

Your document looks similar to the following illustration.

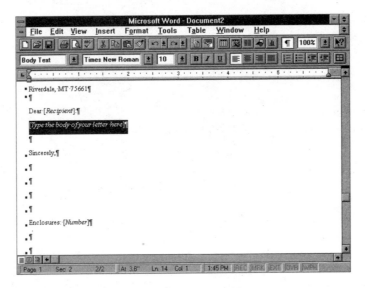

Type your letter

When you first edit a document created by a wizard, the areas in which you enter your own text are shown inside square brackets. This makes it easy to locate where you can enter your own information. You must select and replace both the text inside the brackets and the brackets themselves with your own text for the document.

1 Select the brackets and text after the word "Dear."

2 Type **Julia:**

3 In the next line, select the next set of brackets and text, and then type the following text for the body of the letter:
I thought you would like a preview of last month's sales results. I am developing a new document type that presents the information attractively. What do you think? By the way, can you help out with a chart or some graphics?

4 Select the brackets and text after the word "Enclosures," and then type **1**

Add signature block information

The *signature block* area of a document contains the closing text "Yours truly," followed by three blank lines, allowing room for your signature, your name, and your title. Notice the small squares in the left margin next to the four lines of the signature block. These squares appear when you are working in normal view and indicate that these lines cannot be separated by a page break.

1 Place the insertion point in front of the paragraph mark two lines after the text "Yours truly."

2 Type **Chris Hamilton**

3 With the insertion point in the next line, type **CEO/West Coast Sales**

Switching Document Views

Word provides several *views,* or ways of displaying a document. Each view helps you concentrate on a different aspect of the document. As you work with columns, you will find that certain views better suit the task at hand. For example, normal view, the view you've used most often in the preceding lessons, is best for typing and editing text.

Switch to page layout view

In page layout view, you can edit the document as well as see how it will look when printed.

Page layout view is much like print preview view because it shows how your document will look when it is printed. Unlike print preview, you can see the non-printing characters, which makes this view better for editing and formatting. When you choose page layout view, you'll see the top "edge" of the page.

1 To get a view of the document as it will print, click the Page Layout View button.

2 Scroll up to the first page and examine the envelope that will print when you print this document.

Page Layout View

3 To see the entire envelope, from the Zoom Control drop-down list box in the Standard toolbar, select Page Width.

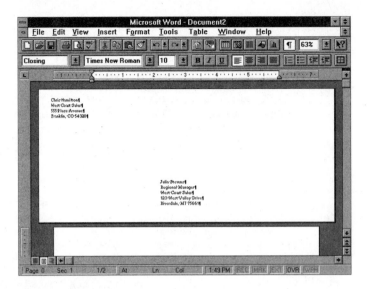

Customize the letter

The letter wizard is a good way to create a basic letter quickly. You can modify this letter just as you can make changes to any document you create. Add visual interest to the letter by placing the date at the right margin.

Align Right

1   With the insertion point in the date paragraph near the top of the letter on the second page, click the Align Right button on the Formatting toolbar.

2   Scroll all the way to the left, so your completed document looks like the following illustration.

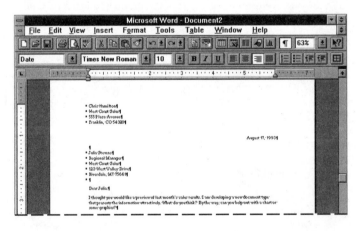

Save the document

1   From the File menu, choose Save As.

2   In the File Name box, type **letter09**

3   Be sure the PRACTICE directory is open, and click the OK button.

4   From the File menu, choose Close to close this document.

Creating a Template

As you saw in the previous exercise, a wizard can help you create standard kinds of business documents quickly. However, if you have document formatting requirements for which no wizards are available, you can create a document from a template. Like a wizard, a template contains all the document and paragraph formatting (in the form of styles) you need in a specific kind of document, plus boilerplate text that you can use or modify as you want. For example, if there is a standard opening or closing paragraph your company uses in all letters, you might prefer to use a template that contains this text. In addition, a template does not ask you questions to help you create a document, as a wizard does.

Word provides several templates for business documents including letters, memos, and press releases. If none of the Word templates provide the kind of document you want, you can create your own template upon which to base future documents.

Creating a Template from an Existing Document

An easy way to create a template is to locate a document that already has many of the formatting features you want. Even if the document does not already have styles applied to the text, you can use the AutoFormat command to analyze the formatting in the document and create styles for you. Then the template you create will have the styles you need in your future documents.

Open a sample document

The document that West Coast Sales uses to create organizational reports can be adapted to create monthly sales reports. Open this document so you can modify it.

Open

1   On the Standard toolbar, click the Open button.

2   In the Directories list, be sure the PRACTICE directory is open. If it is not, select the drive and directory for the Microsoft Word home directory, and then click each subsequent directory until you locate PRACTICE.

3   In the File Name list, double-click 09ORGVW.DOC.

If you do not see 09ORGVW.DOC in the list of file names, check to be sure the correct drive and directory are open.

Save the document with a new name

Save the document with a new name so the changes you make in this lesson will not overwrite the original practice file.

1 From the File menu, choose Save As.

2 In the File Name box, type **orgvw09**

3 Click the OK button.

Switch to normal view

Normal View

▶ For fast editing, click the Normal View button.

Edit the document

Before creating a template from this document, change some of the text so that it reflects sales information. You can also enter placeholder text (xx%) that represents text that must be edited each time you create a document based on the new template.

1 In the first heading, select the text "Organizational Overview" and replace it by typing **Monthly Sales Report**

2 For each division, add the following text to each paragraph: **Growth last month was xx%. Top selling products were:**

3 In place of each category listed, select the text after each hyphen and replace it with **product**

Save your changes

Save

▶ Click the Save button on the Standard toolbar.

Establish styles with AutoFormat

This document has already been formatted, but it does not have styles applied to the text. You can use the AutoFormat command to create styles based on the formatting in the document (as well as new formatting that will improve how your document looks).

The AutoFormat command also looks for "TM" or "(C)" and changes them to the correct symbols, and changes hyphens in a list to bullets. You simply click the AutoFormat button to polish your document.

AutoFormat

▶ Click the AutoFormat button in the Standard toolbar.

Microsoft Word analyzes your document, applies improved paragraph formatting, adds a trademark symbol, replaces hyphens with bullets, and creates styles.

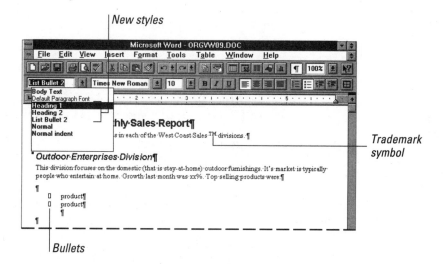

New styles

Trademark symbol

Bullets

Save the document as a template and close it

Now that your document contains the standard text and formatting you need to create sales reports, you can save the document as a template. From this template, you can create standardized sales reports.

1   From the File menu, choose Save As.

2   In the Save File As Type drop-down list, select Document Template.

3   In the File Name box, select the current name and replace it by typing **sales09**

Word adds the template extension DOT when you save the file.

4   Click the OK button to save the new template.

Word stores the template in a subdirectory called TEMPLATE in the Microsoft Word home directory.

5   From the File menu, choose Close.

Creating a New Document Based on a Template

You can get a head start on creating a sales report by using the new SALES09 template you created. With much of the text and the formatting already in the document, you only need to make a few changes to finish the report.

Create a document from a template

1   From the File menu, choose New.

2   In the Template list box, find the new template, SALES09.

If necessary, scroll down to display it.

3   Double-click the template name in the list.

A new document window opens, ready for you to create a new document.

Show paragraph marks

Show/Hide ¶

▶   Click the Show/Hide ¶ button to display paragraph marks if it is not already activated. This makes it easier to format text in your new document.

Enter text in your document

1   In the first heading, select the text "Monthly" and change it by typing **May**

Note   The text changes you make in this document do not affect the template upon which the document was created.

---

2   Select the text "xx" before each percent sign (%) in each paragraph for each division, and enter sales values as indicated here:

Outdoor Enterprises Division   **20**
Great Outdoors Division   **15**
Great Northern Division   **25**

3   Select the text "product" in each category and replace it with the products shown below.

Outdoor Enterprises Division	**Big Plaid oven mitts**
	Big Plaid grill covers
Great Outdoors Division	**D-Lux 5-person tent**
	Kiddie Kamper
Great Northern Division	**Cascade Down comforter covers**
	Sleep Happy Featherbeds

Add text for a new division

Add text announcing a new division. Later you can apply styles to format it properly.

1   Place the insertion point at the end of the document.

2   Type **Great Kitchens Plus Division** and press ENTER.

3   Type **Acquired last month, we are expecting great things from this new division. Hot products coming next month include:** and press ENTER twice.

4   Type **D-Lux Daiquiri Blender**

Apply styles to your text

1   Place the insertion point in the first new line you added, "Great Kitchens Plus Division," and then select the Heading 2 style from the Style drop-down list in the Formatting toolbar.

2   Place the insertion point in the last line of text, "D-Lux Daiquiri Blender," and then select the List Bullet 2 style from the Style drop-down list.

3   With the insertion point at the end of the line, before the paragraph mark, press ENTER.

The text after this style is automatically formatted in the same style as the previous line. The insertion point appears after the bullet.

4   Type **Instant Potato Masher**

The new text in your document looks like the following illustration. As you can see in the Style drop-down list, the List Bullet 2 style has been applied.

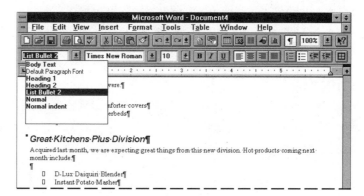

Save and close your new document

1   From the File menu, choose Save As.

2   In the File Name box, type **may09**

3   Click the OK button to save the new document.

4   From the File menu, choose Close.

One Step Further

There are many wizards included with Microsoft Word. To help you prepare for an upcoming meeting, use the Agenda wizard to create an agenda.

1   From the File menu, choose New.

2   In the Template list, select Agenda Wizard.

3   Click the OK button.

Experiment with the different options for creating an agenda. Use your own preferences when selecting options and answering questions posed by the wizard.

If You Want to Continue to the Next Lesson

1   From the File menu, choose Close.

2   If a message appears asking if you want to save changes, click the Yes button.

3   In the Save As dialog box, type **agenda09** and then click OK to save the new agenda document.

If You Want to Quit Microsoft Word for Now

1   From the File menu, choose Exit.

2   If a message appears asking if you want to save changes, click the Yes button.

3   In the Save As dialog box, type **agenda09** and then click OK to save the new agenda document.

Lesson Summary

To	Do this	Button
Create a new document using a wizard	From the File menu, choose New. In the New dialog box, select the wizard upon which you want to base the document. Answer the questions the wizard asks to create a document. Edit the new document so it contains the text you want.	
Create a template	Open the document containing the formatting that you want. Save the document as a template by choosing Save As from the File menu and selecting Document Template from the Save File As Type drop-down list.	
Apply automatic formatting to a document	From the Format menu, choose AutoFormat. *or* Click the AutoFormat button.	
Create a new document using a template	From the File menu, choose New. In the New dialog box, select the template upon which you want to base the document from the Template list box.	

For more information on	See in the *Microsoft Word User's Guide*
Wizards and Templates	Chapter 10, "Document Templates"

Preview of the Next Lessons

The lessons in the next part of this book will show you how you can achieve dramatic results in your documents by formatting text in tables and columns. You will also learn how you can add charts and graphics, and use information from other applications. In the next lesson, you'll learn how to add visual interest to a document with tables and charts.

Review & Practice

The lessons in Part 2 helped you increase your productivity through editing and proofing tools, styles, templates, and wizards. If you want to practice these skills and test your understanding before you proceed with the lessons in Part 3, you can work through the Review & Practice section following this lesson. This less structured activity allows you to increase your confidence using many of the features introduced so far.

Part 2   Review & Practice

In this Review & Practice, you have an opportunity to fine tune the editing and formatting skills you learned in the lessons in Part 2 of this book. Use what you have learned about inserting repeated text, proofing, applying stored formatting, and creating documents from wizards and templates to develop a quarterly report for West Coast Sales.

Scenario

Because you will create these documents four times a year, and they all should contain the same formatting and much of the same text, you will save time by creating a template that has the text and formatting already stored in it. You can use AutoFormat to create styles based on the formatting in an existing document. To increase your productivity even more, add AutoCorrect and AutoText entries to the template document.

You will review and practice how to:

- Save a document as a template.
- Add AutoCorrect entries.
- Add AutoText entries.
- Use AutoFormat to apply styles to an already formatted document.
- Create a document from a template.
- Proof a document.

Estimated practice time: 20 minutes

Step 1:   Create a Template from a Document

1 From the PRACTICE directory, open the document called P2REVIEW.DOC.

2 Save the document as a template called REVIEWP2.DOT.

Be sure to select "Document Template" in the Save As dialog box.

For more information on	See
Creating a template from a document	Lesson 9

Step 2: Add AutoText Entries, Header, and Footer

1 Create AutoText entries for the following words and phrases. Do not include the paragraph mark when you select the text for the entry. Use entry names that make sense to you.

Great Outdoors Division
Outdoor Enterprises Division
Great Northern Division
Great Kitchens PLUS!

2 Create a header that says "WCS Quarterly Report" followed by the date. Create a footer that shows the page number.

For more information on	See
Using AutoText	Lesson 5
Creating headers and footers	Lesson 7

Step 3: Create Styles in the Template

Use existing styles as the basis for new styles. You will apply these new styles when you create a document based on this template.

1 Click the AutoFormat button to create styles based on the formatting in the template.

2 From the Format menu, choose Style, and then create a new paragraph style based on the Heading 2 style, but change the font size so it is 2 points smaller. Call the new style Heading 2a. Do not apply the new style yet.

3 Create another new paragraph style based on the normal indent style, but change the style so it is italic. Call the new style Indent3. Do not apply this style yet.

4 Create a character style to format text in bold and 11-pt Arial. Call this style Numbers. You will use this style to format numbers in the document. Do not apply this style yet.

5 Save the template and close it.

For more information on	See
Using AutoFormat	Lesson 9
Creating Styles	Lesson 8

Step 4:   Create a Document from a Template

1   From the File menu, choose New, and create a new document based on the template called REVIEWP2.

2   Replace each occurrence of the placeholder text "xx" before the "%" with the values shown below. Then apply the character style called Numbers.

Great Outdoors Division	**13**
Outdoor Enterprises Division	**17**
Great Northern Division	**25**
Great Kitchens PLUS	**10**

3   Select the text "product" in each category and replace it with the products shown below. Delete the placeholder text "product" where only one product is listed.

Great Outdoors Division	**D-Lux DomeHome**
	Big Plaid Backpacks
Outdoor Enterprises Division	**Big Plaid Portable Refrigerator**
	Big Plaid Patio Set
Great Northern Division	**Cascade Down Curtains**
Great Kitchens PLUS!	**Big Plaid Toaster Covers**

For more information on	**See**
Applying styles	Lesson 8
Creating a document from a template	Lesson 9

Step 5:   Add Text and Apply New Styles

Add new text below the list of products for each division. You can format the new text in the new styles you created in Step 3.

1   At the paragraph mark under the text "Big Plaid Backpacks," apply the Heading 2a style to the blank line. Then type **Market Focus** and press ENTER.

2   Format the new paragraph in the Indent3 style, before you type the following text. Replace "division" with the actual division name. Save time by using the AutoText entries you created in Step 2 when you first modified the template. **Next quarter's new areas of concentration for the division include:** and press ENTER.

3   Copy the text you entered in 1 and 2 above, and paste it in the corresponding locations under each remaining division. Edit each sentence to contain the correct division name.

4   In the new paragraph after the one formatted in the Indent3 style, type the following areas of concentration for each division. Apply the List Bullet 2 style so that each item appears with a bullet.

Great Outdoors Division	**Active seniors**
Outdoor Enterprises Division	**Affluent singles under 30**
	Active seniors
Great Northern Division	**Empty nesters**
	Telecommuters
Great Kitchens PLUS!	**Affluent singles over 30**

For more information on	**See**
Using AutoText	Lesson 5
Using templates	Lesson 9

Step 6:   Check the Document's Spelling and Grammar

1   Click the Spelling button on the Standard toolbar.

2   Correct any words that are clearly misspelled. Add all proper names to the dictionary, and add AutoCorrect entries for words you misspell frequently.

3   From the Tools menu, choose Grammar. Correct the grammar according to your style and preferences.

4   After you have finished proofing the document, save it with the name REVIEWP2.DOC in the PRACTICE directory.

For more information on	**See**
Proofing a document	Lesson 6

If You Want to Continue to the Next Lesson

1   From the File menu, choose Close.

2   If a message appears asking if you want to save changes, click the Yes button.

If You Want to Quit Microsoft Word for Now

1   From the File menu, choose Exit.

2   If a message appears asking if you want to save changes, click the Yes button.

Creating Tables and Charts

A quick and easy way to arrange columns of numbers in a document is to create a table. You can also use tables to place paragraphs of text side by side. In this lesson, you create a table and apply different formatting options. You adjust column widths, and add and delete columns and rows. Then you experiment with the Table AutoFormat command, and apply your own formatting with borders. After you complete your table, you use the built-in Microsoft Graph application to create and modify a chart based on the information in the table.

You will learn how to:

For instructions about starting Microsoft Word, see "Getting Ready," earlier in this book.

- Insert a table into a document.
- Enter text in a table.
- Adjust the width of table columns.
- Insert rows and columns in a table.
- Merge table cells into one.
- Use Table AutoFormat to modify borders and shading in a table.
- Create a chart from the numbers in the table.

Estimated lesson time: 30 minutes

Open a sample document

Open

1   On the Standard toolbar, click the Open button.

2   In the Directories list, be sure the PRACTICE directory is open. If it is not, select the drive and directory for the Microsoft Word home directory, and click each subsequent directory until you locate PRACTICE.

3   In the File Name list, double-click 10TABLE.DOC.

If you share your computer with others who use Word, the screen display might have changed since your last lesson. If your screen does not look similar to the following illustration, see the Appendix, "Matching the Exercises."

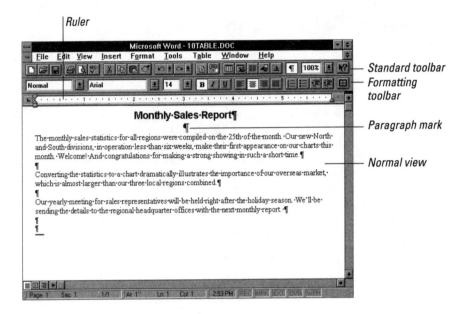

Ruler

Standard toolbar
Formatting toolbar
Paragraph mark
Normal view

Save the document with a new name

Give the document a new name so the changes you make in this lesson will not overwrite the original practice file.

1 From the File menu, choose Save As.

2 In the File Name box, type **table10**

3 Click the OK button.

Display paragraph marks

Show/Hide ¶

▶ If paragraph marks are not currently displayed on the screen, click the Show/Hide ¶ button on the Standard toolbar.

Creating a Table

A table is a grid of rows and columns containing boxes (called *cells*) of text or graphics. Within each cell, text wraps just as it does between the margins in other parts of a document. Unlike a table you might create using tabs, you can easily add or delete text in a table without affecting the arrangement of columns.

When you insert a table, Word outlines each cell with dotted gridlines so you can see the cells when you work in the table. Just as a paragraph mark ends every paragraph, an *end-of-cell mark* shows the end of every cell. Neither gridlines nor end-of-cell marks print.

***If you do not see
the gridlines***
*To display the
gridlines, from the
Table menu, choose
Gridlines.*

Insert a table

1 Position the insertion point in front of the paragraph mark in the last paragraph of text.

Do not place the insertion point in either of the blank paragraphs following the end of the text. These blank lines are needed later in this lesson.

2 Press ENTER twice to insert blank lines between the paragraph and the table you are about to create.

3 On the Standard toolbar, click the Insert Table button to display the grid.

4 Drag across the grid to select two rows and four columns.

Insert Table

When you release the mouse button, Word inserts an empty table that contains the number of columns and rows that you selected.

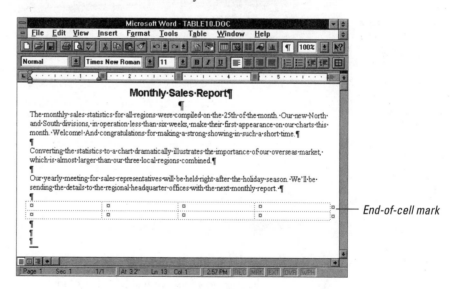

— *End-of-cell mark*

Type the text

When you insert a table, Word positions the insertion point in the first cell, ready for you to type.

1 Type **North**

2 Press TAB to move to the next cell.

3 Type **Central** and press TAB.

4 Type **South** and press TAB.

5 Type **International** and press TAB.

The insertion point moves to the first cell in the next row.

6 Fill in the rest of the table as indicated below. Press TAB to move from cell to cell. A new row of blank cells appears at the bottom of the table when you press TAB in the last cell in the table.

North	Central	South	International
3,209	**1,091**	**2,343**	**7,809**
3,429	**1,908**	**3,485**	**8,988**

Your table looks like this illustration.

If column markers do not appear on the ruler
If you click outside the table, the ruler changes to reflect the indents and margin settings for the paragraph that contains the insertion point. Clicking in the table will display the column markers again.

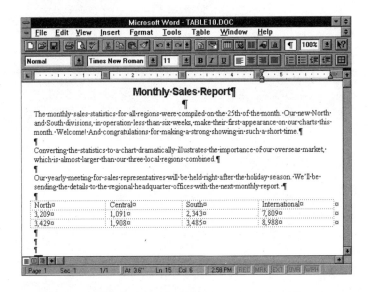

Adjust the width of the columns

You can use the ruler to adjust the width of the columns so they better fit the text. When the insertion point is in a table, the ruler displays a column marker at each column boundary. When you drag a column marker, the column boundary moves. The ruler shows the exact width of the columns.

1   If the ruler is not displayed, from the View menu, choose Ruler.

2   Click in the first cell with the word "North" to display the column markers on the ruler.

3   Drag the first column marker on the ruler to approximately 0.75 inch, so the column boundary is closer to the word "North."

| Column marker on ruler

4   Drag the remaining column markers to make the other columns narrower.

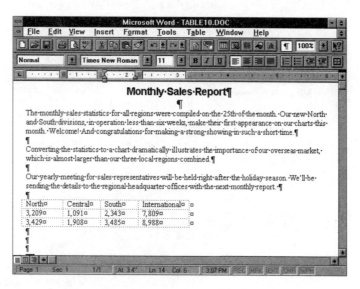

Set the "best fit" for the column width

You can have Word determine the best fit for the width of the columns in the table.

1   Select the entire table by selecting the first cell, and then dragging to the right and down until all the cells are selected.

2   From the Table menu, choose Cell Height And Width.

You can also click the right mouse button when pointing inside a table. This displays a context-sensitive menu from which you can choose the Cell Height And Width command. The dialog box looks like the following illustration.

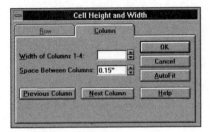

3 Click the AutoFit button.

This option formats each column width to be only as wide as the text in the longest cell in a column without the text appearing on two lines.

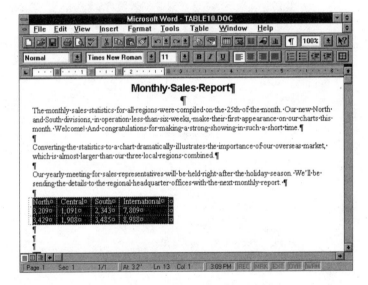

Inserting and Deleting Rows and Columns

As you work in a table you might need to add or delete a column or a row. You can use the commands on the Table menu to add rows and columns, or you can use the Insert Table button on the Standard toolbar. You can use the Cut button on the Standard toolbar to delete selected rows and columns. Or you can use the commands on the Table menu to do the same thing.

Note The function and name of the Insert Table button changes depending on whether rows, columns, or cells are selected in a table. For example, if you select a row, this same button on the Standard toolbar becomes the Insert Rows button. These instructions reflect the name of the button depending on what is selected in the table.

Insert a column

To add a column, you select a column to the right of where you want the new column to appear and click the Insert Columns button on the toolbar. This button is the same as the Insert Table button, except that its effect changes when you select a column.

1   Position the mouse pointer near the top edge of the first column.

2   Click when the pointer changes its shape to a down arrow.

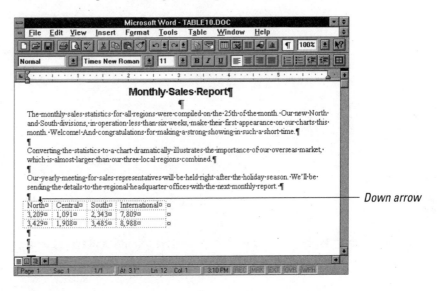
— Down arrow

This selects the entire column.

Insert Columns

3   Click the Insert Columns button on the Standard toolbar.

The remaining columns move to the right to make room for the new column.

Type text in the new column

Earlier in this lesson, you pressed TAB to move from cell to cell. You can also press arrow keys to move directly to a cell.

1   Click in the second cell of the new column, and then type **May**

2   Press the DOWN ARROW key to move down one cell, and then type **June**

Insert a column at the end of the table

Word displays *end-of-row marks* so you can add columns to the right side of a table. You select these marks in the same way you select a column.

1   Position the mouse pointer near the top and to the right of the last column, above the end-of-row marks.

2 Click when the pointer changes its shape to a down arrow.

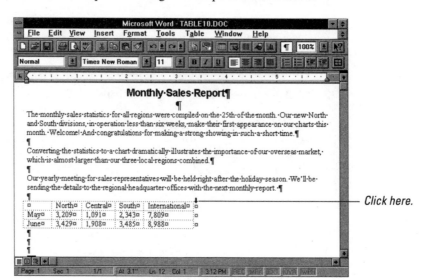

Click here.

Insert Columns

3 Click the Insert Columns button on the Standard toolbar.

A new column appears at the end of the table.

4 Select the first cell of the new column, and type **Totals**

Leave the remaining cells in the column blank for now. Later in this lesson, you learn to calculate totals for all the cells in each row.

Insert a row

To insert a new row, select the row below where you want the new row to appear and click the Insert Table button. When you add a row, existing rows move down to make room for the new row. Word inserts as many rows as you select.

In earlier lessons, you used an invisible selection bar to the left of paragraphs to quickly select lines and paragraphs. There is a selection bar to the left of tables, which you use to select entire rows.

1 Point to the left of the first row.

2 Click when the mouse pointer changes to an arrow pointing upward and to the right.

This selects the entire row.

Each cell also has an invisible selection bar. Be sure you click well to the left of the row so you do not select the first cell by itself.

Insert Rows

3 Click the Insert Rows button on the Standard toolbar.

This is the same button you used previously to insert columns. However, its name becomes "Insert Rows" when you have a row selected.

4   To release the selection, click anywhere outside of the table, and then place the insertion point in the first cell of the new row.

5   Type **Monthly Sales by Region**

The text wraps within the cell as you type. Later in this lesson, you will learn how to center the text in a single cell that spans the width of the table.

Delete a column

Deleting a row or column is as simple as inserting one. In this exercise, you delete the Central column.

1   Select the column labeled "Central" by positioning the mouse at the top edge of the column and clicking when the pointer changes to a down arrow.

Cut

2   Click the Cut button on the Standard toolbar.

You can delete rows in the same way. You select the row, and then choose the Cut button on the Standard toolbar.

Adding Borders and Shading

Although the gridlines you see on your screen make it easy to tell one cell from another, they do not print. If you want table borders to print, you can apply them to the gridlines. You can get a head start on formatting your table by using the Table AutoFormat command. After Word automatically formats your table, you can customize the appearance of your table even further by adding new borders.

Use Table AutoFormat to apply table borders

1   With the insertion point anywhere in the table, from the Table menu, choose Table AutoFormat.

2   In the Formats list box, select Classic 4.

An example of the formatting appears in the Preview area of the dialog box.

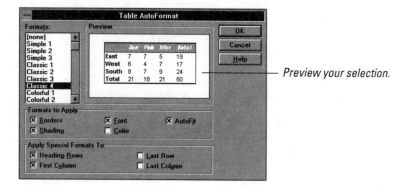

Preview your selection.

3   Click the OK button to return to the document.

Place a border under the second row

To add additional borders to a cell, you can use the Borders button.

1   Select the second row in the table.

2   Click the Borders button on the Formatting toolbar.

Borders

The Borders toolbar appears at the top of the document window above the ruler.

3   Click the Bottom Border button.

Bottom Border

Tip   You can modify the border thickness and shading percentage by selecting an option from the Line Style or Shading drop-down list in the Borders toolbar.

Formatting Text in a Table

With the borders and shading established for your table, you can format the text in individual cells in the same way you format characters and paragraphs in the rest of your document. First you'll merge cells to create a cell that spans all columns of the table. You'll also center text within the table, and then center the table between the document margins.

Merging Cells

You might sometimes want to combine, or *merge*, two or more selected cells within a row to create a single cell. For example, earlier in this lesson, you entered so much text in a cell that it did not fit on one line. By merging cells, you can create a cell wide enough to accommodate a heading that spans several columns.

Note   It's a good idea to insert and format all the columns and adjust their widths before merging cells.

Merge the cells in the top row

1   With the pointer in the selection bar to the left of the first cell, select the first row of the table.

2   From the Table menu, choose Merge Cells.

The selected cells merge into one. Your table looks like the following illustration.

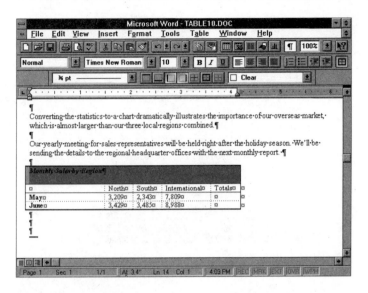

3   To delete the paragraph mark in the first cell, place the insertion point before the end-of-cell mark.

4   Press BACKSPACE to remove the extra paragraph mark.

Format the merged cell borders

The new merged cell does not have a border on the right side, because the border formatting of the first cell (which also did not have a right border) was applied to the new merged cell. This means you need to add a border to the right side of this cell.

1   Select the new merged cell by clicking in the selection bar to its left.

2   Click the Right Border button on the Borders toolbar.

3   Click the Borders button on the Formatting toolbar to hide the Borders toolbar.

Format headings

You edit and format text in a table just as you do any other document text.

1   Select the heading "Monthly Sales by Region," and then from the Font Size drop-down list in the Formatting toolbar, select 12 points.

2   Select the headings in the second row, and then click the Bold button on the Formatting toolbar.

Bold

Center the text in each cell

1   To select all the cells in the table, click with the insertion point anywhere in the table. Then from the Table menu, choose Select Table.

Center

2 Click the Center button on the Formatting toolbar.

Your table looks like the following illustration.

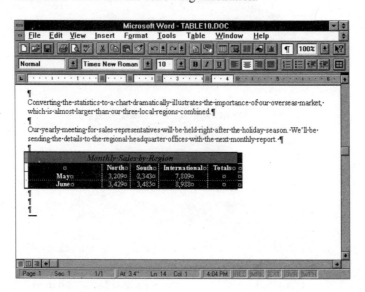

Adjust a column width

Adjust the width of the first column.

▶ With the insertion point in the first column, drag its column marker (the one on the right) to approximately the 1-inch mark.

Center the table between the document margins

You can center one or more selected rows, or you can center the entire table.

1 Select the entire table if it is no longer selected.

2 From the Table menu, choose Cell Height And Width.

3 Click the Row tab if it is not selected.

4 Under Alignment, select the Center option button.

5 Choose the OK button.

The table is centered between the margins of the page.

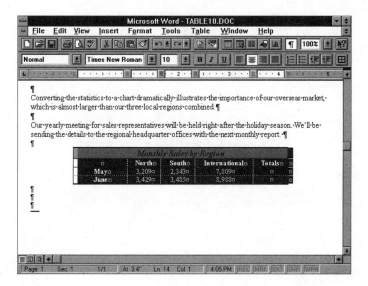

Creating Charts

You can select all or part of a table that contains numbers, and create bar charts, pie charts, and line charts similar to those in the Microsoft Excel spreadsheet program. Unless you specify otherwise, Word creates a bar chart.

The Setup program you use to install Word on your computer gives you the option to install or not install Microsoft Graph. If the feature is not installed, a message will be displayed during the following procedure. You can run the Microsoft Word Setup program again and specify that you want to install Microsoft Graph only.

Create a chart of the sales figures

1 Select the bottom three rows of the table.

2 Click the Insert Chart button on the Standard toolbar.

Insert Chart

Word displays a column chart in its own window, as shown in the following illustration. The window has the title "Microsoft Graph." Microsoft Graph is a special application that comes with Word and that appears with its own title bar and menu bar. You'll use these menus until you return to your document in Word.

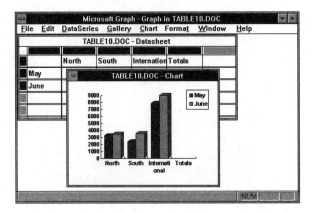

Size the chart

You size a chart in the Microsoft Graph application the same way that you size a window. Drag a border to the size you want.

1 Drag the lower-right corner of the chart window to the right until the word International appears on one line.

When you release the mouse button, Word resizes the chart. If you want to try again, drag the lower-right corner to a new size.

2 Select the legend in the upper-right corner, and drag it to the left, so that it appears to the left of the tallest bar in the chart.

Your chart looks like the following illustration.

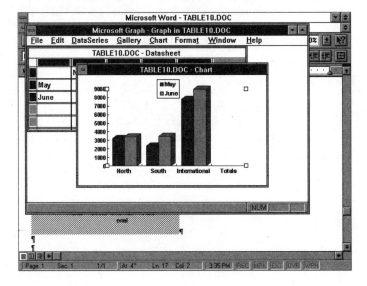

3   From the File menu in the Microsoft Graph window, choose Exit And Return.

4   When Word asks if you want to update the graph in the document, choose the Yes button.

Word inserts a blank line below the table, and then inserts the chart.

Tip   You can position the chart anywhere on the page. Lesson 12, "Adding Graphics and Emphasizing Text," shows you how. For more information, see Chapter 15, "Positioning Text and Graphics with Frames," in the *Microsoft Word User's Guide*.

Save

Save the document

▶   On the Standard toolbar, click the Save button.

Word saves this version of the document in place of the previous version.

One Step Further

You can use Word's Formula command to perform simple calculations in a table, including addition, subtraction, multiplication, and division, as well as basic functions, such as averages. If you are familiar with spreadsheets, such as Microsoft Excel, you can refer to cells by row and column coordinates. The rows are lettered (A, B, C), and so forth, and the columns are numbered (1, 2, 3). For example, the second cell from the left in the third row has the coordinates C2. Even if you are not familiar with spreadsheets, Word makes it easy to calculate totals in a row or column of numbers.

Calculate totals in rows

1   Place the insertion point in the first cell under the Totals column.

2   From the Table menu, choose Formula.

In the dialog box, Word suggests a formula that would sum the values in all cells to the left of the current cell. You can either accept the formula as displayed, or modify it to your needs.

3   Click OK to accept the formula and return to the document.

The total for the cells in this row appear in the current cell.

4   Place the insertion point in the cell below the total you calculated.

5   From the Table menu, choose Formula.

This time, the formula says "SUM(ABOVE)" instead of "SUM(LEFT)." Because you want to sum the row, you must modify the formula.

6   In the formula, select "ABOVE." Type **left** and click OK.

If you need to edit a value in the table, you can quickly recalculate new totals by selecting the cell that contains the total, and pressing F9.

If You Want to Continue to the Next Lesson

1   From the File menu, choose Close.

2   If a message appears asking whether you want to save changes, choose the Yes button.

If You Want to Quit Microsoft Word for Now

1   From the File menu, choose Exit.

2   If a message appears asking whether you want to save changes, choose the Yes button.

Lesson Summary

To	Do this	Button
Insert a table	On the Standard toolbar, click the Insert Table button, and then select the number of columns and rows you want.	🔳
Move to a new table cell	Press the TAB key or use the arrow keys.	
Select an entire column or row	Click above the column or in the selection bar to the left of the row. Select an entire table by choosing the Select Table command on the Table menu.	
Adjust the widths of table columns	Drag the column markers on the ruler.	
Insert a new row or column	Select a row or column in the existing table, and then choose the Insert Rows or Insert Columns command from the Table menu, or click the Insert Table button on the Standard toolbar.	🔳
Delete a row or column	Select the row or column, and then click the Cut button on the Standard toolbar.	
Add pre-defined formatting to a table	From the Table menu, choose Table AutoFormat. Then select the kind of formatting you want.	

To	Do this	Button
Add custom borders to a table	Click the Borders button on the Formatting toolbar, and then select the borders and line width you want.	
Add custom shading to a table row	Click the Borders button on the Formatting toolbar, and then select the shading you want from the Shading drop-down list.	
Merge several cells into one cell	Select the cells, and then choose the Merge Cells command on the Table menu.	
Center text within table cells	Select the table text. On the Formatting toolbar, click the Center button.	
Center a table between the page margins	From the Table menu, choose Select Table. From the Table menu, choose the Cell Height And Width command. On the Row tab, select the Center option under Alignment.	
Create a column chart	On the Standard toolbar, click the Insert Chart button. Resize the chart if needed. From the File menu in the Microsoft Graph menu bar, choose Exit And Return.	

For more information on	See in the *Microsoft Word User's Guide*
Tables	Chapter 13, "Working with Tables"
Sorting a table	Chapter 13, "Working with Tables"
Working with spreadsheet data	Chapter 27, "WordArt, Equation Editor, and Graph"
Positioning charts	Chapter 15, "Positioning Text and Graphics with Frames"

Preview of the Next Lesson

In the next lesson, you'll learn to format text into multiple columns and customize the look of the page by adding vertical lines between columns and breaking columns exactly as you want them. You'll learn the best ways to see the multiple-column document take shape on the screen.

Creating Columns

With Microsoft Word, you can produce "snaking" columns, in which text flows from the bottom of one column to the top of the next, as in newspaper columns. In this lesson you'll format two different documents. In the first, you'll change the number of columns for the entire document. In the second, you'll create a different number of columns for different parts (sections) of the document.

You will learn how to:

For instructions about starting Microsoft Word, see "Getting Ready," earlier in this book.

- Create multiple columns.
- Insert manual column breaks.
- Add lines between columns.
- Vary the number of columns within a document.
- Vary the width of individual columns.
- Reduce or enlarge the display of the document on the screen.

Estimated lesson time: 40 minutes

Open the sample document

Open

1   On the Standard toolbar, click the Open button.

2   In the Directories list, be sure the PRACTICE directory is open. If it is not, select the drive and directory for the Microsoft Word home directory, and click each subsequent directory until you locate PRACTICE.

If the Borders toolbar is still displayed
Click the Borders button on the Formatting toolbar to hide the toolbar. You will not need it in this lesson.

3   In the File Name list, double-click 11COLUMN.DOC.

If you share your computer with others who use Word, the screen display might have changed since your last lesson. If your screen does not look similar to the following illustration, see the Appendix, "Matching the Exercises."

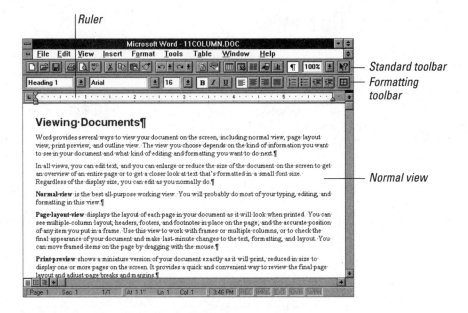

Ruler

Standard toolbar

Formatting toolbar

Normal view

Save the document with a new name

Give the document a new name so the changes you make in this lesson will not overwrite the original practice file.

1   From the File menu, choose Save As.

2   In the File Name box, type **column11**

3   Choose the OK button.

Creating Columns

You can use a button on the Standard toolbar to create columns in a document or to change the number of columns. Word automatically breaks each column at the bottom of the page and moves the remaining text to the top of the page to start a new column. You can also adjust where the columns break by inserting column breaks yourself.

Create multiple columns in a document

When you use the Columns button on the Standard toolbar, Microsoft Word automatically formats the text of the document into the number of columns you specify.

1   On the Standard toolbar, click the Columns button.

2   Point to the left column and drag to select two columns.

Columns

When you release the mouse button, Word creates the number of columns that you specify. You will not see the columns in the document just yet. For now, your document looks like the following illustration.

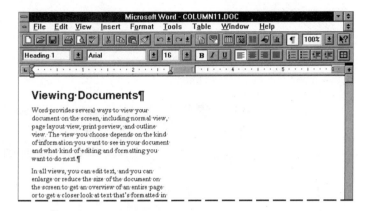

Switch to page layout view

In page layout view, you can edit the document as well as see how it will look when printed.

When you create columns in normal view, Word displays them in their actual width, but not side by side, as they will look when printed. To see the columns side by side, you must switch to page layout view. You can use the Page Layout View button or you can choose the Page Layout command on the View menu.

▶   From the View menu, choose Page Layout.

Columns now appear in your document as shown in the following illustration.

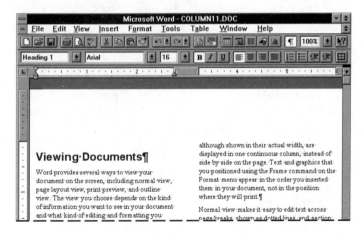

Insert a manual column break

Dragging the scroll box is a quick way to scroll to the end of a document.

Word automatically breaks each column when the text reaches the bottom of the page, moving the text that follows to the top of the next column. If you want to break the columns in another location, you can insert manual column breaks.

1   Scroll down to see the bottom of the page and position the insertion point in front of the heading, "Normal View," which is in bold and italic text.

2   From the Insert menu, choose Break.

3   Select the Column Break option.

4   Choose the OK button.

The text after the column break moves to the top of the next column.

Your document looks like the following illustration.

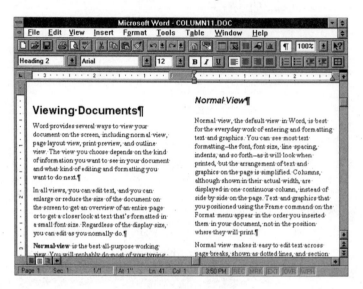

Add lines between columns

The Columns command includes special options for formatting columns. For example, you can use this command to place vertical lines between columns. You can also use this command to specify the space between columns or to create columns of unequal widths. You will learn about these other options later in this lesson.

1   From the Format menu, choose Columns.

2   In the Columns dialog box, click the Line Between check box.

3   Choose the OK button.

Switch to Print Preview

Now switch to print preview to see the whole document.

1   From the File menu, choose Print Preview.

2   Click the One Page button if it is not already selected.

Word displays the document as shown in the following illustration.

One Page

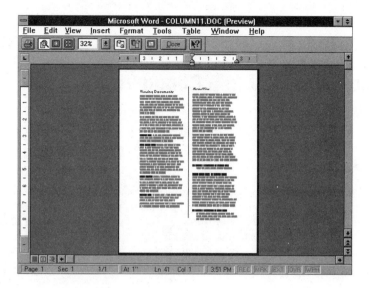

Save the document

▶ From the File menu, choose Save.

Print the document

It's a good idea to check the appearance of a document in print preview before you print it. You can print the document from print preview. Your printed document is the same regardless of which view is on the screen when you print.

▶ Click the Print button at the top of the print preview window.

If you are not connected to a printer, click the Close button.

Close the document

When you return to the document window, close the document.

▶ From the File menu, choose Close, or double-click the document Control-menu box.

Open the second sample document

To get ready for the next part of the lesson, open another sample document.

1 On the Standard toolbar, click the Open button.

2 In the File Name list, double-click **11sect.doc**

Open

Save the document with a new name

Give the document a new name so the changes you make in this lesson will not overwrite the original document.

1 From the File menu, choose Save As.

2 In the File Name box, type **sect11**

3 Choose the OK button.

Varying Columns Within a Document

You've learned all the skills you need to create columns in a document. If you need a more sophisticated page layout, you can vary how many columns appear on a page or in sections of the document. To vary the number of columns, you insert a *section break* before you create your new columns.

When you insert a section break to create multiple columns in a document, indicate that you want a *continuous* break. This means that the next section immediately follows the previous section on the same page. When you insert section breaks, you divide a document into *sections*, indicated by double-dotted lines that do not print. You can then format each section separately. The following illustration shows a page that has been divided into four sections. Each section is formatted with a different number of columns.

Other Useful Views

To work in any of the views described in the following section, you choose the name of the view that you want from the View menu. Your document prints correctly regardless of the view you choose.

Print Preview

Print preview shows you how your document will look when you print it. You can see whole pages one or more at a time and see elements of the document that aren't shown in normal. In addition, you document is displayed without non-printing characters, such as spaces, paragraph marks, or tabs. Your toolbars are also hidden, but you can display them if you wish.

All page elements that appear within the printable area of the page are shown in print preview. When you view your document in print preview, you can specify the number of pages you want displayed at one time. You can also click the Magnifier button to change the pointer to look like magnifying glass. When you click the magnifying pointer on the text of the document, you get a close-up view of the page. With this close-up view, you can read the text clearly. You'll need to click the Magnifier button again if you want to edit your text in print preview. If you click again,

your magnification is restored to the original settings.

When you click the View Rulers button, you can see the horizontal and vertical rulers. By dragging the margin markers, you can insert, move, and delete automatic page breaks.

Other buttons on the Print Preview toolbar allow you to:

- Print the current document.
- Have Word eliminate an extra page by reformatting the document.
- Show the document in Full screen (without menus)
- Set a specific magnification setting.
- Close print preview and return to your document.

Page Layout

After you've typed text and inserted graphics into your document, switch to page layout view. You can see how page elements such as multiple text columns, graphics, headers, footers, and footnotes will be positioned on the printed page.

You can also continue to type, edit, and format text in this view.

Special buttons at the bottom of the vertical scroll allow you to scroll one page at a time. When you reach the bottom of a page, scrolling down changes the display to show the top of the next page. In this view, you can see non-printing characters if you wish.

Outline View

In outline view, you can *expand* and *collapse* the headings in an outline. You expand headings to see more of the outline—main headings, subordinate headings, and any associated body text. You collapse headings to focus more on higher-level structure and less on the detail. You can also use the collapse feature to move large chunks of material efficiently and accurately. Just collapse a heading and move it; all subordinate text moves with the heading. You can also collapse headings to navigate quickly through a long document.

Magnifying or Reducing the Display Size

If you are using a small font and want a closer look at the text in normal view, page layout view, or outline view, you can zoom in the document window. If you open a new window, it will have the level of page you want to see and continue working in the magnified version. Similarly, you can zoom out to see an entire page at once, giving you an overview as you rearrange the headings of an outline or drag framed items such as pictures or tables to a new location on the page.

On the Standard toolbar, you can scroll in the Zoom Control box to one of the preset magnifications. You can also set the magnification to a precise level (such as 47%) if you wish. You can change the magnification for any magnification you last chose. The level of magnification is for your convenience as you edit. It does not affect the actual size of the document to when you print it.

Inserting Section Breaks

In normal view, a section break appears on the screen as a double dotted line extending the width of the page. These lines make it easy to see where section breaks occur, which is helpful when you format the sections. After you insert section breaks and create columns in each section, switch to page layout view to see columns side by side.

Switch to normal view

Normal View

▶ Click the Normal View button on the far left of the horizontal scroll bar.

You must be in normal view to see the section breaks you are creating in the exercise.

Insert a section break

1   Place the insertion point in front of the "Print Preview" heading.

2   From the Insert menu, choose Break.

3   Under Section Breaks, select the Continuous option button so the new section will print right after the previous section on the same page.

4   Choose the OK button.

Word inserts the section mark—a double dotted line. Now the document has two sections: one above the section mark and one below the section mark.

Insert another section break

1   Scroll down and place the insertion point in front of the heading "Magnifying or Reducing the Display Size."

2   From the Insert menu, choose Break.

3   Under Section Breaks, click the Continuous option button.

4   Choose the OK button.

Insert a section break below the heading

1   Place the insertion point in front of the first character in the first line after the "Magnifying or Reducing the Display Size" heading.

2   From the Insert menu, choose Break.

3   Under Section Breaks, select the Continuous option button.

4   Choose the OK button.

Now you can format each section with the number of columns you want.

Creating Columns in Each Section

To create a different number of columns in each section, move to the section in which you want to format in columns. Then use the Columns button on the Standard toolbar. With the document divided into sections, your column formatting affects only the section containing the insertion point.

After you format your columns, you can switch to page layout view to see your columns side by side.

Format each section

1   Scroll to the top of the document.

    The first section should remain formatted as one column. You do not need to do anything to that section.

2   Place the insertion point anywhere in the second section.

3   Click the Columns button on the Standard toolbar, and drag to display three columns.

Columns

4   Scroll down to section 4.

    Be sure the status bar displays the correct section number.

5   Place the insertion point anywhere in section 4 (in the paragraph below the heading "Magnifying or Reducing the Display Size").

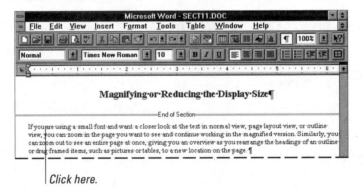

Click here.

The section containing the heading (section 3) is formatted as one column. You do not need to reformat section 3.

6   Use the Columns button on the Standard toolbar to create two columns in the last section.

Note   As you scroll through the sample document, you may notice a single dotted line. That line indicates an automatic page break. You can ignore this page break, because Word will create new page breaks, if necessary, after you finish formatting your columns.

Save

Save the document

▶   Click the Save button on the Standard toolbar.

Getting an Overview of the Layout

The Zoom Control drop-down list on the Standard toolbar is useful when you are working with columns. You can use the selections in the list to change the magnification setting of the document. You can select one of the magnification settings or you can type in an exact value.

When you change the magnification, you are changing only the way the document appears on the screen, not the size of the fonts or the length of the document.

Experiment with zooming in page layout view

Page Layout View

1   Click the Page Layout View button to the left of the horizontal scroll bar.

2   From the Zoom Control drop-down list, select 50%.

3   In the Zoom Control drop-down list, select the existing setting (50%). Type **40** and press ENTER.

Your document looks like the following illustration.

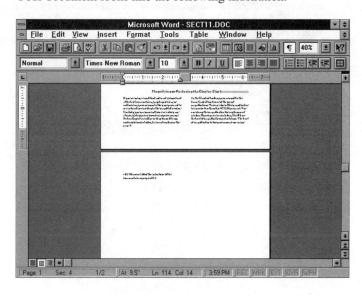

Formatting Columns

In addition to adding lines between columns, you can specify columns of uneven width and can adjust the spacing between columns.

Make uneven columns

To add visual interest to your document, you can make one column narrower than the other.

If you get unexpected results
Click the Undo button and place the insertion point again, this time taking care not to select any text.

1   Place the insertion point in the last section of the document.

Be sure you do not select any text when you place the insertion point, because Word will attempt to insert new columns inside an existing one.

2   From the Format menu, choose Columns.

3   In the Presets area, select the Left box.

This selection makes the left column narrower than the right column.

4   Click the OK button.

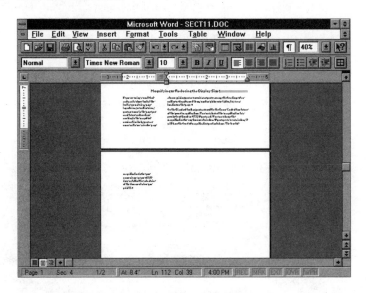

Specify spacing between columns

1   Place the insertion point in section 2.

2   From the Format menu, choose Columns.

3   In the Width And Spacing box, click the down arrow under Spacing to specify a 0.3-inch space between columns.

4   Click the OK button.

Your document looks like the following illustration.

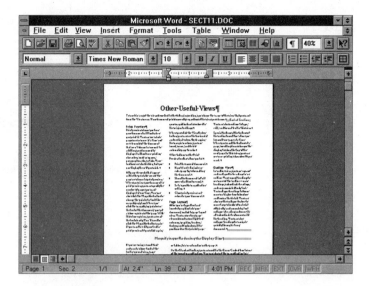

Save

Save the document

▶ From the File menu, choose Save.

One Step Further

For even faster formatting, you can use the column markers in the ruler to adjust the column width and spacing between columns. If the current section is formatted for columns that have the same width, dragging the column markers changes the width of the columns as well as the spacing between them. If the current section is formatted for uneven columns, dragging column markers changes only the width of the column.

Change column width using the ruler

1 Be sure the insertion point is in the wider column in section 4.

2 Drag the right edge of the column marker in the ruler to the left until the column's left edge aligns with the left edge of the second column in section 2 (the one containing three columns).

Tip Increase the magnification to make finer adjustments to the column width.

Justify

3 Improve the appearance of the document by selecting the last two paragraphs of the document, and clicking the Justify button on the Formatting toolbar.

If You Want to Continue to the Next Lesson

1   From the File menu, choose Close.

2   If a message appears asking whether you want to save changes, choose the Yes button.

If You Want to Quit Microsoft Word for Now

1   From the File menu, choose Exit.

2   If a message appears asking whether you want to save changes, choose the Yes button.

Lesson Summary

To	Do this	Button
Create columns	On the Standard toolbar, click the Columns button, and then drag to select the number of columns you want.	
Insert manual column breaks	From the Insert menu, choose the Break command, and then select Column Break.	
View a single page of the document as it will look when printed	From Print Preview, click the One Page button	
Add lines between columns	From the Format menu, choose Columns, and then select the Line Between option.	
Divide a document into sections	From the Insert menu, choose Break, and then select the option you want under Section Breaks.	
Format each section in a document separately	Click in the section you want to format, and then apply formatting.	

To	Do this	Button
Increase or decrease the magnification of a document	From the View menu, choose Zoom. In the Zoom dialog box, specify the magnification you want. *or* On the Standard toolbar, click the Zoom Control button and select the magnification you want.	

For more information on	See in the *Microsoft Word User's Guide*
Columns, column breaks, and lines between columns	Chapter 12, "Newspaper-Style Columns"
Working with sections	Chapter 11, "Page Setup: Margins, Page Numbers, and Other Items"
Changing the view of a document	Chapter 1, "The Word Workplace "

Preview of the Next Lesson

In the next lesson, you will learn to emphasize important text by adding borders and shading. You'll also try your hand at turning words into art. And you'll learn to insert and size graphics, and position them exactly where you want them on the page.

Adding Graphics and Emphasizing Text

You can add graphics to Word documents to illustrate a point or to add interest to a document. In this lesson, you learn to work with the tools on the Drawing toolbar with which you create and modify graphics that you can insert into your Word documents. You also learn to use WordArt, another built-in application in which you can create special effects with text, such as curving, rotating, flipping, or stretching the text. You learn to position text and graphics on the page and to wrap text around them. In the One Step Further, you can explore inserting data or graphics from other applications, such as Microsoft Excel or Paintbrush.

You will learn how to:

For instructions about starting Microsoft Word, see "Getting Ready," earlier in this book.

- Insert, size, and edit a graphic.

- Insert a Drop Cap.

- Drag graphics and text to a new location on the page.

- Add shading, borders, and special effects to text.

Estimated lesson time: 40 minutes

Open a sample document

Open

1 On the Standard toolbar, click the Open button.

2 In the Directories list, be sure the PRACTICE directory is open. If it is not, select the drive and directory for the Microsoft Word home directory, and click each subsequent directory until you locate PRACTICE.

3 In the File Name list, double-click 12ART.DOC.

   If you share your computer with others who use Word, the screen display might have changed since your last lesson. If your screen does not look similar to the following illustration, see the Appendix, "Matching the Exercises."

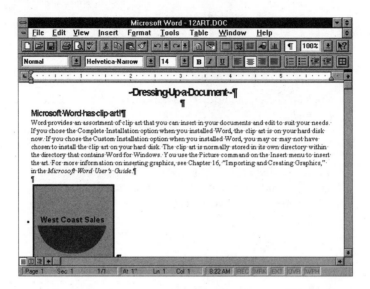

Save the document with a new name

Give the document a new name so the changes you make in this lesson will not overwrite the original practice file.

1   From the File menu, choose Save As.

2   In the File Name box, type **art12**

3   Choose the OK button.

Inserting and Sizing Graphics

You can import graphics from many graphics programs into Word. When you insert a graphic into a Word document and then click the graphic, eight sizing handles appear around it. You can use the sizing handles to make the graphic larger or smaller. You can also use the handles to trim, or *crop,* the graphic, hiding the portions you don't want to be displayed or printed. The sizing handles do not print.

Insert a graphic

Word provides a collection of clip art—graphics that you can insert in documents and then edit to suit your needs. The exercise disk included with this book contains a graphic of three-dimensional arrows you can insert into your document.

1   Position the insertion point at the beginning of the line below "Microsoft Word has clip art!" as shown in the following illustration.

If Word displays a message that the filter is unavailable Word requires a filter to display the graphic. Run the Microsoft Word Setup program again, choose Custom Installation, and choose the Conversions button. Select the Windows Metafile Filter to install the correct filter for this graphic.

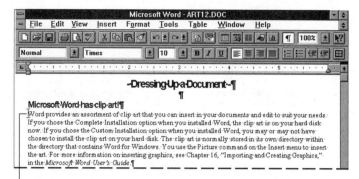

Click here.

2   From the Insert menu, choose Picture.

3   Double-click the PRACTICE directory.

4   In the File Name list, double-click 12ARROWS.WMF.

Word inserts the graphic in the document at the location of the insertion point.

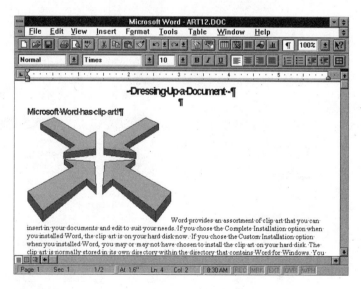

Crop the graphic

The graphic shows four arrows. You need only the one on the upper left. You can use the cropping tool to hide the others. When you drag a sizing handle while holding down the SHIFT key, you *crop* the graphic, hiding part of it. Dragging in the other direction reveals any hidden parts of the graphic.

1   Click the graphic once to select the graphic and display the sizing handles.

If the Drawing
toolbar appears
Clicking a graphic
once selects the
graphic. Double-
clicking a graphic
displays the Drawing
toolbar with which
you can edit the
graphic. To return to
the document, click
the Close Picture
button on the floating
toolbar.

2   Hide the right half of the graphic by first holding down the SHIFT key and then pointing to the middle sizing handle on the right, as shown in the following illustration. When the pointer changes to a cropping tool, drag to the left.

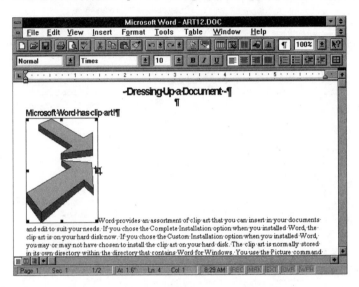

3   Hold down the SHIFT key and drag the middle sizing handle on the bottom of the graphic upward until the graphic looks like the following illustration.

Experiment with the sizing handles

Dragging a sizing handle without holding down the SHIFT key changes the size of the graphic. You can drag any side to stretch the graphic, and drag a corner to make the graphic smaller or larger proportionally.

1   If the ruler is not displayed, from the View menu, choose Ruler.

> **Tip**   If you want to see the vertical ruler, you can view the document in page layout view.

2   With the graphic selected, drag the middle handle on the bottom of the graphic downward about 1 inch to see the effect on the graphic.

Undo

3   Click the Undo button on the Standard toolbar to reverse the stretch.

4   Drag the middle handle on the right toward the right to stretch the graphic.

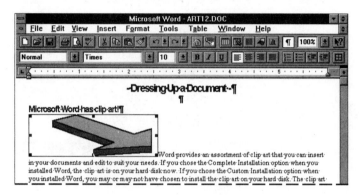

5   Click the Undo button after you've seen the effect.

6   Make the graphic larger proportionately by dragging the lower-right corner until the graphic is about 3 inches wide. Use the ruler at the top of the screen to determine the width of the graphic.

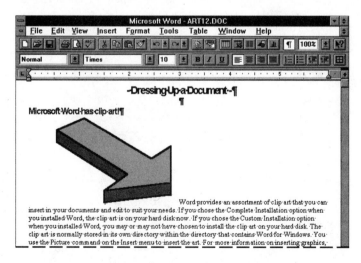

7   Make the graphic smaller proportionately by dragging the lower-right corner until the graphic is approximately 1 inch wide.

Framing a Graphic

You can create interesting visual effects in your document, such as allowing the text to wrap around a picture, by inserting a *frame* around the graphic. When you work with framed items, it's best to work in page layout view. Page layout view displays framed items in their correct location on the page. In normal view, framed items appear aligned with the left margin, marked by small, nonprinting bullets.

Insert a frame around the graphic

You must select the graphic before you can insert a frame around it. If you can see the sizing handles, the graphic is selected.

Page Layout View

1   Click the Page Layout View button in the lower-left corner of your screen.

2   If you cannot see the sizing handles, click the graphic once to select it.

Drawing

3   Click the Drawing button on the Standard toolbar.

This button displays the Drawing toolbar at the bottom of the screen.

Insert Frame

4   Click the Insert Frame button on the right end of the Drawing toolbar.

You can also insert a frame by choosing the Frame command from the Insert menu.

If you do not see the anchor
See the Appendix, "Matching the Exercises."

Framing an object allows text to flow around it. The framed object is surrounded by a shaded border that marks the frame. You also see an anchor icon next to the paragraph. The anchor indicates that the graphic is "anchored" to this paragraph. If you increase (or decrease) the amount of text before this paragraph, the framed graphic moves as well. Neither the anchor nor the shaded border around a graphic object prints.

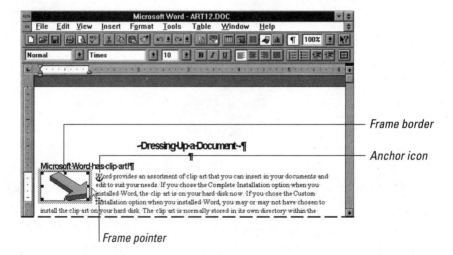

Frame border

Anchor icon

Frame pointer

Tip   If you decide you don't want text to flow around a graphic, you can choose that option using the Frame command on the Format menu.

Position the graphic on the page

In addition to allowing text to flow around an object, frames allow you to drag an object anywhere on the page, using a special, four-headed pointer.

1   If the graphic is not currently selected, click it once to display the sizing handles.

2   Drag the graphic to the position shown in the following illustration. Adjust the position of the frame as necessary.

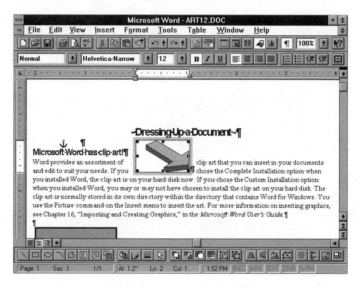

3   Click outside the graphic to hide the sizing handles and view the overall effect.

Save the document

Save

▶   On the Standard toolbar, click the Save button.

Word saves this version of the document in place of the previous version.

Making Changes to Graphics

In addition to inserting, sizing, cropping, and positioning graphics, you can edit them using the Drawing toolbar. You use this toolbar to create graphics of your own and to edit graphics that you've imported. You can also draw your own art. For more information about creating your own graphics, see Chapter 16, "Importing and Creating Graphics" in the *Microsoft Word User's Guide*.

Display the Drawing toolbar

With the Drawing toolbar, you can edit graphics, create special effects, and add text to graphics. This part of the lesson shows you how to edit a graphic already inserted in your document.

1   Double-click the West Coast Sales logo in the second paragraph to display the Drawing toolbar.

2   In the window, locate the small, floating toolbar window titled "Picture" and drag it to the upper-right corner of the screen.

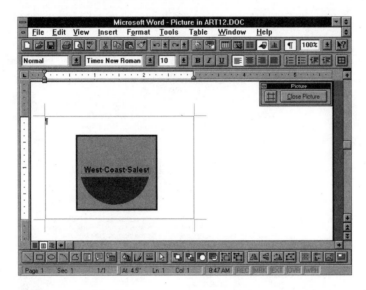

Edit the graphic

1   Select the half-circle below the text in the graphic.

Flip Vertical

2   Click the Flip Vertical button on the Drawing toolbar.

The graphic flips over.

Fill Color

3   With the half-circle still selected, click the Fill Color button on the Drawing toolbar, and then select the color yellow from the color palette.

Select Drawing Objects

4   Click the Select Drawing Objects (pointer) button in the Drawing toolbar, and then drag the half-circle so it appears above the text, as shown in the following illustration.

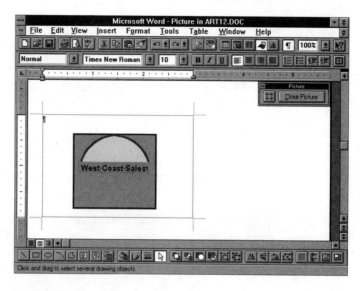

Turn off Snap To Grid

If you are having trouble positioning the object exactly where you want it, you can turn off the Snap To Grid option. When the Drawing toolbar first appears, this option is in effect to make it easy to line up objects evenly. However, if you need to make finer adjustments as you position an object, you can turn off this option to move your object freely.

Snap To Grid

1   In the Drawing toolbar, click the Snap To Grid button.

2   In the Snap To Grid dialog box, clear the Snap To Grid check box.

3   Click the OK button to return to your drawing.

4   Position the half-circle just below the top border of the square, and center it over the text.

5   Select the entire square object.

6   Drag the middle sizing handle at the bottom of the square upward to directly below the text in the logo.

Return to the document

▶   Click the Close Picture button on the floating toolbar to return to your document.

The Draw window closes and the edited graphic replaces the previous version.

Crop the graphic

You can eliminate the extra white space around the logo by using the cropping tool.

1 If the sizing handles aren't displayed, click the graphic once.

2 Hold down SHIFT and drag the sizing handles on the top, bottom, and each side of the graphic to remove as much white space as you can without hiding the logo itself.

When you edit a graphic, a frame is automatically applied to it and text wraps around it.

3 Drag the logo graphic to the middle of the paragraph as shown in the following illustration.

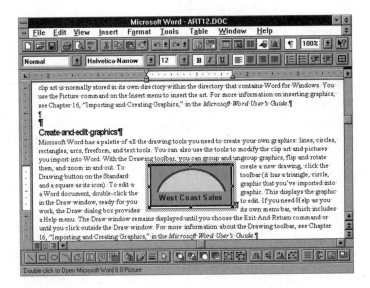

4 Click outside the graphic to hide the sizing handles and see the overall effect.

Save the document

Save

▶ On the Standard toolbar, click the Save button.

Creating Drop Caps

You can create additional effects with text using the Drop Caps feature. This command, on the Format menu, automatically inserts a large, uppercase character as the first character of a paragraph, and aligns the top edge of the character with the first line of the paragraph.

Insert a drop cap

1   Place the insertion point anywhere in second paragraph (the one that contains the West Coast Sales logo).

2   From the Format menu, choose Drop Cap.

3   Under Position, click the Dropped option.

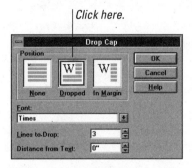

Click here.

4   Click the OK button.

The first character in the paragraph appears enlarged in a frame, as shown in the following illustration.

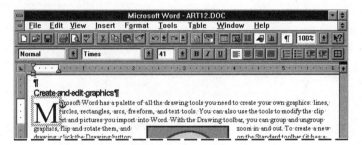

Working with WordArt

With WordArt, you can create graphic effects with text, such as flipping, rotating, and curving. After you insert a WordArt object in a document, you can work with it as you work with graphics. You can drag sizing handles to stretch or crop the WordArt object. You can frame a WordArt object so that text flows around it, and then drag it to other locations on the page. In the next exercises, you apply some of the WordArt effects and create a WordArt object for the sample document.

Display the WordArt dialog box

Cut

1   Select the heading "Turn text into art with WordArt," and then click the Cut button on the Standard toolbar.

2   From the Insert menu, choose Object.

Word displays a dialog box that lists optional applications you can use to create objects, such as equations, graphs, charts, or drawings.

If you do not see Microsoft WordArt 2.0 in the list

WordArt is an optional feature that you might not have installed during setup. For information about installing WordArt, see Microsoft Word Quick Results.

3   Scroll down, if necessary, and double-click Microsoft WordArt 2.0.

Word displays the WordArt toolbar and the Enter Your Text Here dialog box.

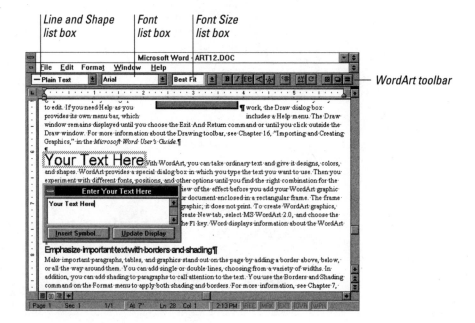

Create a WordArt object

1   In the Enter Your Text Here dialog box, select and delete any text.

2   With the insertion point in the text box, press CTRL+V to paste the heading text.

3   Select the text "with WordArt" and then press DEL.

4   Click the Update Display button.

Your text is inserted into the document.

Modify the WordArt object

1 Click the down arrow next to the Line and Shape list box, and then choose the third shape from the left in the fifth row down.

If the Enter Your Text Here dialog box obscures your view of the WordArt object, drag the box to the upper-right corner of the screen.

Note The text in the Line And Shape list box should read "Inflate (Bottom)." The selected text in the document changes shape as you select different options.

---

2 In the Font list box, select Arial, if it is not already selected.

3 In the Font Size list box, select Best Fit, if it is not already selected.

Alignment

4 On the WordArt toolbar, click the Alignment button, and then select Center.

Special Effects

5 On the toolbar, click the Special Effects button.

The Special Effects dialog box appears.

6 In the Special Effects dialog box, change the rotation to 30º, and then click OK.

Shading

7 On the toolbar, click the Shading button.

The Shading dialog box appears.

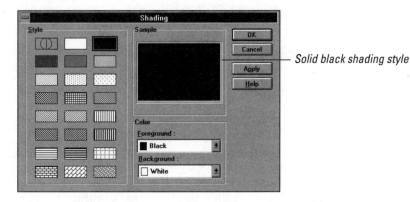

— *Solid black shading style*

8 In the Shading dialog box, be sure that the solid black shading style is selected, and then click OK.

Shadow

9 On the toolbar, click the Shadow button, and then click MORE in the lower-right corner of the options display.

10 In the Shadow dialog box, select the second shadow from the left, and then click OK.

Return to your document

If the WordArt object appears in a black bar
Click outside the bar to clear it.

▶ Click anywhere in the document to close the WordArt application.

Your screen should look similar to the following picture.

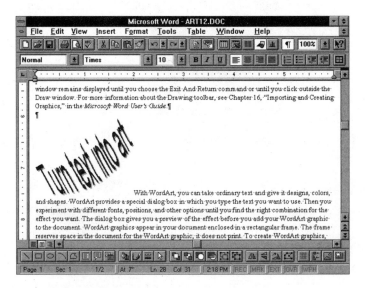

Save

Save the document

▶ On the Standard toolbar, click the Save button.

It's a good idea to save your work often when you are making complicated changes.

Insert a frame around the WordArt graphic

You can insert a frame around the WordArt graphic, so that text flows around it and you can drag it to a new location.

1   Click the WordArt graphic once to select it.

Insert Frame

2   On the Drawing toolbar, click the Insert Frame button. If a message appears asking whether you want to switch to page layout view, choose the Yes button.

Text wraps around the WordArt graphic and the frame appears.

Size the WordArt object

▶   Drag the middle sizing handle on the right side until the WordArt graphic is about 1.75 inches wide, as shown in the following illustration.

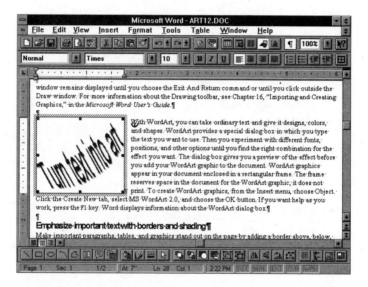

Save

Save the document

▶   On the Standard toolbar, click the Save button.

Word saves this version of the document in place of the previous version.

Framing and Sizing Text

You can insert a frame around regular text, just as you do around a graphic. If you size the frame, the text wraps within it. When you frame text, Word automatically provides a box border around the text; the border will print. If you prefer a different style of border—perhaps a double line instead of a single line—or if you do not want a border, you can change it. You can format framed text just as you normally format text.

1   Scroll to the bottom of the document, if necessary, to display the last heading and paragraph in the document. The heading begins "Emphasize important text."

2   Drag in the selection bar to select the heading and final paragraph as shown in the following picture.

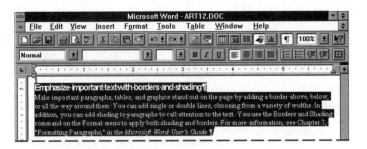

Insert Frame

3 On the Drawing toolbar, click the Insert Frame button.

The text now has a border that will print and sizing handles that will not print.

4 With the two-headed arrow, drag the right side of the frame toward the left until it is slightly wider than the heading, as shown in the following picture.

5 Click outside the frame to hide the sizing handles and view the overall effect.

Add shading and lines to the text

You can add shading to a paragraph and change the style of border around framed paragraphs. In this exercise, you apply 20 percent shading and place a double-line border around the heading and paragraph.

1 Click the framed text with the four-headed arrow to display the sizing handles.

You'll need to point to the shaded border of the frame.

Borders

2 Click the Borders button in the Formatting toolbar.

3 In the Borders toolbar (just below the Formating toolbar), the Shading box currently shows "Clear." Display the list of shading choices by clicking the down arrow.

4 Select 20%.

5 From the Line Style drop-down list box in the Borders toolbar, select the thick double-line (2¼ pt).

To change the line around the text, you must first select the line style, and then identify what parts of the paragraph should contain the line.

Outside Border

6 Click the Outside Border button on the Borders toolbar.

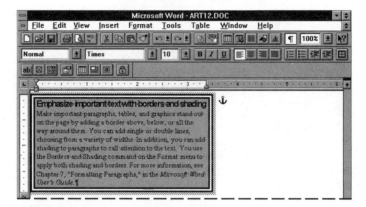

Fine-tune the layout

1 In the Zoom Control box on the Standard toolbar, type **35** and press ENTER.

2 Click each framed item in turn to display the sizing handles, and then, with the four-headed arrow, drag to position each item on the page so the document looks similar to the illustration that follows step 4. If necessary, also adjust the sizing and cropping.

3 With the two-headed arrow, drag the right side of the shaded paragraph frame until it extends from margin to margin.

4 With the paragraph selected, select 2¼ pt single line from the Line Style drop-down list box, and then click the Outside Border button.

This changes the double border to a single-line border around the paragraph. Your complete document, when printed, would look like the following picture.

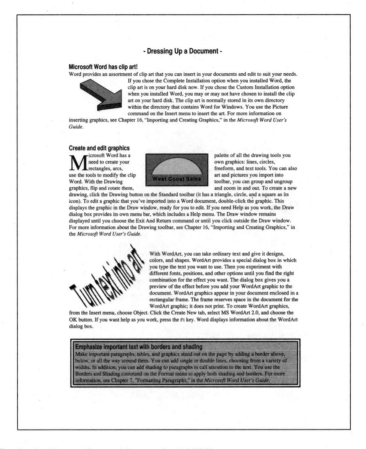

5   In the Zoom Control box, select 100%.

Create a shadow box for the title

You can add preset borders and shading to any text by using the Borders And Shading command on the Format menu. In this exercise, you add a shadow to the document title.

1   Place the insertion point in the title of the document.

2   From the Format menu, choose Borders And Shading.

3   Under Presets, click the Shadow option.

4   Under Line, select the 2¼ pt single line style, and click OK.

Save and close the document

Save

1   On the Standard toolbar, click the Save button.

2   From the File menu, choose Close.

One Step Further

WordArt is an example of subsidiary applications in which you can create objects and insert them in your documents. However, you are not limited to using objects from those applications that are only available from the Standard toolbar. In fact, you can insert information from other Windows-based applications, such as spreadsheets from Microsoft Excel or Paintbrush graphics.

Suppose you would like to display, in a Word document, a table of information taken from an Excel spreadsheet. Suppose, further, that you'd like the data in the Word document to be updated automatically whenever the spreadsheet data is changed. Using a special version of the Paste command, you can set up an active link between the Excel spreadsheet (called the *source*) and the Word document (called the *destination*). In this One Step Further, you'll copy an object consisting of a range of data from an Excel spreadsheet and link it to a Word document. Then you'll modify some of the data in the source spreadsheet and observe the changes in the destination document.

Note   If you do not have Microsoft Excel installed on your computer, you can try this exercise using Paintbrush instead. Refer to the margin notes to guide you through the differences between Microsoft Excel and Paintbrush.

Create a destination document

1   From the File menu, choose New, and then click OK in the New dialog box.

In Paintbrush, type this text for step 2:
Here is the new logo for Great Kitchens Plus. *Save the file as LOGO.DOC.*

2   Type the following text, and then press ENTER three times.

   Below is a WCS budget summary for Q1 and Q2 of FY 1994.

3   From the File menu, choose Save As and save the file with the name BUDGET12.DOC.

4   Reduce the size of the Word application window and move it to the right half of the screen.

   This will allow you to view both the source and the destination files at the same time.

Tip   If your application window is maximized, click the topmost Restore button on the window, and then drag the window border to size it.

Copy a source object

1   Press SHIFT+TAB to switch to Program Manager.

2   From Program Manager, start Excel.

In Paintbrush, use the file 12LOGO.BMP and save it as LOGO12.BMP Use the Pick tool to select the logo.

3 Open the file 12SPREAD.XLS in your PRACTICE directory, and maximize the document window within Excel.

4 Save the file as SPREAD12.XLS.

5 Select the range A11 to E16.

This range contains the data that you want in your Word document.

6 From the Edit menu, choose Copy.

7 Reduce the Excel window and move it to the left half of your screen. If necessary, minimize Program Manager so that both your Word and Excel windows are visible. (They can partially overlap.)

Link the object data from the source to the destination

1 Click in the Word document, and be sure the insertion point is two lines below the text.

2 From the Edit menu in Word, choose Paste Special.

The Paste Special dialog box appears.

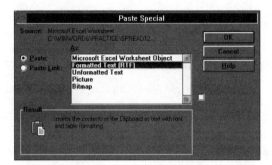

3 At the left side of the dialog box, click the Paste Link option button.

4 In the As list box, select Microsoft Excel Worksheet Object, and then click OK.

The copied portion of the spreadsheet appears in the Word document, as shown in the following illustration.

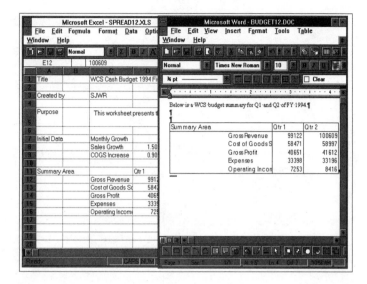

Modify the linked object

Tip   If the source application is not running, you can usually open the application and the source document by double-clicking the destination object in the Word document.

In Paintbrush, use the Paint Roller tool to change the color of the logo.

1   In the Excel spreadsheet, select cell D12. Type **100000** and press ENTER.

2   Select cell E12. Type **150000** and press ENTER.

3   Select the Word destination document.

The gross revenue numbers in the Word document have been automatically updated, as in the following illustration.

In Paintbrush, the color of the logo is automatically updated.

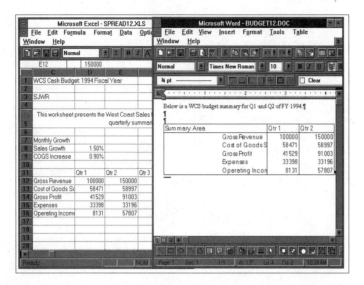

4   In Excel, save the SPREAD12.XLS file, and then exit Excel.

If You Want to Continue to the Next Lesson

1   From the File menu in Word, choose Close.

2   If a message appears asking if you want to save changes, click the Yes button.

If You Want to Quit Word for Now

1   From the File menu in Word, choose Exit.

2   If a message appears asking if you want to save changes, click the Yes button.

Lesson Summary

To	Do this	Button
Insert a graphic	From the Insert menu, choose Picture. Select the name of the graphic you want to insert.	
Size a graphic	Select the graphic. Drag the corner handles to size the graphic proportionately, or drag the middle handles to stretch the graphic.	

To	Do this	Button
Display the Drawing toolbar	Click the Drawing button on the Standard toolbar.	
Frame and position a graphic	Select the object you want to position. On the Drawing toolbar, click the Insert Frame button. With the four-headed arrow, drag the item to position it on the page.	
Edit a graphic	Double-click the graphic in the document. The application in which the graphic was created opens so you can edit the graphic. Exit the application to return to the document.	
Crop a graphic	Hold down the SHIFT key as you drag a sizing handle.	
Insert a drop cap as the first character in a paragraph	From the Format menu, choose Drop Cap. In the Drop Cap dialog box, click the style of drop cap you want. Click the OK button to return to the document.	
Start WordArt	Select the text to modify, and then click the Cut button on the Standard toolbar. From the Insert menu, choose Object. Choose Microsoft WordArt 2.0.	
Create a WordArt object	Start WordArt. Delete any text in the dialog box. Paste the WordArt text into the dialog box. Click the Update Display button to make any changes in the text. Click in the document to exit WordArt.	
Add shading to text	Select the text. From the Format menu, choose Borders and Shading. Choose the Shading tab. In the Shading box, select the percent of shading that you want. You can also click the Shading box on the Borders toolbar.	
Display the Borders toolbar	Click the Borders button on the Formatting toolbar.	

To	Do this	Button
Change the border of a framed text paragraph	Click the frame to select it. From the Format menu, choose Borders And Shading. Under Line, click the type of line you want, and then click OK. *or* Click the Outside Border button on the Borders toolbar. Then select a line style from the Line Style drop-down list.	
Link an object from Excel	In the Excel source file, copy the data you want to link. In the Word document, position the insertion point, and then choose Paste Special from the Edit menu. Select the options for Paste Link and for Microsoft Excel Worksheet Object, and then click OK.	

For more information on	See in the *Microsoft Word User's Guide*
Inserting, editing, and sizing graphics	Chapter 16, "Importing and Creating Graphics"
Positioning graphics and text on the page	Chapter 15, "Positioning Text and Graphics with Frames"
Creating WordArt	Chapter 27, "WordArt, Equation Editor, and Graph"
Adding borders and shading	Chapter 7, "Formatting Paragraphs"
Linking data between applications	Chapter 28, "Exchanging Information with Other Applications"

Preview of the Next Lessons

In the next lesson, you'll learn to locate files that you have very little information about. For example, you'll find files when you know only two letters of the file name, or when you know only one word that it contains. You'll also learn how you can open, copy, delete, or print more than one file at a time. Finally, you can print either of the two documents you find, or you can print both—at the same time.

Review & Practice

The lessons in Part 3 provided you with advanced skills to enhance your documents by adding tables and charts, creating multiple columns, adding graphics, and linking objects. If you want to practice these skills and test your understanding before you proceed with the lessons in Part 4, you can work through the Review & Practice section following this lesson. This less structured activity allows you to increase your confidence using many of the features introduced so far.

Part 3   Review & Practice

In this Review & Practice, you have an opportunity to fine tune the graphics and advanced layout skills you learned in the lessons in Part 3 of this book. Use what you have learned about creating and formatting tables, and creating columns to develop an executive summary for West Coast Sales' quarterly report.

Scenario

After gathering information from various regions in the company, you have found two documents that contain the financial and product information you need for the executive summary. Your task is to enhance the appearance of these documents to give them greater impact.

You will review and practice how to:

- Create a table and format it.
- Create a chart from a table.
- Create columns in a document.
- Use special effects with text, such as WordArt and Drop Caps.
- Use lines and shading to draw attention to important information in a frame.
- Modify graphics to enhance the appearance of the document.

Estimated practice time: 20 minutes

Step 1:   Create a Table and Format It

1   From your PRACTICE directory, open the document called P3REVEWA.DOC.

2   Save the document as REVEWAP3.DOC.

3   With the insertion point in front of the existing paragraph mark under the heading "Financial Results," create a two-column table. Enter the following information:

Division	First Quarter
Outdoor Enterprises	22.8
Great Outdoors	17.1
Great Northern	16.3

4   Size the columns to make them narrower.

5   Add a new column in the table to report this quarter's results.

Division	Second Quarter
Outdoor Enterprises	**32.4**
Great Outdoors	**17.9**
Great Northern	**18.6**

6   Add a new row to the bottom of the table and add the new division's results.

Great Kitchens PLUS   **81.3**

You can manually size the new column so the text fits on one line, or you can use the AutoFit option when you use the Table AutoFormat command in the next step.

7   Add borders and shading to the table using the Table AutoFormat command from the Table menu. Select any formatting option you want. You can select the AutoFit check box to automatically adjust the column width to fit the text in the cells, if you have not already sized the new column manually.

8   Add a new row to the beginning of the table, merge the cells in the new row, and give your table the title **Second Quarter Results (in Thousands)**. Add new borders as necessary to the merged row, and then center the table title.

For more information on	See
Creating tables	Lesson 10
Formatting tables	Lesson 10

Step 2:   Create a Chart from the Table

1   Select the data in the table, and then click the Insert Chart button in the Standard toolbar. Adjust the width of the Chart and position the legend as needed.

2   Close the Microsoft Graph window, and update the document with the chart.

For more information on	See
Creating charts	Lesson 10

Step 3:   Add a Frame to Text

1   Add a frame around the paragraph below the chart, which begins "This Executive Summary."

2   Using the Borders And Shading command from the Format menu, create a Shadow box around the text.

3   Use the Shading drop-down list on the Borders toolbar to apply a 10 percent shading pattern to the framed text.

4   Center the text in the box.

For more information on	See
Adding a frame	Lesson 12
Shading and borders	Lesson 12

Step 4:   Create Columns in a Document

1   From your PRACTICE directory, open the document called P3REVEWB.DOC, and save it as REVEWBP3.DOC.

2   Select the first line in the report, and create a Shadow box as you did in Step 3 of this Review & Practice.

3   With the insertion point at the beginning of the heading "Exciting New Products," insert a continuous section break.

4   With the insertion point at the beginning of the heading "Outdoor Enterprises Division," insert another continuous section break.

5   With the insertion point below the section break and at the beginning of the heading "Outdoor Enterprises Division," format the text into two columns.

For more information on	See
Adding section breaks	Lesson 11
Creating columns	Lesson 11

Step 5:   Create Special Effects with Text

1   Use WordArt to create a special effect for the heading "Exciting New Products."

Use the picture at the end of Step 6 as a guide. If the heading is not centered over the bulleted list after you exit WordArt, make sure the WordArt object is selected and click the Center button.

2   Add a drop cap to each of the headings in section 3.

For more information on	See
Using WordArt	Lesson 12
Inserting Drop Caps	Lesson 12

Step 6:   Modify Graphics

▶ Double-click the West Coast Sales logo, and then double-click the elements in the logo to change their color. Return to the document.

Your final, report pages should look similar to the following.

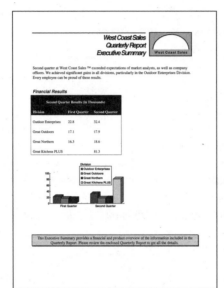

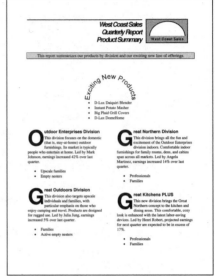

Organizing a Document with Outlining

When you work with a document that is several pages long and contains many different topics, or that has a hierarchical structure (with main topics and subtopics), you will find Microsoft Word's outlining feature a valuable tool. In this lesson, you display a document in outline view to add an outline structure to your document. You promote and demote heading levels, and view only specific levels of the document. In outline view, you also reorganize your document quickly by moving headings.

You will learn how to:

For instructions about starting Microsoft Word, see "Getting Ready," earlier in this book.

- Switch to outline view.

- Use the Outline toolbar to promote and demote headings.

- View only selected heading levels and body text.

- Rearrange blocks of text by moving headings.

Estimated lesson time: 35 minutes

Open a sample document

Open

1   On the Standard toolbar, click the Open button.

2   In the Directories list, be sure the PRACTICE directory is open. If it is not, select the drive and directory for the Microsoft Word home directory, and click each subsequent directory until you locate PRACTICE.

3   Double-click 13VIEWS.DOC.

If you share your computer with others who use Word, the screen display might have changed since your last lesson. If your screen does not look similar to the following illustration, see the Appendix, "Matching the Exercises."

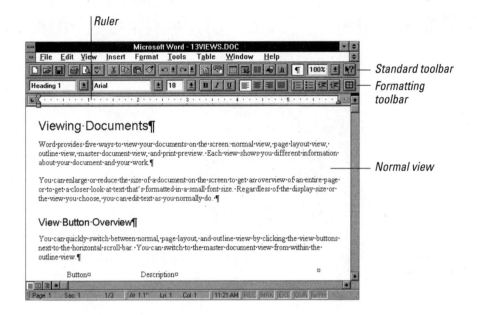

Ruler

Standard toolbar

Formatting toolbar

Normal view

Save the document with a new name

Give the document a new name so the changes you make in this lesson will not overwrite the original practice file.

1 From the File menu, choose Save As.

2 In the File Name box, type **views13**

3 Click the OK button.

Working in Outline View

To use the Word outline feature, you need to display your document in *outline view*. The fastest way to switch between views, including outline view, is to click the view buttons just above the status bar.

Switch to outline view

Outline View

▶ Click the Outline View button to the left of the horizontal scroll bar.

The Outline View button is to the left of the horizontal scroll bar. When you are in outline view, the Outline toolbar appears below the other toolbars already displayed. Here is an overview of the buttons on the Outline toolbar.

To do this	Use these buttons
Promote and demote headings	
Demote heading to body text	
Move heading and associated subheadings and text up or down one line	
Expand a heading to reveal its immediate subheadings and associated text	
Collapse a heading to hide its immediate subheadings and associated text	
Show all levels through the selected level	1 2 3 4 5 6 7 8 All
Show only the first line of body text in a paragraph. This button toggles to display all lines	
Show outline with or without formatting	
Display Master Document toolbar	

Understanding Outline View

When you first display your document in outline view, any text that has a heading style appears with an outline symbol (a plus sign) next to it. Lower-level headings appear indented under higher-level headings. A minus sign next to a heading indicates that there are no subheadings or text under this heading. Text that is not formatted with a heading style (that is, without a plus or minus outline symbol in front of it) is called body text and appears with a small square next to it. In an outline, text is associated with the preceding heading, so you can work with *blocks* of information. The following illustration identifies what you see in outline view.

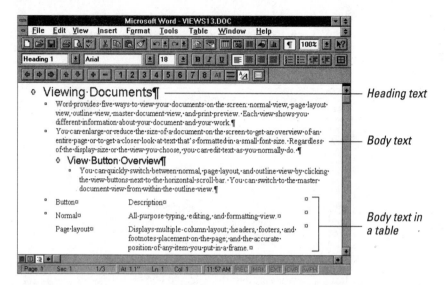

— Heading text

— Body text

— Body text in
a table

Outline view shows that the text "Viewing Documents" is already assigned an outline heading. When you select the heading, the Style box in the Formatting toolbar indicates this is a heading 1. The text "View Button Overview" is assigned a heading 2. These headings already have heading styles applied to them, and this outline reflects that structure. The remaining text you see in the window is body text. Body text is usually indented under its heading. Text in a table, however, is not indented.

Promoting and Demoting Headings

In outline view, you can quickly change the heading levels. You can either promote a heading to a higher level or demote it to a lower level. When you promote or demote a heading, any subordinate subheadings and text are likewise affected. You can change body text to a heading level in the same way you promote or demote a heading. You can also change a heading level to body text with the Demote To Body Text button.

Promote headings

To organize this document, use the Promote and Demote buttons to establish a hierarchical structure to the remaining topics.

1 Scroll downward until you see the text "Normal View" on a line by itself.

You will need to scroll about one-third of the way down the vertical scroll bar, or click once below the scroll box in the vertical scroll.

Promote

2 Place the insertion point in this heading, and then click the Promote button on the Outline toolbar.

This text is promoted to a heading 2, the same as the heading "View Buttons Overview" and subordinate to the heading "Viewing Documents."

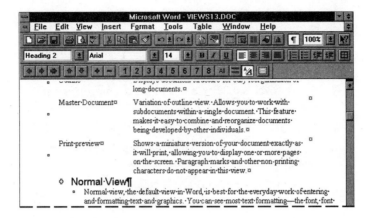

3 Scroll to and select the text "Print Preview."

You can also place the insertion point anywhere in the line you want to promote.

4 Click the Promote button to assign this text a heading 2.

5 Scroll to and select the text "Page Layout."

6 Click the Promote button to assign this text a heading 2.

7 Scroll to and select the text "Outline View."

8 Click the Promote button to assign this text a heading 2.

9 Scroll to and select the text "Master Document View."

10 Click the Promote button to assign this text a heading 2.

11 Scroll to and select the text "Magnifying or Reducing the Display Size."

12 Click the Promote button twice to assign this text a heading 1.

Your outline looks like the following illustration.

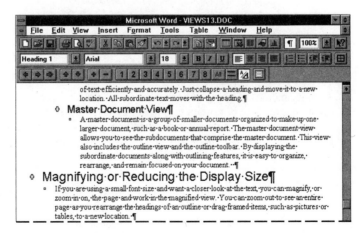

Demote headings

When you want to adjust an existing heading level to a lower level, use the Demote button on the Outline toolbar. Using the Demote To Body Text button, you can change a heading to body text.

1 Scroll towards the beginning of the document, and select the text "Using the Draft Font in Normal View."

Demote

2 Click the Demote button to assign this text a heading 3.

3 Scroll down to "1   From theTools menu, choose Options," and place the insertion point in the heading.

Demote To Body Text

4 Click the Demote To Body Text button on the Outline toolbar.

This text is now body text.

Your outline looks like the following illustration.

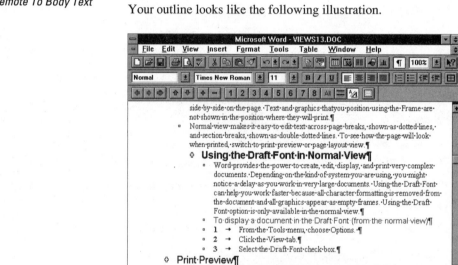

Viewing Specific Parts of the Outline

A major benefit of using outline view is that you can focus on only those parts of the document that are important to you at the moment. You can view a specific range of heading levels, and hide all the subheadings and text that are subordinate. When you are ready to focus on the details of a topic, you can view lower level headings and body text. You can also specify how much of the body text you want to see when viewing body text.

You can view a range of heading levels for the entire document, or you can expand or collapse the individual headings.

Viewing Specified Heading Levels

When you want to focus on the higher level structure of your document or work on overview information, you might want to see only the first two or three heading levels. When you click a heading button on the Outline toolbar, you see only those headings through the level you select. You can click any heading level button that corresponds to the level of detail you want to see. For example, if you click the Show Heading 3 button, you see heading levels 1, 2, and 3.

View first-level headings

Show Heading 1

You can click the Show Heading 1 button to get the highest level view of your document. Use this setting when you want to focus on only the major elements in your document.

▶ Scroll to the beginning of the document and click the Show Heading 1 button on the Outline toolbar.

Your document looks like the following illustration.

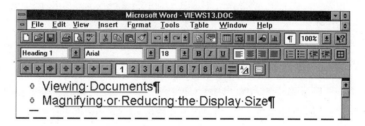

View the first three heading levels

Show Heading 3

Use lower level settings when you want to focus on specific details or individual topics in your document. Viewing only a few levels helps you see the overall structure and organization of your document without seeing more text than you need.

▶ Click the Show Heading 3 button on the Outline toolbar.

Your document looks like the following illustration.

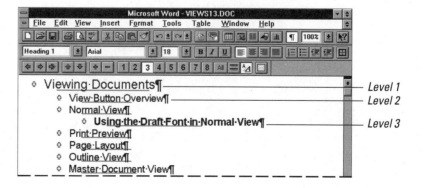

View all heading levels and body text

When you want to see all the information in your document, you can click the All button on the Outline toolbar.

All

▶ Click the All button on the Outline toolbar.

All levels and text in your document are displayed.

View two heading levels

Show Heading 2

▶ Click the Show Heading 2 button on the Outline toolbar.

The first two levels in your document are displayed.

Expanding and Collapsing Headings

The heading level buttons on the Outline toolbar affect the number of heading levels displayed for the entire outline. When you want to display more (or fewer) heading levels under a single heading, you can *collapse* or *expand* headings. The Expand and Collapse buttons on the Outline toolbar display (or hide) subordinate headings and text of the heading containing the insertion point.

Expand a heading

You can use the Expand button to see more detail about a topic in your document. Click the button repeatedly until you see all the subordinate text.

1 Place the insertion point in the heading "Normal View."

Expand

2 Click the Expand button on the Outline toolbar.

The next level of subheading under this heading is displayed.

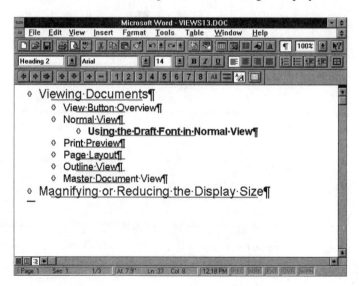

3   Click the Expand button until all subordinate text and headings are displayed.

Notice that the other headings in the document remain collapsed.

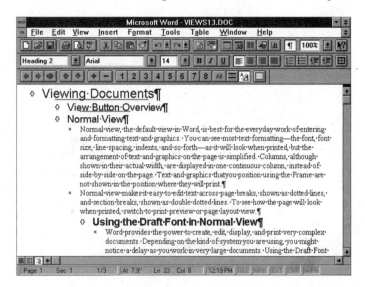

Collapse a heading

Collapse

Use the Collapse button to hide details for this topic in your document.

▶   With the insertion point still in the heading "Normal View," click the Collapse button on the Outline toolbar once.

The lowest level of subheadings and text under this heading are hidden.

Viewing Body Text

When you display body text in outline view, you can specify how much of the body text you want to see. You can choose to see all the body text, which is useful for editing. Or you can choose to see only the first line of individual paragraphs of body text, which is useful for helping you recall the content of a paragraph without displaying all of the text.

Display the first line of body text

The Show First Line Only button on the toolbar toggles to display the first line of a paragraph or to display all body text for an expanded heading. For example, when all the body text is displayed, clicking this button hides all but the first line of text. When you click it again, it displays all the text.

Expand

1   With the insertion point still in the heading "Normal View," click the Expand button once.

Show First Line Only

2 Click the Show First Line Only button.

Only the first line of text in each paragraph appears.

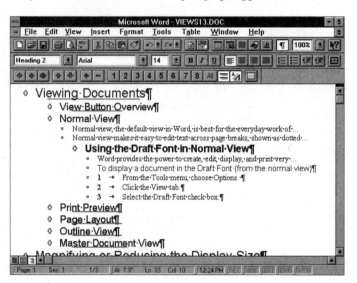

Moving Blocks of Text

Using the outline view to reorganize a document ensures that all the text associated with a heading stays together as you move text around in your document. You can rearrange large blocks of text in your document without selecting all the text you want to move. In outline view, when you move a collapsed heading, all the subordinate headings and text move with the heading. If you select an expanded heading, however, only the selected text moves.

Move a block of text

Show Heading 2

To move a block of text in an outline, collapse the heading so that all the subordinate headings are hidden. Then use the buttons on the Outline toolbar to move the heading up or down one line at a time. When you move the heading, the subordinate headings and body text move as well.

1 Click the Show Heading 2 button on the Outline toolbar.

2 Select the heading "Print Preview."

Move Down

3 Click the Move Down button on the Outline toolbar three times to move the selected heading after the heading "Master Document View."

Expand

4 Click the Expand button to see that all the subordinate text also moved.

Your outline looks like the following illustration.

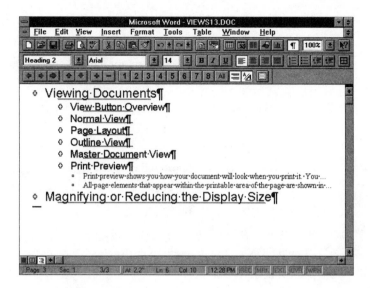

Normal View

5   Click the Normal View button next to the horizontal scroll bar.

Your document appears in normal view.

One Step Further

An added benefit of using outline view to organize your document is that assigning heading levels also applies heading styles to the text. With heading styles (such as heading 1 and heading 2) applied to the text, Word makes it easy to create a table of contents for your document. When you choose the Index And Tables command from the Insert menu, you can create a table of contents that includes the range of heading levels you specify.

Set page numbering

You will insert a table of contents at the beginning of the document. Because you want the first topic to appear on page 1, not on page 2, you can specify page number-ing to start at "0." This setting ensures that the table contents page itself does not affect the page numbering of the following pages.

1   Move to the beginning of the document and place the insertion point before the title.

2   Press CTRL+ENTER to insert a hard page break at the beginning of the document.

3   With the insertion point on the page break line, choose Page Numbers from the Insert menu.

4   In the Page Numbers dialog box, clear the Show Number On First Page check box.

5 Click the Format button, and then type **0** in the Start At box.

6 Click the OK button until you return to your document

With the page numbering format set for the table of contents page, you are ready to insert a table of contents.

Create a table of contents

Creating a table of contents is easy when you base the table of contents on heading styles you created in outline view.

1 From the Insert menu, choose Index And Tables.

2 Click the Table Of Contents tab to display the table of contents options.

3 Click the Options button.

4 Be sure the Styles check box is selected.

5 Click the OK button to return to the Table Of Contents tab.

6 Select the Classic style.

You can select and preview the other table of contents styles if you want.

7 Click the OK button to return to the document and generate a table of contents.

Your table of contents appears at the beginning of the document.

If You Want to Continue to the Next Lesson

1 From the File menu, choose Close.

2 If a message appears asking if you want to save changes, click the Yes button.

If You Want to Quit Microsoft Word for Now

1 From the File menu, choose Exit.

2 If a message appears asking if you want to save changes, click the Yes button.

Lesson Summary

To	Do this	Button
Display the document in outline view	Click the Outline View button next to the horizontal scroll bar.	
Promote or demote a heading	Click the Promote or Demote button.	
Demote a heading to body text	Click the Demote To Body Text button.	
Display specific headings for the entire document	Click the heading level button that corresponds to the headings you want to see.	
Hide subheadings and text for selected headings	Select the heading and click the Collapse button.	
Display subheadings and text for selected headings	Select the heading and click the Expand button.	
Display all headings and body text	Click the All button.	
Toggle the display to show the first line or all lines of body text	Expand the heading and click the Show First Line Only button.	
Move a collapsed heading	Select the heading and click the Move Up or Move Down button to move one line at a time.	
Set page numbers	From the Insert menu, choose Page Numbers. Click the Format button, and type the starting page number in the Start At box.	
Create a table of contents	Place the insertion point where you want the table of contents to appear. From the Insert menu, choose Index And Tables. Select the Table Of Contents tab. Click the Options button, and select any desired options. Click OK. Select a format for the table, and then click OK.	

For more information on	See in the *Microsoft Word User's Guide*
Outlining	Chapter 17, "Outlining and Organizing a Document"

Preview of the Next Lesson

In the next lesson, you'll learn efficient ways to manage your documents and work with several documents open at once. Word provides easy ways to search for documents even if you have forgotten what you've named them. You will also learn a fast way to copy files into a new directory and to open more than one file at a time.

Working with Multiple Documents

After creating many documents, it can often be a challenge to locate and retrieve documents when you need them again. In this lesson, you learn to search for files three different ways. First, you search for files when you know only a few letters of the file name. Next, you search for a file by specifying a word that the file contains. Finally, you search for files based on a keyword that was entered in the Summary Info dialog box. With several files open at once, you learn how to copy files to a new directory and open two files.

You will learn how to:

For instructions about starting Microsoft Word, see "Getting Ready," earlier in this book.

- Search for an incomplete file name.
- Search for text in a document.
- Search for summary information.
- Copy documents to a new directory.
- Open multiple documents at once.

Estimated lesson time: 25 minutes

Using the Find File Command

The Find File command on the File menu, gives you the flexibility to locate a document even if you don't know its name or much else about it. You can locate a document by searching for almost any information you can recall—or guess—about the document.

For example, if you remember only part of the name of the document, you can search for that document by the part of the name you can remember. If you want to find a document that contains a phrase, such as "annual income," you can search specifically for that phrase. If you need to recall information from a memo written by a colleague last May, you can search for documents based on the subject entered in the Summary Info dialog box.

From the Find File dialog box, you can learn a file's location, display its contents, and view other information about the file without opening it. You can also perform file-management tasks such as opening, printing, copying, and deleting one or more files.

Open the Find File dialog box

▶ From the File menu, choose Find File.

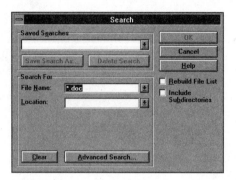

The first time you choose the Find File command, Word displays the Search dialog box. In this dialog box, you see information about previous search settings, if any. To change the path or specify search criteria other than the file name, you click the Advanced Search button.

Searching for Documents

In the Search dialog box, you need to provide two types of information: what to search for and where to search. The information you use to locate a document—file name, author, subject, and so on—is called the *search criteria*. Each time you change the search criteria, a list of the files that meet the new criteria appear in the Find File dialog box. The criteria remain active until you change them.

Specify the search path

The *path* is the sequence of drives and directories in which you want Word to search. You can type the path in the Search dialog box, or you can click the Advanced Search button to select drives and directories on the Location page. Using the Advanced Search button is faster than typing and you are less likely to make mistakes as you specify the path name. The path you specify for a search appears in the Location box of the Search dialog box.

You can search through several drives and directories at once by adding more paths on the Location page of the Advanced Search dialog box. You can also remove paths to restrict your search.

The path displayed in the Location box of the Search dialog box is the current search path. It is the one Word will search to locate your documents. If you exited Word at the end of the previous lesson, you will need to change the search path so that Word searches for documents in the PRACTICE directory.

If you are continuing directly from the previous lesson, the correct search path is probably already displayed, but you can follow these steps to learn how you can change the search path when necessary.

1   In the Search dialog box, click the Advanced Search button.

2   Click the Remove button to remove any existing search path from the Search In list.

3   In the Drives list box, select the drive where Microsoft Word is stored.

4   In the Directories box, double-click the directory where Microsoft Word is stored.

This is usually named WINWORD.

5   In the Directories box, click the PRACTICE directory.

If you click the Include Subdirectories check box, Word will search all the subdirectories under the current directory. Do not click this check box now.

6   Click the Add button to add the PRACTICE directory to the search path.

The Advanced Search dialog box looks like the following illustration.

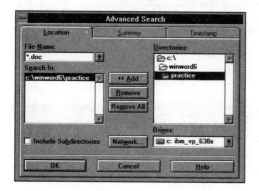

7   Click the OK button to return to the Search dialog box.

The Location box reflects the new search path.

Search using an incomplete file name

Now that you've identified where to search, you need to specify your search criteria. Suppose you want to locate a document, but you cannot recall its exact file name. Even if you can remember only part of the name, you can find all the files that begin with the characters you can remember by using *wildcards*—placeholders—for the rest of the name.

1   In the File Name box, place the insertion point in front of the asterisk, and type **sbs**

The asterisk (*) is a wildcard character that indicates you want to find file names that start with "sbs" followed by any other character.

2   Select the Rebuild File List check box.

This option gives you a fresh start by displaying only those file names that match this criterion rather than adding these files to those displayed in a previous search.

The dialog box should look similar to the following illustration. Depending on your particular configuration of drives and directories, the exact path you see might be different.

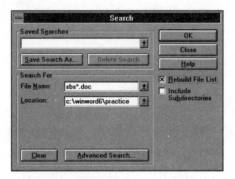

3   Click the OK button.

Word closes the Search dialog box and displays a list of the files that match the criterion you specified in the Find File dialog box. The Preview window displays the contents of the first file in the list.

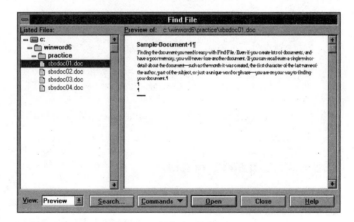

Tip   You need to click the Preview button to display the contents of files that are not Microsoft Word documents, such as graphics or files created in other applications.

Search based on the contents of a file

Suppose that a co-worker needs a letter that someone in your office wrote to someone in Paris. You do not remember the file name or author, or even when the letter was written, but you guess that the letter contains the word "Paris." That's all you need to know to search for the file.

The Search dialog box still contains the information you used in your last search. In this exercise, you clear the previous search information and use instead the new search criterion—"Paris."

1 In the Find File dialog box, click the Search button.

2 Click the Advanced Search button.

3 Click the Summary tab.

On the Summary page, you can specify search criteria based on information in the Summary Info dialog box for a document or based on text in the document itself.

4 In the Options drop-down list, be sure the Create New list option is selected.

This option gives you a fresh start by displaying only those file names that match this criterion rather than adding these files to an existing search.

5 In the Containing Text box, type **Paris**

6 Select the Match Case check box.

This option ensures that Word searches for "Paris" as a proper noun and not part of another word, such as "com*paris*on."

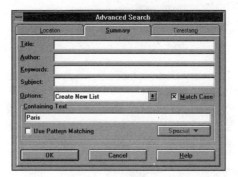

7 Click the OK button to return to the Search dialog box.

8 Open the File Name drop-down list box and select "Word Documents (*.DOC)" as the type of file you want to find.

The File Name box displays "*.doc" so that any file name with a ".doc" extension will be included in the list of files.

9 Click the OK button.

Word displays the names of any files that contain the word "Paris." The list should include 02BASICS.DOC and 06LETTER.DOC. If you completed Lesson 2 and Lesson 6 in this book, you should also see the files BASICS02.DOC and LETTER06.DOC.

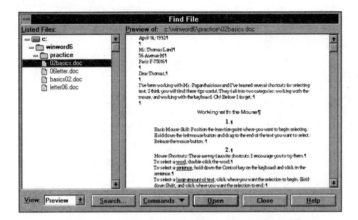

Searching for Files with Summary Information

Several types of search criteria are stored as part of the file—the file name, text, the date a file was created, the date a file was last saved, and even the author's name as it was entered when you set up Word. But you can also have the option to provide additional information about your document when you save a file.

You provide the optional information in the Summary Info dialog box. If you fill in the dialog box when you save the file, later you can search for the file based on the information you provided—a title of the document, a description of the subject, or keywords that remind you of the file. You can type as many as 255 characters, including spaces and punctuation, for each category of information.

The documents you used in these lessons have several types of information stored in the Summary Info dialog box.

Title   The title of the active document. Because the title can be longer and more descriptive than the eight-character file name, be sure to enter enough text to make it easy for you to remember.

Subject   A description of the document's contents.

Author   By default, the name assigned to your copy of the Word program during setup. You can change the author for the active document by typing a new name. You can change the author for all future documents by choosing Options from the Tools menu, selecting the User Info tab, and then typing a new name in the Name box.

Keywords   General topics in the document or other important information, such as client names and account numbers.

Comments   Comments are notes you type to yourself or to a co-worker. You cannot use Comments as a search criterion.

Search using a keyword

Included in the Step by Step practice files are documents that contain information about working with multiple documents. When the documents were created, the word "multiple" was entered as a keyword. In this exercise, you specify a search criterion based on this keyword.

1   Click the Search button.

2   Click the Advanced Search button.

3   Be sure the Summary tab is selected.

4   In the Containing Text box, select the text remaining from the last search and press the BACKSPACE or DEL key.

5   In the Keywords box, type **multiple**

6   Clear the Match Case check box.

   The case of the text in the Keyword box can be either uppercase or lowercase to match this search criterion.

7   Click the OK button to return to the Search dialog box.

8   Be sure the Rebuild File List check box is selected.

9   Click the OK button to start the search.

   Word locates the files 14COPY.DOC and 14OPEN.DOC because they have the keyword "multiple" in the Summary Info dialog box. The first page of the first document appears in the Preview window.

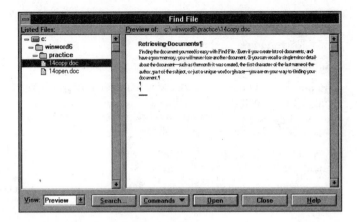

Viewing Other Information

The View drop-down list in the Find File dialog box includes other kinds of information you can get about a document in the file list. In addition to the Preview option, you can select File Info to see basic technical information about the document. You can also select the Summary option to get more detail about the document.

View file information

You can select the File Info option from the View drop-down list to get basic information about the name, title, size, author, and date the document was last saved. Use this option when this information helps you identify the document better than a picture of the first page.

▶ From the View drop-down list, select File Info.

The Find File dialog box looks like the following illustration.

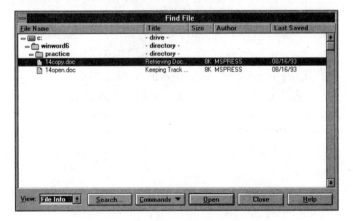

View summary information

You can select the Summary option from the View drop-down list to get more details about a document including information from the Summary Info dialog box, as well as the date the document was created, the date it was last saved, and the date it was last printed. You also see the number of times the document was revised, the amount of editing time, and the size of the document in terms of four measures: bytes (the amount of disk space), characters, words, and pages. Use this option when you need these details to help you identify the document.

▶ From the View drop-down list, select Summary.

The Find File dialog box looks like the following illustration.

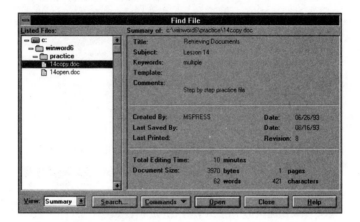

Working with Multiple Files

In this lesson, you've used only one of the many capabilities of the Find File dialog box. In addition to searching for files, you can open, print, copy to another directory, or delete more than one file at a time simply by selecting the file names from the list, and then choosing the appropriate option from the Commands button.

In the following exercise, you select two files to copy, create a new subdirectory to copy them into, and then open both files at once.

Copy multiple files

1   In the Listed Files box, select the document 14COPY.DOC.

2   Hold down the CTRL key and select the document 14OPEN.DOC.

To select two or more file names at once, first select one file name. Then hold down CTRL while you select the second file name you want.

3   Click the Commands button to display a list of commands.

4 Choose Copy.

The Copy dialog box appears.

5 Specify a path for the directory you are about to create by double-clicking each directory and subdirectory in the Directories list up to and including the PRAC-TICE directory.

Because you cannot copy files into the same directory in which the original files are located, you need to specify the path for the new directory. Your new directory will be under the PRACTICE directory.

6 In the Copy dialog box, click the New Folder button.

This selection creates a new directory (or folder) into which you can copy these files.

7 In the Name box, type **direct14**

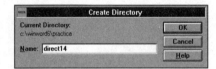

8 Click the OK button to return to the Copy dialog box.

9 Click the OK button to copy the selected files into the new directory you just created.

Locate documents in the new directory

To locate the documents you copied in the new directory, you need to specify a new search path.

1 Click the Search button in the Find File dialog box.

2 Click the Advanced Search button.

3 Click the Location tab.

4 Click the Remove button to remove the existing search path.

5 In the Directories list, select the new directory DIRECT14 under the PRACTICE directory.

6 Click the Add button.

7 Click the OK button to return to the Search dialog box.

8 Select the Rebuild File List check box.

9 Click the OK button to locate the Word documents in the new directory.

The copied files appear in the Find File dialog box.

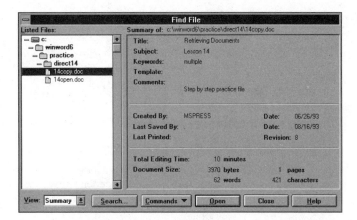

Note If you want to print both documents, select each document, click the Commands button, and then choose Print.

Open multiple files

1 Select the document 14COPY.DOC.

2 Hold down the CTRL key and select the document 14OPEN.DOC.

3 Click the Open button.

Both documents are now open.

4 Choose the Window menu.

Notice in the following illustration that both file names appear in the open document list at the bottom of the Window menu.

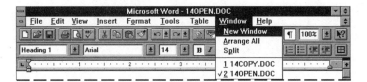

5 Click anywhere in the document window to close the menu.

6 Press CTRL+F6 to alternate displaying the two documents.

One Step Further

With two documents open at once, you can display both of them at the same time using the Arrange All command on the Window menu. Then you can scroll through both documents independently. With both documents displayed, you can use drop and drag techniques to copy information from one document to another.

Display two documents at once

1   From the Window menu, choose Arrange All.

The document window is split into two windows. Each one contains a document. You can scroll through each window independently.

2   Scroll through the document called 14OPEN.DOC, and select the sentence that begins "Find File is like."

This text is the second to last sentence in the document.

3   Hold down the CTRL key and drag the selected text to the 14COPY.DOC document in the other window.

4   With the insertion point at the beginning of the first paragraph, release the mouse.

If You Want to Continue to the Next Lesson

1   To close each document, from the File menu, choose Close.

2   If a message appears asking if you want to save changes, choose the Yes button.

3   Repeat steps 1 and 2 to close the other document.

If You Want to Quit Microsoft Word for Now

1   From the File menu, choose Exit.

2   If a message appears asking if you want to save changes, choose the Yes button.

Lesson Summary

To	Do this
Find a file	From the File menu, choose Find File. If the path is not what you want, choose Edit Path and select the drives and directories you want to search. Specify any search criteria, such as date or author. Choose the Search button.
Select multiple file names in the Find File dialog box	From the File menu, choose Find File. Search, if necessary, to display the file names you want to use. Hold down the CTRL key and click to select the files you want. If you accidentally select a file name that you do not want, hold down the CTRL key and click the file name again to remove the highlighting.
Open multiple files	From the File menu, choose Find File. Search, if necessary, to display the file names of the files you want to open. Select the file names and choose the Open button in the Find File dialog box.
Display two files at once	From the Window menu, choose Arrange All.

For more information on	See in the *Microsoft Word User's Guide*
Finding files or working with multiple files	Chapter 22, "Locating and Managing Documents"

Preview of the Next Lesson

In the next lesson, you'll learn to create an attractive, easy-to-complete online form. Using an online form in which you supply choices of answers and easy-to-use selection options ensures that the information entered in the form can be organized consistently. Plus, a form completed online is always legible—you never have to decipher someone's bad handwriting. After you create a simple form, you will enter information in it.

Working with Forms

Paper forms are often known for being difficult to complete, and sometimes difficult to read after they are completed. An online form minimizes many of the disadvantages of paper forms. With Word, you can design an online form to ensure that your forms are completed quickly and accurately.

In this lesson, you'll combine many of the features you have learned about in this book—tables, templates, frames, and borders—to create an online form, that is, a form you can fill in as a Word document. After you create an online form, you will complete the form so that it looks similar to the following illustration.

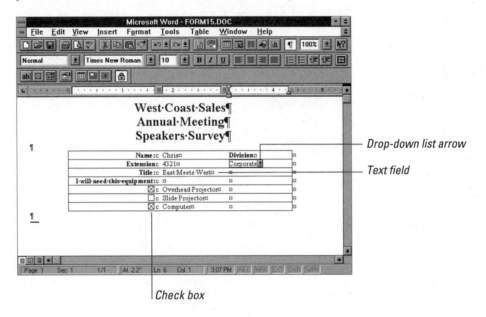

Drop-down list arrow

Text field

Check box

You will learn how to:

For instructions about starting Word, see "Getting Ready," earlier in this book.

- Create a form template.

- Insert text fields, drop-down lists, and check boxes for easy data entry.

- Protect a form for online completion.

- Enter information in an online form.

Estimated lesson time: 35 minutes

Understanding Online Forms

You are probably already familiar with many different kinds of paper forms: purchase order forms, expense forms, tax forms, and so on. Although there are forms too numerous to count, they all have a few things in common:

- All forms contain both text and blank areas, or *fields*, in which people enter information.

- Text and fields are usually arranged in a grid, allowing space for individuals to enter information in the fields.

- Paper forms are usually known for being difficult to complete ("What am I supposed to enter here?") and, in the case of forms completed by hand, difficult to decipher ("Is this a 'one' or an 'L'?") after they are completed.

An online form minimizes many of the disadvantages of paper forms. With Word, you can design an online form to display Help information that guides people through the process of completing the form. Your online form can also contain either text fields of a fixed length, or they can be of unlimited length. A drop-down list field provides a list of options from which the user can choose. For "yes" or "no" responses, you can create check box fields in which the user can place an "X" by clicking in the box. You can also specify the "default" answer in specific fields, to make the form even easier to complete.

Because a user completes your form online, you don't need to try to decipher someone's handwriting. In addition, if your computer is connected to a network, online forms can be completed and shared in the same way you share other documents, eliminating the need for paper forms entirely.

Creating an Online Form

You create a form by first creating a template. This template contains the arrangement of text and fields you want for your form. You specify the types of fields you want and format the form. Finally, before you save the template, you protect the form elements so that when people complete the form they change only the information in the fields and not the text or format of the form.

Create an online form

Suppose you have been asked to help coordinate speakers for an upcoming annual company meeting. To enlist the aid of your colleagues, you need to create a form in which the speakers complete a short survey.

If you are continuing from Lesson 14, you might need to maximize the document window. Before you begin this lesson, click the Maximize button in the document window, so that the document window appears full size.

1 From the File menu, choose New.

2 From the Template list, select Normal.

3 In the New area, select the Template option button.

Your online form is a template document.

4 Click the OK button.

5 Click the Save button on the Standard toolbar.

Save

6 In the File Name box, type **form15**

Word automatically supplies the .DOT extension and stores the template in the TEMPLATE directory in the Word home directory. All templates must be stored in this directory for the name of the template to appear in the Templates list of the New dialog box.

7 Click the OK button.

Design your form

Using the illustration at the beginning of this lesson as your guide, enter text for the top part of the form. Later you can format the text to make your form more attractive.

1 At the insertion point, type **West Coast Sales** and press ENTER.

2 In the next line, type **Annual Meeting** and press ENTER.

3 In the third line, type **Speakers Survey** and press ENTER twice.

These three lines of text are the title of the form. Pressing ENTER twice creates an extra line between the title and the next part of the form.

Display the Forms toolbar

The Forms toolbar contains buttons that make it easy to create a form.

1 From the View menu, choose Toolbars.

2 In the Toolbars dialog box, select the Forms check box.

3 Click the OK button.

The Forms toolbar appears. You might need to double-click in a gray area on the Forms toolbar to move it above the workspace.

If you are unfamiliar with tables in Word, see Lesson 10.

Insert a table

Use a table to arrange the text and fields for your form. Later you can format your table.

Insert Table

▶ Click the Insert Table button on the Forms toolbar and drag a grid that is seven rows down by three columns across as shown in the following illustration.

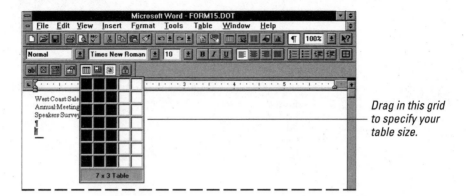

Drag in this grid to specify your table size.

Add text to the table

1   With the insertion point in the first cell, type **Name:**

This text is the label for the field you will create in the next step.

Tip   To make it easier to work in the table as you create your form, display the table gridlines if they are not already displayed. You can display the gridlines by choosing Gridlines from the Table menu.

---

2   Press TAB to move to the next field.

Insert a text field

A text field is a field in which the user can enter text. You can allow users to enter an unlimited amount of text, or you can restrict the number of characters they are able to enter. Create a text field in this cell in which users will enter a name.

Text Form Field

1   On the Forms toolbar, click the Text Form Field button.

A shaded rectangle appears in the cell. This is a text field.

2   Double-click the shaded text field.

Double-clicking a text field displays the Text Form Field Options dialog box. In this dialog box, you specify the options you want for the field.

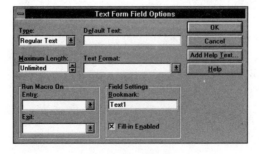

3   In the Maximum Length area, be sure Unlimited is selected.

If it is not selected, use the arrows to select Unlimited. This selection allows the user to enter an unlimited amount of text in the field.

4   Click the OK button.

You won't see any change to the field in the table.

5   Place the insertion point in the second row of the first column.

Insert text and another text field

1   Type **Extension:**

2   Press TAB to move to the next field.

3   On the Forms toolbar, click the Text Form Field button.

A shaded rectangle appears in the cell.

4   Double-click the text field.

5   In the Maximum Length area, use the scroll up arrow to select 4.

This selection allows the user to enter only four characters in this field when filling out the form. If the user attempts to enter more characters, the program beeps.

6   Under Type, click the drop-down list and select Number.

This selection verifies that the user has entered a number (not a letter). If the user attempts to enter a character that is not a number, the program beeps.

7   Click the OK button to return to the form.

8   Place the insertion point in the third row in the first column.

Insert text and another text field

1   Type **Title:**

2   Press TAB to move to the next field.

3   On the Forms toolbar, click the Text Form Field button.

4   Double-click the text field.

5   In the Maximum Length area, use the scroll arrows to select 30.

This selection allows the user to enter 30 characters in this field. You also type the number of characters you want for the field length. If the user attempts to enter more characters, the program beeps.

Assign help to a field

To make it easier for a user to enter the correct information in a field, you can provide information as a message that appears in the status bar, or as a Help window that appears when the user presses F1. In this exercise, you create a message in the status bar for the current field, clarifying how long the title of the speech can be.

1   In the Text Form Field Options dialog box, click the Add Help Text button.

2   In the Form Field Help Text dialog box, be sure the Status Bar tab is selected.

3   Select the Type Your Own option button.

4   Type **Enter the exact title of your speech. You are limited to 30 characters.**

This message will appear in the status bar when the user moves to this field in the form.

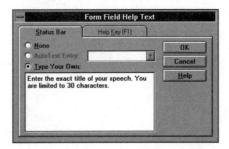

5   Click the OK button to return to the Text Form Field Options dialog box.

6   Click the OK button to return to the form.

7   Place the insertion point in the fourth row in the first column.

Add text to the form

Enter a heading that describes the fields in the next part of the form.

1   Type **I will need this equipment**:

2   Press the DOWN ARROW key to place the insertion point in the cell below (the fifth row in the first column).

Insert a check box field and text

When you want the user to specify a "yes" or "no" response in a form, you can insert a check box field.

Check Box Form Field

1   On the Forms toolbar, click the Check Box Form Field button.

A check box appears in the cell.

2   Press TAB to move to the cell in the next column.

3   Type **Overhead Projector**

4   Place the insertion point in the first cell of the next row.

Insert two check box fields and text

1   On the Forms toolbar, click the Check Box Form Field button.

A check box appears in the cell.

2   Press TAB to move to the cell in the next column, and then type **Slide Projector**

3   Place the insertion point in the first cell of the next row.

4   On the Forms toolbar, click the Check Box Form Field button.

A check box appears in the cell.

5   Press TAB to move to the cell in the next column, and then type **Computer**

6   Click the Save button to save the work you have completed so far.

Save

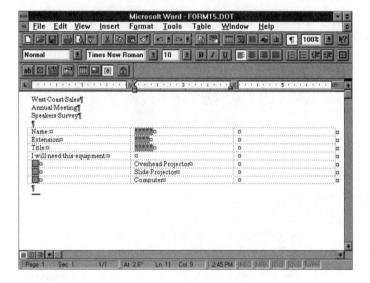

Add text to the form

Enter a label that describes the field you will create next.

1   Place the insertion point in the cell at the first row of the third column.

2   Type **Division:**

3   Press the DOWN ARROW key to place the insertion point in the field below (the second field in the third column).

Insert a drop-down list field

To make it easy for the user to specify the division name to which he or she belongs, you can create a drop-down list of selections. The user will click this field and make a selection from the list.

Drop-Down Form Field

1   On the Forms toolbar, click the Drop-Down Form Field button.

A drop-down list field appears in the cell.

2   Double-click the drop-down list field you just created.

Double-clicking a drop-down form field displays the Drop-Down Form Field Options dialog box. In this dialog box, you can specify the options you want for the field.

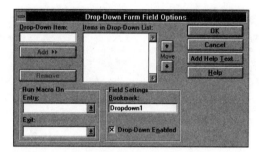

Specify selections in a drop-down list field

Enter the list of choices from which the user will choose when he or she completes the form.

1   In the Drop-Down Item box, type **Outdoor Enterprises**

2   Click the Add button.

The item "Outdoor Enterprises" appears in the list to the right. The first item in the list will be the default selection.

3   Type **Corporate**

4   Click the Add button.

The item "Corporate" appears in the Items in the Drop-Down List box to the right.

5   Type **Great Outdoors** and then click the Add button.

6   Type **Great Northern** and then click the Add button.

7   Type **Great Kitchens PLUS** and then click the Add button.

8   Click the OK button to return to the form.

Your form looks like the following illustration.

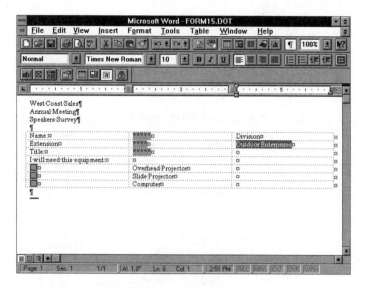

Format the table

Format the table to make it more attractive and easier to read.

1   From the Table menu, choose Select Table.

2   From the Table menu, choose Table AutoFormat.

3   From the Formats list, select the List 5 format.

4   Clear the Heading Rows check box, and then click OK.

5   From the Table menu, choose Cell Height And Width.

6   Click the Row tab, if it does not appear foremost in the dialog box.

7   In the Alignment area, select the Center option button, and then click OK.

Format cells

In this exercise, you use the Align Right button on the Formatting toolbar to align the text and fields in the first column. You also change a cell's text style to bold, and hide paragraph marks and gridlines.

1   Position the pointer near the top edge of the first column.

2   When the pointer changes shape to a down arrow, click the mouse button to select the first column.

3   On the Formatting toolbar, click the Align Right button.

4   Select the first-row cell in the third column (the one that contains the text "Division:"), and then click the Bold button on the Formatting toolbar.

Align Right

Show/Hide ¶

5   Click the Show/Hide ¶ button on the Standard toolbar to hide paragraph marks.

6   From the Table menu, choose Gridlines to hide the gridlines.

When you are making the finishing touches to your form, you might prefer to hide both the non-printing characters and the gridlines.

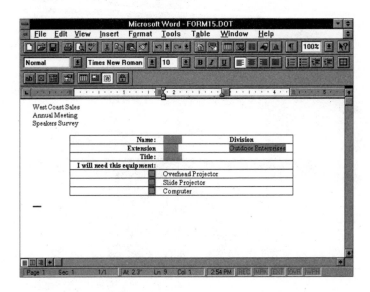

Format the title of the form

Center

1   Select the three lines of text at the top of the document (outside the table), and click the Center button on the Formatting toolbar.

2   With the text still selected, click the Bold button on the Formatting toolbar.

3   From the Font Size drop-down list on the Formatting toolbar, select 18 to create 18-point type.

Bold

Hide form shading

The default setting for the fields is shaded. You can hide the shading to improve the appearance of the form.

Form Field Shading

▶   Click the Form Field Shading button on the Forms toolbar to hide the shading.

Your form looks like the following illustration.

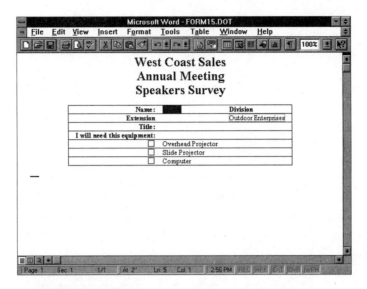

In this illustration, the extra toolbars and the ruler are hidden to display more of the form in the document window.

Protect the form

So that people do not inadvertently change the form when they complete it online, you can protect the form.

Protect Form

▶ Click the Protect Form button on the Forms toolbar.

Save and close the form

1 From the File menu, choose Close.

2 When a message appears asking if you want to save changes, click the Yes button.

   Your form is saved as a template.

Using an Online Form

Now that you have created a form, you can use Word to complete it. To complete an online form, you create a new document based on the form template. Each completed form is a Word document.

Open an online form

To start your presentation planning on the right track, complete an online form to identify your preferences for your presentation.

1 From the File menu, choose New.

2 From the Template list, select FORM15.

3 Be sure the Document option button is selected.

4 Click the OK button.

Complete the form online

To move from field to field, you can press TAB. Notice that because the form is protected, you cannot move to cells that do not contain fields.

1 In the Name field, type **Chris,** and then press TAB to move to the next field.

2 In the Extension field, type **4321,** and then press TAB to move to the next field.

3 Click the arrow to open the Division drop-down list.

Your screen should look like the following illustration.

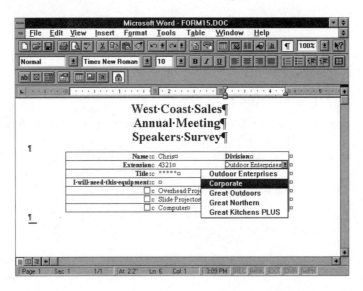

4 From the list, select Corporate.

5 Press TAB to move to the Title field, and then type **East Meets West**

6 Click both the Overhead Projector and the Computer check boxes.

7 Click the Save button on the Standard toolbar.

8 In the Save As dialog box, double-click the appropriate directories until PRAC-TICE is the current directory.

The current path changed when you created the template document earlier in this lesson. Templates are automatically stored in the TEMPLATE subdirectory in the Microsoft Word home directory.

Save

9   In the File Name box, type **form15** and then click OK.

Your responses in the form are saved in this document. The original form template is unaffected.

10   From the File menu, choose Close.

One Step Further

You can improve the appearance of the form by increasing the row height of the rows in the table, and adjusting the spacing of the text in each row.

Open another form template

1   On the Standard toolbar, click the Open button.

2   In the Directories list, be sure the PRACTICE directory is open. If it is not, select the drive and directory for the Microsoft Word home directory, and click each subsequent directory until you locate PRACTICE.

3   Click the down arrow next to List Files Of Type, and select Document Templates (*.DOT).

4   Double-click 15OSF.DOT.

This practice template was copied to the PRACTICE directory. To use it as a template, you need to save it in the TEMPLATE directory.

Save the template in the TEMPLATE directory with a new name

1   From the File menu, choose Save As.

2   In the File Name box, type **osf15.dot**

Be sure the TEMPLATE directory is open. If it is not, select the drive and directory for the Microsoft Word home directory, and click each subsequent directory until you locate TEMPLATE.

3   Click the OK button.

Format the table rows

1   Click in the table and then, from the Table menu, choose Select Table.

2   From the Table menu, choose Cell Height And Width.

3   Click the Row tab, if it does not appear foremost in the dialog box.

4   In the At box, type **30pt**

5   Click the OK button.

Format the text

1   With the entire table still selected, choose Paragraph from the Format menu.

2   In the Before box under Spacing, type **6pt**

3   Click the OK button.

If You Want to Continue to the Next Lesson

1   From the File menu, choose Close.

2   When a message appears asking if you want to save changes, click the Yes button.

If You Want to Quit Microsoft Word for Now

1   From the File menu, choose Exit.

2   If a message appears asking if you want to save changes, click the Yes button.

Lesson Summary

To	Do this	Button
Create a form	From the File menu, choose New. Select Normal, and click the Template option button. Click OK, and then save the form with a new name.	
Display the Forms toolbar	From the View menu, choose Toolbars, and select the Forms check box.	
Insert a text field	On the Forms toolbar, click the Text Form Field button. Double-click the text field. Specify the desired options in the dialog box, and click OK.	ab
Insert a check box	On the Forms toolbar, click the Check Box Form Field button.	⊠
Insert a drop-down list field	On the Forms toolbar, click the Drop-Down Form Field button.	
Protect a form	Click the Protect Form button on the Forms toolbar.	🔒
Complete an online form	From the File menu, choose New. Select a form template.	

For more information on	See in the *Microsoft Word User's Guide*
Working with templates	Chapter 10, "Document Templates"
Creating forms	Chapter 14, "Forms"

Preview of the Next Lesson

If you need to create many documents that are nearly identical, you can use Word's Mail Merge feature to insert the variable information where you need it. In the next lesson, you will learn how to use the Mail Merge Helper to combine documents in a way that creates personalized form letters.

Creating and Printing Merged Documents

Suppose you want to mail out several letters that are nearly identical. With Word, you can create a *merged document*, in which customized information is combined with standard or boilerplate text, as in form letters. In this way, you can create many letters efficiently, each with a personal touch. In this lesson, you learn to create a main document that contains standard text. Then you create a data source, the document that contains the individualized information. Finally, you merge the main document and the data source to create your customized form letters. You also learn how to attach an existing data source to a main document.

You will learn how to:

For instructions about starting Microsoft Word, see "Getting Ready," earlier in this book.

- Create a main document with instructions for inserting variable information, such as names and addresses.

- Create a data source of names and addresses.

- Merge the data source information into the main document.

- Attach an existing data source to a main document.

Estimated lesson time: 35 minutes

Merging Documents: Basic Techniques

Preparing any type of merged document involves two files: a *main document* and a *data source*. The main document contains the standardized text and graphics you want in each version of the merged document. The *data source* contains only the information that varies with each version—such as names, addresses, account numbers, and product codes. In the main document, you insert special instructions, called *merge fields*, to indicate where you want the variable information to appear. When you merge the data source and the main document, Word inserts the appropriate information from the data source into the merge fields to create a merged document.

Whether you're printing mailing labels or personalizing a form letter, you use the same basic techniques to create the final, merged documents. The *Mail Merge Helper,* available with the Mail Merge command on the Tools menu, guides you through the following sequence of major steps:

- Open a new or existing document and attach a data source to it. You can attach an existing data source or you can attach a new one that you fill in. Attaching the data source makes the active document the *main document.*

- Insert merge field names into your main document to indicate where you want the variable information such as names and addresses. The field names must exactly match those in the data source.

- Merge the main document with the data source, and either print the merged documents or store them in a new file for viewing on the screen and editing.

Create a main document

Suppose you want to send letters to several individuals who you met at a recent trade show, informing them of your upcoming visit to their town. You can create a main document containing boilerplate text to this effect, and later merge in their names and addresses. In this exercise, you create a form letter main document. For the time being, you will not type any text in the main document until you've created the data source.

New

1   If you don't see a blank document, then click the New button on the toolbar to create a new document.

If you share your computer with others who use Microsoft Word, the screen display might have changed since your last lesson. Be sure your screen displays the Standard and Formatting toolbars, the ruler, and normal view. (If you need help, see the Appendix, "Matching the Exercises.")

2   From the Tools menu, choose Mail Merge.

3   In the Main Document area of the Mail Merge Helper window, click the Create button.

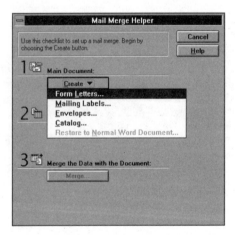

Clicking this button reveals a list of main document options from which you can choose.

4   Select Form Letters.

A message window appears.

5   In the dialog box, click the Active Window button.

This selection creates a main document in the currently active document window, rather than opening a new document window.

Creating a Data Source

Now that you've created an empty main document, you're ready to create a data source. A data source contains all the text and graphics that have changed with each version of a merged document. Each set of related information (for a specific customer, for instance) makes up one *data record* in the data source. The different categories of information in each record—title, first name, last name, company, street address, city, state, postal code, and product—are called *fields*.

Each field name in a data source must be unique and can have as many as 32 characters. You can use letters, numbers, and underscore characters, but not spaces. The first character must be a letter.

Create and attach a data source

From the Mail Merge Helper dialog box, you can either open an existing data source or create a new one. In this exercise, you create a new data source and select the field names to be included.

1   In the Mail Merge Helper dialog box, under Data Source, click the Get Data button.

2   Select Create Data Source.

Word displays the Create Data Source dialog box in which you can specify the field names to include in the data source. You can start with the suggested fields already provided, remove the ones you won't use, or add your own.

3   Because you will use all but a few of the field names in the Field Name list, you can remove the ones you don't want. For each of the following field names, first select the field, and then click the Remove Field Name button to remove it from the list.

JobTitle
Address2
Country
HomePhone
WorkPhone

You will need to scroll downward to select field names further down in the list.

4 In the Field Name box, type **Product**

You can type over any text already selected in the Field Name box.

5 Click the Add Field Name button.

Your new field appears at the bottom of the list of field names.

6 Click the OK button.

The Save Data Source dialog box appears.

7 Under Directories, be sure the PRACTICE directory is open. If it is not, select the drive and directory for the Microsoft Word home directory, and click each subsequent directory until you locate PRACTICE.

8 In the File Name box, type **data16**

9 Click the OK button.

A dialog box informs you that this data source has no records in it. You can choose to add records right away, or you can return to the main document and begin adding merge fields.

10 Click the Edit Data Source button.

The Data Form dialog box appears.

Entering Data Records

The Data Form dialog box contains the fields you specified in the data source. You enter a set of fields (that is, a data record) for each individual you want to receive this letter. You can enter as many data records as you wish.

Complete the data source form

Now you can enter the name and address (plus product information) for the first person to whom you want to send a form letter.

1   Type the following information in the form. As you complete each field, press ENTER to move to the next field. Press SHIFT+TAB to move to a previous field. When you have completed entering a data record and want to enter another data record, click the Add New button. Click the OK button when you have finished entering data records.

Title	**Mr.**
FirstName	**Guy**
LastName	**Barton**
Company	**Victory Sports**
Address1	**1234 Central Avenue**
City	**Cascade Views**
State	**WA**
PostalCode	**98076**
Product	**camping and adventure gear**

Your completed dialog box looks like the following illustration.

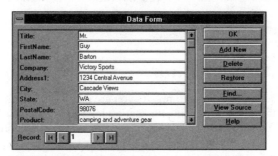

2   Click the Add New button.

You can also press ENTER to enter a new record.

3 Add new data records for the following individuals. Notice that, for one of them, you will not enter a company name. By default, Word will skip blank fields, so it does not affect the merge to have blank entries in the data form. Remember to click the Add New button to add another data record.

Title	**Ms.**
FirstName	**Julia**
LastName	**Nelson**
Company	**Valley Sports Center**
Address1	**43908 West Old Highway 904**
City	**Riverdale**
State	**WY**
PostalCode	**87087**
Product	**camping gear**

Title	**Mr.**
FirstName	**James**
LastName	**Lee**
Company	
Address1	**Valley Heights Mall**
City	**Appleton**
State	**GA**
PostalCode	**06578**
Product	**outdoor cooking gear**

4 Click the OK button.

You return to the main document. Notice the new Mail Merge toolbar. Use the buttons on this toolbar when you are working with merged documents.

Working with Main Documents

Now that the data source is complete, you are ready to complete the main document with standard text, spaces, and punctuation to print in all versions of the merged document. You also need to specify where you want variable information to appear. To do this, you insert merge fields. These fields correspond to fields in the data source. When you merge the main document with the data source, Word replaces the merge field names with the corresponding information from each data record in the data source.

Display paragraph marks

The merge field names act as *placeholders*, that is, they reserve a place for the data source text. You must insert the same spacing and punctuation between the merge field names as you would between words. Displaying paragraph marks makes it easier to see the spaces between words and the "empty paragraphs," or blank lines, in the document.

Show/Hide ¶

▶ If paragraph marks are not currently displayed on the screen, click theShow/Hide ¶ button on the Standard toolbar.

Insert the date

Use the Date And Time command to insert the current date into the main document. Word automatically updates the information each time you print the document.

If you see "{TIME_}" on the screen instead of a date

This means you are viewing the main document with the field codes displayed. These codes instruct Microsoft Word to insert information into the document. To hide them, select Options from the Tools menu and click Field Codes on the View tab to remove the check mark.

1 From the Insert menu, choose Date And Time.

2 Select the date format that shows the date like this: June 29, 1994.

3 Click the OK button.

Word inserts the date into the document. Each time you print the main document, Word will insert the current date.

4 Press ENTER twice to leave a blank line below the date.

Inserting Field Names in the Main Document

When you insert the merge field names into the main document, you are telling Word where you want the variable information from the data source to appear. Word encloses each field name in chevrons (« »).

Insert the title, first name, and last name

1 On the Mail Merge toolbar, click the Insert Merge Field button.

When you click this button, a list of field names that you can insert in your main document appears. You select field names from this list.

Insert Merge Field

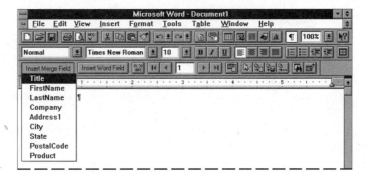

2 The merge field name Title is already selected. Click the field to insert it into the document.

3 Press the SPACEBAR to insert a blank space between the title and the first name.

4 Click the Insert Merge Field button to insert the next field name, and select FirstName.

5   Press the SPACEBAR to insert a blank space between the first name and the last name.

6   Click the Insert Merge Field button, and select LastName.

7   Press ENTER to move to the next line.

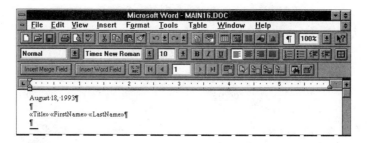

Insert the company name and address

1   Click the Insert Merge Field button, select Company, and press ENTER.

2   Click the Insert Merge Field button, select Address1, and press ENTER.

3   Click the Insert Merge Field button, and select City.

4   Type a comma and press the SPACEBAR so that the punctuation will be correct between the city and state.

5   Click the Insert Merge Field button, and select State.

6   Press the SPACEBAR to insert a blank space between the state and the postal code.

7   Click the Insert Merge Field button, and scroll downward, if necessary, to select PostalCode.

8   Press ENTER twice to leave a blank line.

Type the salutation

You can use a merge field name as many times as you want in a document. In this exercise, you type the boilerplate salutation "Dear" followed by the Title and LastName merge fields, and finally a comma.

1   Type **Dear** and press the SPACEBAR. Do *not* press ENTER yet.

2   Click the Insert Merge Field button, and select Title.

3   Press the SPACEBAR to leave a space between the title and the last name.

4   Click the Insert Merge Field button, and select LastName.

5   Type a comma, and then press ENTER twice to leave a blank line.

Your document looks like the following illustration.

Finish typing the letter

You can use a merge field name within the body of the letter to customize the text. The following procedure inserts the name of the city in each letter.

1 Type **Thank you for attending our trade show. We will be in**

Do *not* press ENTER yet.

2 If you have not already typed a space following "We will be in," press the SPACEBAR now.

3 Click the Insert Merge Field button, select City, and press the SPACEBAR.

4 Type **next month. We would like to show you our new** and press the SPACEBAR.

5 Click the Insert Merge Field button, and select Product.

6 Type a period. Then press ENTER twice to create a blank line between the body of the letter and the signature that you will type next.

7 Type **Sincerely,** and press ENTER three times.

8 Type **Chris Hamilton**

Your completed document looks like the following illustration.

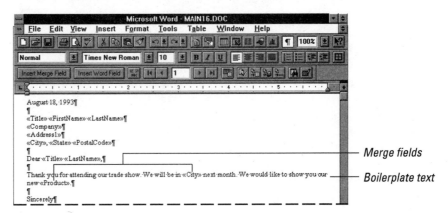

— Merge fields

— Boilerplate text

Save the main document

1 From the File menu, choose Save.

2 Under Directories, be sure the PRACTICE directory is open. If it is not, select the drive and directory for the Microsoft Word home directory, and click each subsequent directory until you locate PRACTICE.

3 Under File Name, type **main16** and press ENTER.

Merging Documents

Once you've attached a data source to a main document and inserted merge field codes into the main document, you are ready to combine the main document with the data source. You have three choices; each is available by clicking one of the following buttons on the Mail Merge toolbar.

- Use the Check For Errors button to have Word check the main document and the data source, and alert you to errors.

- Use the Merge To Printer button to merge the main document with the data source, and immediately print each resulting document.

- Use the Merge To New Document button to merge the main document and data source, and store the resulting documents in a new document called Form Letters1. You can then view each version of the merged document on your screen and check formatting, spacing, and other details. This is what you will do in the following exercise. You can save this document if you want and print it later.

Merge the information into one file

Merge To New Document

▶ To merge the main document and the data source and store the results in a new file, click the Merge To New Document button.

Each form letter is separated with a double dotted line that indicates a section break. Each section is automatically formatted to begin on a new page as shown in the following illustration.

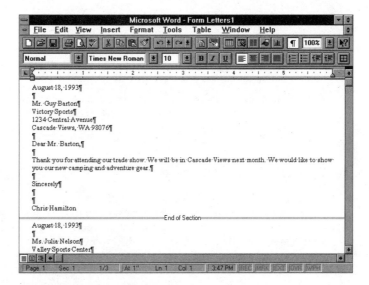

View and edit the letters

As you scroll through the letters, note that the first two letters have a company name in the address, but that the third letter does not. Word skips this field in the third letter because you left the company field blank in the data source. You can edit any of the text as you would edit any other document.

1 Click the down arrow on the scroll bar to examine each letter.

2 In the last letter, select the word "month" and type **week** instead. Then position the insertion point at the end of the last sentence, press the SPACEBAR, and type **Please contact Maria Mendel to set up an appointment.**

Print the merged letters

Print

▶ If you have a printer connected to your computer, be sure it is turned on, and then click the Print button on the Standard toolbar.

If you don't have a printer, continue with the next exercise.

Close the merged document file

1 From the File menu, choose Close.

2 When a message appears asking if you want to save this document, click the No button. You do not need to save this file.

You can quickly generate another merged document whenever you want to print these documents. The main document called MAIN16.DOC is still open in the document window.

Attaching an Existing Data Source

You can use other existing data sources with your main documents, provided that the data source contains the same field names found in the main document. Suppose a co-worker also has a list of individuals to whom you want send your letter, and has already entered the data records into a data source. You can attach your main document to that data source using the Mail Merge Helper.

Attach an existing data source

Included on the Step by Step practice disk is a file called 16MORE.DOC. This data source contains additional data you can merge with your main document.

Mail Merge Helper

1 Click the Mail Merge Helper button on the Mail Merge toolbar.

2 In the Data Source area, click the Get Data button.

3 Select Open Data Source.

4 In the Open Data Source dialog box, double-click 16MORE.DOC.

5 When you return to the Mail Merge Helper dialog box, click the Close button.

6 Click the Merge To New Document button.

Word merges the main document with the data source and displays letters in a new document window called Form Letters2.

Close the merged document file

1 From the File menu, choose Close.

2 Click the No button. You do not need to save this file.

One Step Further

Your simple and straight-to-the-point letter could be used by your sales force, all of whom have customers to whom they also want to send customized form letters. So that they can use your letter without making additional revisions, you can substitute a field that inserts the salesperson's name in the signature. Using Word's Author field instead of your name in the signature is an additional way to customize form letters efficiently.

Insert Word's author field

Be sure the main document called MAIN16 is still open.

1   Select the name in the signature at the bottom of the document.

2   From the Insert menu, choose Field.

3   In the Field Names box on the right, select the Author field.

4   Click the OK button.

Word inserts the name that appears on the User Info tab of the Options dialog box. If you are working with your own copy of Microsoft Word, the author field will supply your name.

When you share this document with someone else who works on another computer, his or her name will appear in the main document.

If You Want to Continue to the Review & Practice

1   From the File menu, choose Close.

2   When a message appears asking if you want to save changes, click the Yes button.

If You Want to Quit Word for Now

1   From the File menu, choose Exit.

2   If a message appears asking if you want to save changes, click the Yes button.

Lesson Summary

To	Do this	Button
Create a main document	Choose Mail Merge from the Tools menu. In the dialog box, click the Create button and select a document type. Make a selection in the dialog box, and then click Close.	
Create and attach a data source	Be sure the document you want to use as the main document is open. From the Tools menu, choose Mail Merge. Click the Get Data button, and select Create Data Source to open the dialog box where you add or remove field names. After you name and save the data source, a data form opens where you type the information for each field.	

To	Do this	Button
Insert merge fields in a main document	With the main document open, click the Insert Merge Field button on the Mail Merge toolbar. Select the name of each field you want to insert.	Insert Merge Field
Merge a main document and a data source, and save the merged documents to a new file	With the main document open, click the appropriate button on the Mail Merge toolbar. Click the Merge To New Document button to merge the information into one file that you can view and print later.	

For more information on	See in the *Microsoft Word User's Guide*
Merging documents	Chapter 29, "Mail Merge: Step by Step"
Merging specific data records	Chapter 30, "Mail Merge: Advanced Techniques"

Review & Practice

The lessons in Part 4 familiarized you with some the more sophisticated Word features for accomplishing special projects with your documents. If you want to practice these skills and test your understanding before you go on to work with special projects of your own, you can work through the Review & Practice section following this lesson. This less structured activity allows you to increase your confidence using many of the features introduced so far.

Part 4 Review & Practice

In this Review & Practice, you have an opportunity to fine tune the document management skills you learned in the lessons in Part 4 of this book. Use what you have learned about outlining documents, locating files, creating forms, and merging documents to complete several special projects for West Coast Sales marketing efforts.

Scenario

To help the West Coast Sales marketing department prepare for a nationwide sales campaign, you need to modify a long document by rearranging text. Because you can't recall the document name, you need to use Find File to locate and open it. In addition, you have been asked to prepare an online form to help the sales force keep track of sales calls. Finally, to help the sales representatives prepare for a series of sales meetings, you will create and modify a main document that you can merge with sales information.

You will review and practice how to:

- Locate a document using Find File.
- Use outlining techniques to reorganize a document.
- Create an online form.
- Add merge fields to a main document and attach a data source.
- Merge documents.

Estimated practice time: 30 minutes

Step 1: Locate a Document

You need to locate a document in your practice directory, but you cannot remember the exact name. You do recall, however, some of the text in the keyword field.

1 Locate the document that has the word "review04" in the keyword field of the Summary Info dialog box.

2 Open the document and save it as REVIEWP4.DOC.

For more information on	See
Locating a document using Find File	Lesson 14

Step 2:   Reorganize a Document

Because you want to rearrange "chunks" of information in the document, use the outline feature to reorganize the document more efficiently.

1   Display the document in outline view.

2   Promote the first line of the document to a heading 1.

3   Promote all the division headings to level 2 headings.

4   Collapse the document to display only the first two heading levels.

5   Move the heading "Great Kitchens PLUS" to before the heading "Outdoor Enterprises Division."

6   Expand this heading so you see all the subordinate text.

7   Return to normal view, and then save and close your document.

For more information on	See
Outlining a document	Lesson 13
Promoting headings	Lesson 13

Step 3:   Create an Online Form

The sales force needs a way to summarize sales meetings. The following online form with default answers will encourage sales representatives to use the form and keep accurate records of their meetings.

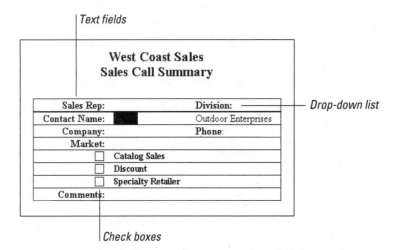

1   Create a new template based on the Normal template.

2   Type in the two-line table title followed by a few blank lines. Format the title similar to the above illustration. Display the Forms toolbar, and insert a table three columns by eight rows. In column one, enter the field names and the three check boxes. Select column one, and right align the text. In column two, insert the text fields and enter the check box field names. In column three, create a drop-down list for Division names and a text field for Phone.

3   Select the table. From the Table menu, choose Table AutoFormat and select a table format. From the Table menu, select Cell Height And Width and select Center on the Row tab to center the table. Turn off the display of gridlines (from the Table menu) and form field shading (from the Forms toolbar).

4   Protect the document so that the user can modify the form fields only.

5   Save the form template with the name RPSALE04.

For more information on	See
Creating an online form	Lesson 15

Step 4: Complete an Online Form

1   Create a new document based on the form template.

2   Complete the form with the following information.

Sales Rep	**Julia Martin**
Division	**Great Northern**
Contact Name	**Darrell James**
Company	**Home At Last**
Phone	**(555)888-1234**
Market	**Catalog Sales**
	Specialty Retailer
Comments	**Wants to know about discounts.**

3   Save the form document with the name **rpsale04** in the PRACTICE directory.

For more information on	See
Completing an online form	Lesson 15

Step 5: Create a Main Document and Attach a Data Source

1   Create a new copy of the form document by saving it as **rpmain04**

2   Unprotect the document by choosing Unprotect Document from the Tools menu.

3   From the Tools menu, display the Mail Merge Helper.

4   Create a main form document based on the document in the active window.

5   Attach the data source document called RPDATA04.DOC from your PRACTICE directory.

For more information on	See
Protecting a document	Lesson 15
Creating main documents and attaching a data source	Lesson 16

Step 6: Modify the Main Document and Merge Documents

1   Select the text in what had been form fields (and the check boxes) and replace them with the merge fields according to the following table:

Existing text	Replace with this merge field
Julia Martin	**SalesRep**
Great Northern	**Division**
Darrell James	**ContactName**
Home At Last	**Company**
(555)888-1234	**Phone**
Catalog Sales	**Market1**
Discount	**Market2**
Specialty Retailer	**Market3**
Wants to know about discounts.	**Comments**

2   Save your work in the main document.

3   Merge your documents to another document or directly to an attached printer. You don't need to save your merged document.

For more information on	See
Adding merge fields	Lesson 16
Merging documents	Lesson 16

If You Want to Quit Microsoft Word for Now

1   From the File menu, choose Exit.

2   If a message appears asking if you want to save changes, choose the Yes button.

Appendix

Matching the Exercises

Word has many optional settings that can affect either the screen display or the operation of certain functions. Some exercise steps, therefore, might not produce exactly the same result on your screen as shown in the book. For example, if you could not find the PRACTICE subdirectory or if your screen did not look like the illustration at a certain point in a lesson, a note in the lesson might have directed you to this appendix for guidance. Or, if you did not get the outcome described in the lesson, you can use this appendix to determine if the options you have selected are the same as the ones used in this book.

Displaying the Practice Files

You begin most of the lessons by opening one of the sample documents that came on the Step by Step Practice Files disk. The practice files should be stored on your hard disk, in a subdirectory called PRACTICE. The PRACTICE subdirectory is located in Word's home directory. If you cannot locate the practice files you need to complete the lesson, follow these steps.

Open the PRACTICE directory

1   On the Standard toolbar, click the Open button.

    Clicking the Open button displays the Open dialog box, where you select the name of the document to open. You must tell Word on which drive and in which directory the document is stored.

2   If the Drive box does not display the drive where the practice files are stored, click the arrow next to the box and then click the name of the correct drive.

    Most users have the PRACTICE subdirectory stored on drive C.

3   In the Directories box, find the name of the directory where the PRACTICE subdirectory is stored. You might need to click the up or down arrow in the scroll bar to see all the directories in the list. When you find the name of the directory, double-click it to open the directory and display the PRACTICE subdirectory.

    The Word for Windows home directory (typically WINWORD or WINWORD6) is the usual location for the PRACTICE subdirectory.

4   Double-click the PRACTICE subdirectory to open it.

    When you open the PRACTICE subdirectory, the names of the Step by Step practice files (the sample documents) appear in the File Name box. Click the up or down arrow in the scroll bar to see all the names.

    Once you open the correct directory, you are ready to open a practice file. Return to the lesson to learn which file you need to open to complete the lesson.

Matching the Screen Display to the Illustrations

Word makes it easy for you to set up the application window to suit your working style and preferences. If you share your computer with others, previous users might have changed the screen setup. You can easily change it back, so that the screen matches the illustrations in the lessons. Use the following methods for controlling the screen display.

If you change the screen display as part of a lesson and leave Word, the next time you open Word, the screen looks the way you left it in the previous session.

Display toolbars

If toolbars are missing at the top of the screen, previous users might have hidden them to make more room for text. You can easily display the toolbars that contain the buttons you need in these lessons.

1   From the View menu, choose Toolbars.

2   In the Toolbars dialog box, click the check boxes for the toolbars you need.

Most of the lessons require that the Standard and Formatting toolbars appear.

Display the ruler

If the ruler is missing from the top of the screen, previous users might have hidden it to make more room for text. Although the ruler is not required in all lessons, it is usually displayed in the illustrations. To display the ruler, do the following.

▶   From the View menu, choose Ruler.

Hide extra toolbars

To use specific features in some of the lessons, additional toolbars appear in the application window. If, after completing the lesson, you no longer want these toolbars to appear, use the Toolbars dialog box to hide toolbars you do not want to see. However, most of the lessons require that the Standard and Formatting toolbars appear.

1   From the View menu, choose Toolbars.

2   In the Toolbars dialog box, clear the check boxes for the toolbars you do not want to see.

If the vertical scroll bar does not display

If you do not see the vertical scroll bar, a previous user might have hidden the scroll bar to make more room for text. You can easily display it again.

1   Click the Tools menu, then choose Options.

2   Click the View tab to display the view options in the dialog box.

3   In the Window area, click the Vertical Scroll Bar check box so that an "X" appears, indicating it is selected.

If the Vertical Scroll Bar option was previously selected, complete step 4 and then see the following procedure, "If the Word for Windows application window does not fill the screen."

4   Click the OK button.

If the Word for Windows application window does not fill the screen

A previous user might have made the Word application window smaller to allow quick access to another application. You can enlarge the document window by doing the following.

Maximize

▶   Click the Maximize button in the upper-right corner of the Microsoft Word title bar.

If the right edge of the Word window is hidden so that you cannot see the Maximize button, point to "Microsoft Word" in the title bar at the top of the screen, and then drag the title bar to the left until you see the Maximize button.

If the document does not fill the space that Word allows

The last time Word was used, the user might have displayed the document in a smaller size to get an overview of a document. To see your document at the normal size, use the Zoom drop-down list on the Standard toolbar.

▶   Click the down arrow next to the Zoom Control drop-down list, and select 100%.

If you see the top edge of the page on the screen

The last person to use Word might have worked in page layout view, which displays one page of text on the screen. Return to normal view for the lesson.

▶   Click the Normal View button to the far left of the horizontal scroll bar.
or
From the View menu, select Normal.

If spaces appear before periods when moving text

A previous user might have preferred not to use the smart-cut-and-paste feature. Because all the lessons after Lesson 1 assume that this feature is active, you can turn this feature back on.

1   From the Tools menu, choose Options.

2   Click the Edit tab to display the edit options in the dialog box.

3   Click the Use Smart Cut And Paste check box.

4   Click the OK button.

If you see words in brackets

If you see {TIME...} or {SYMBOL..} or {DATE...} in the document, you are looking at the codes that instruct Word to insert a certain type of information. You can hide the codes and view the information that Word inserts in place of them without changing the document in any way.

1 From the Tools menu, choose Options.

2 Click the View tab to display the view options in the dialog box.

3 Click the Field Codes check box to clear it.

4 Click the OK button.

If you see "¶" in the document

Show/Hide ¶

You are viewing the paragraph marks that indicate the end of paragraphs. You might also be viewing other nonprinting symbols that mark spaces or locations where the TAB key was pressed. The symbols do not affect the way the document prints. Many users work with the symbols on all the time. If you prefer to hide the symbols, you can do so without affecting the document in any way. Some of the instructions in the lessons require you to locate a specific paragraph mark in the document. In this case, be sure to click this button on the Standard toolbar.

To hide the symbols, click the Show/Hide ¶ button on the Standard toolbar.

Changing Other Options

If you are not getting the results described in the lessons, follow the instructions in this section to verify that the options set in your application are the same as the ones used in this book.

Review each of the following dialog boxes to compare settings for those options that users change most often and are most likely to account for different results. You can view these dialog boxes by choosing the Options command from the Tools menu. Then you click the tab corresponding to the options you want to see.

View Options

Click the View tab to change options that affect the appearance of the document window. Here are the View settings used in this book.

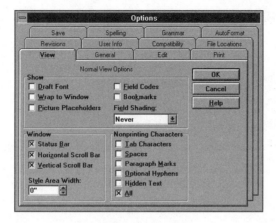

General Options

Click the General tab to change options that affect the operation of Word in general. Here are the General settings used in this book.

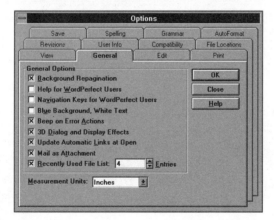

Edit Options

Click the Edit tab to change options that affect how editing operations are performed. Here are the Edit settings used in this book.

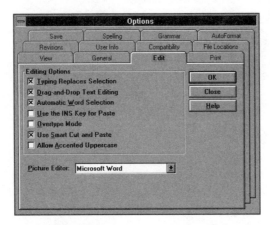

Print Options

Click the Print tab to change options that affect how printing operations are performed. Here are the Print settings used in this book.

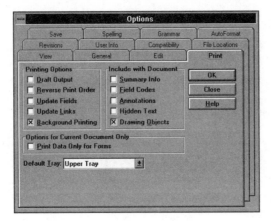

Spelling Options

Click the Spelling tab to change options that affect how the spelling check feature works. Here are the Spelling settings used in this book.

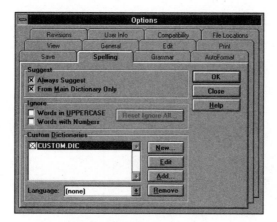

Grammar Options

Click the Grammar tab to change options that affect how the grammar check feature works. Here are the Grammar settings used in this book.

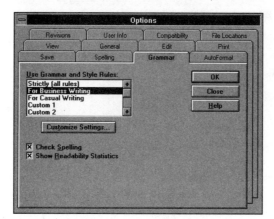

AutoFormat Options

Click the AutoFormat tab to change options that affect how the AutoFormat feature works. Here are the AutoFormat settings used in this book.

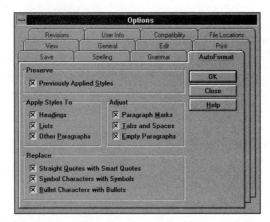

Save Options

Click the Save tab to change options that affect how your documents are saved to disk. Here are the Save settings used in this book.

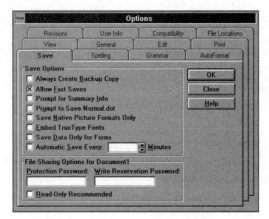

Glossary

alignment   The horizontal position of text within the width of a line or between tab stops. There are three kinds of alignment in Word.

Alignment	Determines
Paragraph	Whether the lines in a paragraph are aligned with the left indent (flush left), aligned with the right indent (flush right), aligned with both indents (justified), or centered between indents (centered).
Tab	Which direction text extends from a tab position.
Section	How paragraphs are placed vertically on a page.

application   Software, such as Microsoft Word or Microsoft Excel, that helps a user create documents or perform work.

application Control menu   A menu that includes commands with which you can control the size and position of the Word window and switch to another application. To display the menu with keys, press ALT+SPACEBAR.

application window   A window that contains a running application. The window displays the menus and provides the workspace for any document used within the application. The application window shares its borders and title bar with document windows that are maximized.

arrow keys   The UP ARROW, DOWN ARROW, LEFT ARROW, and RIGHT ARROW keys. Used to move the insertion point or to select from a menu or a list of options.

automatic save   An option that automatically saves your document at specified intervals. You can select or clear the Automatic Save option with the Options command on the Tools menu.

AutoText entry   A place you store text or graphics you want to use again. Each piece of text or graphics is stored as an AutoText entry and assigned a unique name. Global AutoText entries are available to all documents.

border   A line that goes around text or tables. You can assign a variety of widths to a border. *See also* Rule.

bullet   A mark, usually a round or square dot, often used to add emphasis or distinguish items in a list.

cell The basic unit of a table. In a table, the intersection of a row and a column forms one cell. You type text into cells.

click To press and release a mouse button in one motion.

Clipboard A temporary storage area in the computer's memory for cut or copied text or graphics. You can paste the contents of the Clipboard into any Word document or into a file of another application, such as Microsoft Excel. The Clipboard holds the information until you cut or copy another piece of text or a graphic.

column break A place in text where you designate the end of one column and the beginning of another. In page view and print preview, and when you print your document, text after a column break appears in a new column. A column break appears as a dotted line. A break you insert is called a hard break; a break determined by the page layout is called a soft break.

Control Panel The Microsoft Windows Control Panel adjusts operations and formats, such as the insertion point blink rate, date and time formats, and communications setup. The settings affect both Word and Windows.

crop To trim away the parts of a graphic you don't want to display.

cut To remove selected text or a graphic from a document so you can paste it to another place in the document or to another document. The cut information is placed in a temporary storage area called the Clipboard. The Clipboard holds the information until you cut or copy another piece of text or a graphic.

data source A document that contains text to be merged into a main document to create form letters or other merged documents. For example, a data source for a form letter may contain names and addresses that vary for each letter. If you want to use data from another word-processing program, database, or spreadsheet, you first convert the file to Word format.

defaults Predefined settings, such as page margins, tab settings, and shortcut key assignments, which are stored in the default template. The default template when you create documents is NORMAL.DOT, whose default settings include margins of 1.25 inches and no indents.

dialog box A box that displays the available command options or list selections for you to review or change.

directories Subdivisions of a disk that work like a filing system to help you organize your files. For example, you can create a directory called LETTERS for all of your form letters.

document Control menu   A menu with commands that control a document window. For example, you can size, position, and split a document window. To display the menu with keys, you press ALT+HYPHEN.

document window   A rectangular portion of the screen in which you view and edit a document. You can have multiple document windows open in the Word window. Each document window can be divided horizontally into two parts, called panes. When you enlarge a document window to maximum size, it shares its borders and title bar with the Word window.

drag   To hold down the mouse button while moving the mouse.

drive   The mechanism in your computer that contains a disk to retrieve and store information. Personal computers often have one hard disk drive labeled C and two drives labeled A and B that read removable floppy disks.

drop cap   A text formatting effect in which the first character of a paragraph is significantly larger than the surrounding text. The top of the character is aligned with the text at the top of paragraph, while the bottom of the character "drops" into the body of the paragraph.

edit   To add, delete, or change text and graphics.

extend selection   To lengthen a selection. When you extend a selection, it grows progressively larger each time you press F8. For example, if you select a word, you can extend the selection to a sentence by pressing F8 once. To shrink the selection, you press SHIFT+F8.

field   The coded instructions that insert many types of information into your document, including the variable data inserted into form letters during printing. You can update fields to insert new information into your document automatically.

field codes   A field that appears as instructions enclosed by field characters ({ }).

field result   Text or graphics inserted into a document because of the action of a field.

file   A document that has been created, and then saved, under a unique filename. In Word, all documents are stored as files.

file format   The format in which data is stored in a file. Word usually stores a document in Word's "Normal" file format, which includes the text and all the formatting applied to the document. Word can read and save in several file formats, such as Microsoft Excel BIF, Windows Write, RTF, and WordPerfect.

font   A family of type styles, such as Geneva and Modern. Effects, such as bold or italic, are possible within one font, and various point sizes can be applied to a font.

form letter or document   A document consisting of boilerplate text and personalized information, such as names and addresses. A form letter is created by merging the main document and the data document. The main document contains basic text that is the same in every copy of the letter. The data document contains the information that varies for each letter, such as names and addresses.

format   The way text appears on a page. The four types of formats are character, paragraph, section, and document. Styles can be applied to any of these formats.

forms   A special document template in which form fields allow the user to complete the form online without affecting the text and formatting of the form.

formula   A mathematical statement or expression, such as $3x = \frac{1}{2}y$. Word provides special codes to create formulas.

frame   A box you add around an area of your document—for example, a block of text, a graphic, or a chart—so that you can easily change its position on a page. Once you insert an object into a frame, you can drag it to the position you want in page layout view. Word automatically makes room for the frame at the new location.

global template   In Word, a template with the filename NORMAL.DOT that contains default menus, dialog box settings, and styles. Documents use the global template unless you specify a custom template.

hanging indent   A paragraph format in which the first line of a paragraph starts farther to the left than subsequent lines.

header and footer   A header is text or graphics that appear at the top of every page in a section. A footer appears at the bottom of every page. Headers and footers often contain page numbers, chapter titles, dates, and author names. Headers and footers appear in the header or footer pane for editing.

header file   In a print merge process, a document containing a header record that Word substitutes for the header record in a data document.

heading   A title for a part of a document (for example, a chapter title).

hidden text   A character format that allows you to show or hide designated text. Word indicates hidden text by underlining it with a dotted line. You can select or clear the Hidden Text option with the Options command on the Tools menu. You can omit hidden text during printing.

icon   A graphical representation of a file-level object—that is, a disk drive, a directory, an application, a document, or other object that you can select and open.

indent   The distance between text boundaries and page margins. Positive indents make the text area narrower than the space between margins. Negative indents allow text to extend into the margins. A paragraph can have left, right, and first-line indents. Indents can also be measured relative to columns in a section, table cells, and the boundaries of positioned objects.

insertion point   The vertical blinking line on the Word screen that shows your current location and where text and graphics you type or paste will be inserted. The insertion point also determines where Word will begin an action, such as checking spelling.

landscape   A term used to refer to horizontal page orientation; opposite of "portrait," or vertical orientation.

leader characters   Characters, usually dots or hyphens, that fill the space between words separated by tabs to draw the reader's eye across a line. Leader characters are often used in tables of contents. Example: Chapter 1.................Page 5

line break   A break you insert when you want to end one line and start another without starting a new paragraph. A line break is represented by the newline character, which you can display by selecting options from the Tools menu, clicking on the View tab, and then selecting the All option.

line spacing   The height of a line of text, including extra spacing. Line spacing is often measured in lines or points. The following table shows the approximate point equivalents for standard line spacing set with the ruler for 12 point type.

Spacing	Line height in points
Single	12
One-and-one-half	18
Double	24

Note: Two lines = double-spaced; 72 points = 1 inch.

list box   Part of a dialog box that contains a list of possible selections for an option. Some list boxes stay the same size; others drop down to display the list of items.

main document   In a form letter or document, the main document contains text and graphics that are the same for all the merged documents. Within the text, you insert fields that are replaced by information specific to each of the merged documents when you print.

measurement A measured distance. In Word, you type measurements in a dialog box with one of the following units.

Unit	Equivalent measurements
Centimeters (cm)	2.54 cm = 1 in
Inches (in or ")	1 in = 72 pt = 6 pi
Lines (li)	1 li = 1/6 in = 12 pt
Picas (pi)	1 pi = 1/6 in = 12 pt
Points (pt)	1 pt = 1/12 pi = 1/72 in

menu   A list of commands that drops down from the menu bar. The menu bar is displayed across the top of an application window and lists the menu names, such as File and Edit.

merge   To combine one or more sources of text into a single document, such as a form letter.

message   A notice on the screen that informs you of a problem or asks for more information. Messages appear in the status bar at the bottom of your screen, in a message box, or as bold text in your document. When Word displays a message, you can press F1 for immediate help, with the following exceptions: field error messages that appear as bold text in your document, or some low-memory messages. You can get help on all messages by pressing F1 and choosing the Index button. Choose Messages under Reference Information.

normal view   The view you see when you start Word. Normal view is used for most editing and formatting tasks.

object   A table, chart, graphic, equation, or other form of information you create and edit with an application other than Word, but whose data you insert and store in a Word document.

options   The choices you have in a dialog box.

outline view   An outline shows the headings of a document indented to represent their level in the document structure. In Word, you can display the structure of your documents in outline view. Outline view makes it easy to move quickly through a document, change the importance of headings, and rearrange large amounts of text by moving headings.

overtype   An option for replacing existing characters one by one as you type. You can select overtype by pressing the INS key, or by selecting the Overtype option with the Options command on the Tools menu. When you select the Overtype option, the letters "OVR" appear in the status bar at the bottom of the Word window.

page break   The point at which one page ends and another begins. In page view and print preview, and when you print your document, text after a page break appears on a new page. A break you insert, called a hard break, is created by pressing CTRL+ENTER. A break inserted automatically, as determined by the page layout, is called a soft break.

page layout view   A view that displays your document as it will appear when you print it. Items, such as headers, footnotes, and framed objects, appear in their actual positions, and you can drag them to new positions. You can edit and format text in page layout view. You can only view certain elements in this view, such as page headers and footers, and multiple columns.

paste   To insert cut or copied text into a document from the temporary storage area called the Clipboard.

path   Drive, directory, and filename. For example, the complete path for the Word for Windows program file might be C:\WINWORD\WINWORD.EXE.

point size   A measurement used for the size of text characters. There are 72 points in an inch.

portrait   A term used to refer to vertical page orientation; opposite of "landscape," or horizontal orientation.

position   The specific placement of graphics, tables, and paragraphs on a page. In Word, you can assign items to fixed positions on a page.

repaginate   To calculate and insert page breaks at the correct point in your document. By default, Word repaginates whenever you make a change in your document.

rule   A straight vertical or horizontal line between columns in a section, next to paragraphs, or in a table. You can assign a variety of widths to a rule. *See also* Border.

ruler   A graphical bar displayed across the top of the document window. You can use the ruler to indent paragraphs, set tab stops, adjust page margins, and change column widths in a table.

scale   To change the height or width of a graphic by a certain percentage. You can choose to preserve or change the relative proportions of elements within the graphic when you scale it.

scroll bar   A graphical device for moving vertically and horizontally through a document with a mouse. Scroll bars are located at the right and bottom edges of the document window. You can display or hide scroll bars with the Horizontal Scroll Bar and Vertical Scroll Bar check boxes, on the View tab in the Options dialog box (Tools menu).

section   A portion of a document in which you set certain page formatting options. You create a new section when you want to change options, such as line numbering, number of columns, or headers and footers. Until you insert section breaks, Word treats your document as a single section.

section break   The point at which you end one section and begin another because you want some aspect of page formatting to change. In normal or draft view, a section break appears as two dotted lines.

selection bar   An invisible area at the left edge of a document window used to select text with the mouse. In a table, each cell has its own selection bar at the left edge of the cell.

soft return   A line break created by pressing SHIFT+ENTER. This creates a new line without creating a new paragraph. *See also* Line break.

special characters   Symbols displayed on the screen to indicate characters that do not print, such as tab characters or paragraph marks. You can control the display of special characters with the Options command on the Tools menu, and the Show/Hide ¶ button on the ribbon.

status bar   A bar at the bottom of the Word window that displays information about the current status of the document and application.

style   A group of formatting instructions that you name and store. When you apply a style to selected characters and paragraphs, all the formatting instructions of that style are applied at once.

style area   An area to the left of the selection in which the names of applied styles are displayed. You can display the style area using the Options command for View options on the Tools menu.

summary information   Descriptions and statistics about a document such as title, author, comments, and revision number. You can view or change summary information with the Summary Info command on the File menu.

tab stop   A measured position for placing and aligning text at a specific place on a line. Word has four kinds of tab stops, each with a different alignment: Left extends text to the right from the tab; Center centers text at the tab; Right extends text to the left from the tab until the tab's space is filled, and then extends text to the right; and Decimal extends text before the decimal point to the left, and then extends text after the decimal point to the right.

table   One or more rows of cells commonly used to display numbers and other items for quick reference and analysis. Items in a table are organized into rows and columns. You can convert text into a table with the Insert Table command on the Table menu.

template   A special kind of document that provides basic tools and text for shaping a final document. Templates can contain the following elements: text that is the same in every document, styles, glossary items, macros, menu and key assignments.

text box   A box within a dialog box where you type information needed to carry out a command.

title bar   The horizontal bar at the top of a window that shows the name of the document or application that appears in that window.

toolbar   A graphical bar with buttons that perform some of the most common commands in Word, such as opening, copying, and printing files. The toolbars you can display include: Standard, Formatting, Outline, Forms, Borders, Database, Word 2.0, and Drawing.

vertical alignment   The placement of text on a page in relation to the top, bottom, or center of the page.

view   A form of screen display that shows certain aspects of the document. Word has six views: normal, draft, outline, page layout, full screen, and print preview.

widow and orphan   A widow is the last line of a paragraph printed by itself at the top of a page. An orphan is the first line of a paragraph printed by itself at the bottom of a page. The default settings in Word prevent widows and orphans.

window   A rectangular area on your screen in which you view and work on documents. You can have up to nine different document windows open at one time.

wizard   An online coach you use to create documents. When you use a wizard to create a document, you are asked questions about your document preferences, and the wizard creates the document according to your specifications.

wordwrap   Automatic placement of a word on the next line. When you type text and reach the right margin or indent, Word checks to see if the entire word you type fits on the current line. If not, Word automatically places the word on the next line.

Index

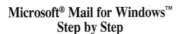